Symbols of Law

Itero

Reprints in the Service of the Scholarly Community
www.ehs.se/itero

Series Editor

Thomas Kazen

No. 1

Åke Viberg

Symbols of Law

A Contextual Analysis of Legal Symbolic Acts
in the Old Testament

Enskilda Högskolan Stockholm
2021

Itero – Reprints in the Service of the Scholarly Community

Books still in demand should not get out of print, and with today's techniques there is no defence. With the reprint series *Itero*, the Biblical Studies department at Stockholm School of Theology would like to make books available for free online and at a very low cost in print. Part of the background is the fact that several faculty members have published their studies in series that were cancelled. With the publishing market in constant flux, series migrate, and volumes still in demand can suddenly become unavailable. This is unsatisfactory. In collaboration with the authors, we are now republishing a number of such volumes and we will consider publishing other out-of-print titles, for which authors hold the copyright. This is entirely a non-profit project. Files may be downloaded at www.ehs.se/itero and books can be bought through most major internet bookshops.

University College Stockholm – Stockholm School of Theology

University College Stockholm (Enskilda Högskolan Stockholm) is a major Swedish provider of education in Human Rights and Democracy, as well as in Theology/Religious Studies. EHS offers Bachelor's Master's and Doctoral programmes. The university college was founded in 1993 through a merger of educational institutions with roots dating back to 1866. Stockholm School of Theology is the common designation for the two theological departments: Religious Studies and Theology, and Eastern Christian Studies. Stockholm School of Human Rights and Democracy is the designation for the programmes in Human Rights and Democracy.

ISBN: 978-91-88906-13-7

Cover design by Carl Johan Berglund. Typeset in EB Garamond. Printed by BoD – Books on Demand, Norderstedt, Germany.

Stockholm School of Theology
University College Stockholm
Åkeshovsvägen 29, 168 39 Bromma, Sweden
www.ehs.se

Preface to the Itero Reprint Edition

It is not without some mixed feelings I return to my dissertation, written almost thirty years ago. But still, I am grateful for the opportunity to make it available in print yet again, especially since it has not been available for purchase for some time.

Stockholm, 26 October 2021

Åke Viberg

Table of Contents

Preface V

1 Introduction 1
1.1 Aim and Method of the Analysis 1
1.2 What is a Legal Symbolic Act? 8
   1.2.1 A Definition of 'Legal Symbolic Act' 9
   1.2.2 Conventional and Innovative Acts 11
   1.2.3 Legal Symbolic Acts and Performatives 12
1.3 What Makes a Symbolic Act Legal? 14
   Excursus: Customary Law in the OT 15
1.4 A Variety of Legal Functions 17

2 Analysis of Legal Symbolic Acts 19
2.1 **Raising the Hand** 19
   2.1.1 Introduction 19
   2.1.2 Procedure 19
      Excursus: Deuteronomy 32:40 According to the LXX 20
   2.1.3 Legal Function 21
      2.1.3.1 Introduction 21
      2.1.3.2 Genesis 14:22 21
         Excursus: The Constituents of Oaths in the OT 22
      2.1.3.3 Daniel 12:7 25
      2.1.3.4 Deuteronomy 32:40 26
      2.1.3.5 Ezekiel 20:5-6 et al. 27
         Excursus: Why Does God Raise His Hand? 29
   2.1.4 Historical Explanation 31
   2.1.5 Summary and Conclusions 32

2.2 **Shaking the Hand** 33
   2.2.1 Introduction 33
   2.2.2 Procedure 33
   2.2.3 Legal Function 36
      2.2.3.1 Introduction 36
      2.2.3.2 2 Kings 10:15 36
      2.2.3.3 Ezekiel 17:18 37
         Excursus: A Diplomatic Handshake 38
      2.2.3.4 Ezra 10:19 39
      2.2.3.5 Proverbs 6:1 40
      2.2.3.6 Job 17:3 42
   2.2.4 Historical Explanation 43
   2.2.5 Summary and Conclusions 44

2.3 **Putting the Hand Under the Thigh** 45
   2.3.1 Introduction 45
   2.3.2 Procedure 45

2.3.3 Legal Function 47
    2.3.3.1 Genesis 24:9 47
    2.3.3.2 Genesis 47:29 48
2.3.4 Historical Explanation 49
2.3.5 Summary and Conclusions... 51

2.4 Walking Through a Divided Animal **52**
2.4.1 Introduction 52
    Excursus: Some Alleged Parallels 53
2.4.2 Procedure.. 57
2.4.3 Legal Function 59
    2.4.3.1 Jeremiah 34:18-19 59
        Excursus: Is Jeremiah 34:18 in Need of Repair? 59
    2.4.3.2 Genesis 15:17 63
        Excursus: Judges 19:29 and 1 Samuel 11:7 65
2.4.4 Historical Explanation 67
2.4.5 Summary and Conclusions... 68

2.5 Sharing a Meal **70**
2.5.1 Introduction 70
2.5.2 Procedure.. 70
2.5.3 Legal Function.. 71
    2.5.3.1 Genesis 26:30 71
    2.5.3.2 Genesis 31:46, 54.. 73
    2.5.3.3 2 Samuel 3:20 74
2.5.4 Historical Explanation 75
2.5.5 Summary and Conclusions... 76

2.6 Piercing the Ear of the Slave **77**
2.6.1 Introduction 77
2.6.2 Procedure.. 77
2.6.3 Legal Function 83
2.6.4 Historical Explanation 86
    Excursus: Driving in the Nail: A Connection? 86
2.6.5 Summary and Conclusions... 88

2.7 Anointing the Head with Oil **89**
2.7.1 Introduction 89
    Excursus: Earlier Views on Anointing in the OT 89
2.7.2 Procedure.. 91
2.7.3 Legal Function 92
    Excursus: Anointing Outside the OT 92
    2.7.3.1 Judges 9:8, 15 94
    2.7.3.2 1 Samuel 10:1 95
    2.7.3.3 1 Samuel 16:13 97
    2.7.3.4 2 Samuel 2:4 98
    2.7.3.5 2 Samuel 5:3 99
    2.7.3.6 2 Samuel 19:11 103
    2.7.3.7 1 Kings 1:39 103
        Excursus: Problem with Numbers in 1 Kings 1:34, 45 104
    2.7.3.8 1 Kings 19:15-16 and 2 Kings 9:3, 6 109

2.7.3.9 2 Kings 11:12 110
Excursus: An Implicit Plural Subject of 'Anoint' in the LXX ...112
2.7.3.10 2 Kings 23:30 113
Excursus: Anointing in Psalms 45:8; 89:21 and 105:15 114
Excursus: Priestly Anointing 116
2.7.4 Historical Explanation 117
2.7.5 Summary and Conclusions....................................118

2.8 Grasping the Horns of the Altar 120
2.8.1 Introduction 120
2.8.2 Procedure...120
2.8.3 Legal Function 121
2.8.3.1 Exodus 21:12-14 121
2.8.3.2 1 Kings 1:50 122
2.8.3.3 1 Kings 2:28 123
2.8.4 Historical Explanation 124
2.8.5 Summary and Conclusions...................................126

2.9 Transferring the Mantle 127
2.9.1 Introduction 127
2.9.2 Performance...127
2.9.3 Legal Function 128
Excursus: The Covenant Between Jonathan and David 130
2.9.4 Historical Explanation 134
2.9.5 Summary and Conclusions...................................135

2.10 Covering a Woman with the Mantle 136
2.10.1 Introduction...136
2.10.2 Performance 136
2.10.3 Legal Function 138
2.10.3.1 Ezekiel 16:8 138
*Excursus: Removing the Mantle and Uncovering
the Nakedness* 139
2.10.3.2 Ruth 3:9 141
2.10.4 Historical Explanation 142
2.10.5 Summary and Conclusions 144

2.11 Removing the Sandal......................................145
2.11.1 Introduction..145
2.11.2 Procedure 145
2.11.2.1 Ruth 4:8 145
2.11.2.2 Deuteronomy 25:9 147
2.11.3 Legal Function 148
2.11.3.1 Ruth 4:8 148
Excursus: Technical Terminology in Jeremiah 32:8 151
2.11.3.2 Deuteronomy 25:9 156
Excursus: Amos 2:6; 8:6 and 1 Samuel 12:3 157
Excursus: Walking Through the Land..........................160
2.11.4 Historical Explanation 161
Excursus: Removing the Sandals in Testament of Zebulon 3:2-7 163
2.11.5 Summary and Conclusions 165

2.12 Putting a Child on the Knees............................**166**
    2.12.1 Introduction...166
    2.12.2 Procedure 167
    2.12.3 Legal Function..168
        Excursus: Adoption in the OT?........................168
        Excursus: Earlier Views on Naomi's Act in Ruth 4:16.....................169
    2.12.4 Historical Explanation 175
    2.12.5 Summary and Conclusions 176

3 Concluding Remarks...............................**177**

4 Abbreviations and Technical Remarks......................**180**

5 Bibliography **181**
5.1 Sources...181
5.2 Literature 183

6 Indexes **201**
6.1 Biblical, Apocryphal and Jewish Sources 201
6.2 Ancient Near Eastern Sources 205
    6.2.1 Syro-Palestine and Mesopotamia 205
    6.2.2 Hatti 206
6.3 Classical Sources 206

1 Introduction

1.1 Aim and Method of the Analysis

"Spread your mantle over me!" This urgent request was made by Ruth, the young Moabite woman, to the older and well-established Boaz on the local threshing-floor. Earlier the same night, Ruth had covered herself with Boaz' mantle as he lay sleeping. What was the intention of her request as well as her act? Was there more than meets the eye? Indeed there was, since Ruth was aiming at something which went beyond the mere procedure of her act, something which lay hidden in the symbolic value of the act itself. She was in fact referring to a particular symbolic act to be performed by Boaz. What is more, the symbolic act which Ruth alluded to was generally known to have a particular legal function, making it a legal symbolic act. When Boaz was to perform the act of covering Ruth with his mantle, a profound change of legal status would occur, for Ruth as well as for Boaz.

There are several more examples from the OT of similar symbolic acts with a legal function. It is the aim of this analysis to understand more fully some of them as they are described in the OT.

What, then, is a legal symbolic act? Awaiting a more comprehensive definition, it can be defined simply as *an act by which a legal function is symbolized and effected*. There are certain restrictions connected to this definition, which will be returned to below.

Until now, the legal symbolic acts in the OT have not received a thorough study of their own. There have been earlier studies specifically related to some of these acts, such as Malul's studies of the acts of putting the hand under the thigh and covering a woman with the mantle, and Kruger's studies related to various acts in relation to the mantle.[1] These studies, which are related to specific acts, will be taken up below in the analysis of each particular act. Legal symbolic acts are naturally commented upon in various other works as well. What has been lacking so far, however, is a thorough analysis of legal symbolic acts in the OT, together with a theoretical base upon which to establish a method for analyzing these acts. The latter is the intention of this introduction. This introduction owes a great deal to the theoretical base in Malul's analysis of legal symbolic acts in Babylonian legal texts, although the differences between the two are just as significant.[2] So far, Malul's analysis is the only thorough study of legal

---

[1] Malul (1985; 1985b; 1987; 1990a), Kruger (1984; 1986).

[2] Malul (1988). In relation to this, see also Malul (1985a; 1987a).

symbolic acts from the ancient Near East outside the OT. Its value for this work can be evidenced by its use throughout the following analysis. Malul's study was preceded by some articles by Munn-Rankin, Greengus and in particular one article by Draffkorn Kilmer, in which a list was drawn up of legal symbolic acts from the ancient Near East.[3]

If the legal aspect is omitted and the more general study of symbolic acts is focused upon, the most thorough and recent study is that of Gruber.[4] Gruber studies symbolic acts, or more correctly, non-verbal communication in three semitic languages, namely biblical Hebrew, Ugaritic and Akkadian. Gruber is primarily interested in the emotional aspects of the non-verbal communication. Although his purpose is different in principle from both this analysis as well as that of Malul, there are some relevant points of contact, as will be noted throughout this analysis. Another study of non-verbal communication in the OT is the study by Carena. However, Carena's study is of more limited use for this analysis.[5] An older study of non-verbal communication, or body language, in the OT was made by Vorwahl, which includes a short section on legal symbolic acts.[6] A similar, yet more comprehensive work related to ancient Greece and Rome was made by Sittl.[7]

In the light of this overview of earlier studies, more or less related to the subject, it is clear that there definitely is a place for a thorough study of legal symbolic acts in the OT.

The method which is used in order to achieve the aim, as stated above, is to analyse each legal symbolic act in the literary context in which it is described. The analysis will be performed by asking three basic questions in relation to the texts which describe the acts:

1. How is the act performed?
2. What is the legal function of the act?
3. Why was the legal function once connected to this performance?

These three questions will be used to structure the presentation of the analysis of each act in three parts, namely 'Performance', 'Legal Function' and 'Historical Explanation'.[8]

The main effort is spent on answering the second question concerning the legal function. However, in order to understand the legal function of an

---

[3] Munn-Rankin (1956), Greengus (1966), (1969) and Draffkorn Kilmer (1974).

[4] Gruber (1980). See also Gruber (1975; 1978; 1983) and Kruger (1989).

[5] Carena (1981).

[6] Vorwahl (1932).

[7] Sittl (1890).

[8] Malul (1988:30-3) has a similar tripartite structure, made up of "morphology", "semantics" and "etymology".

act it must also be understood how the act was performed, since any doubt as to how the act was performed also raises doubts as to whether the act is supposed to be performed. The question of performance will therefore sometimes include the more basic issue of whether a text actually describes the performance of an act.

The third question concerns the historical explanation for the connection between the performance of an act and its legal function. This is only made tentatively in this analysis, since such an endeavour deserves its own study, not the least because of the theoretical difficulties involved. In answering this question, various symbols are of particular importance. 'Symbol' is then used in the very wide and simple sense of *one entity which stands for and represents another entity*.[9] These symbols can be of various kinds, e.g. the acts themselves, various parts of the body,[10] clothing, such as a sandal or a mantle,[11] and other items such as the horns of the altar. In the attempt to explain the acts historically, it must be asked whether the legal function of an act was once connected to a particular performance because of some symbolism related to that performance. If so, that symbolic meaning related to the performance could be used to explain how the legal function came to be related to a particular performance. It should also be noted that the relationship between the symbolic meanings connected to the performance and the legal function is most often characterized by analogy. One example is when Jonathan turns over his mantle, among other things, to David in 1 Sam 18:4. As the analysis below will attempt to show, this act is based on a legal symbolic act which had as its legal function to transfer a certain legal status, such as being heir to the throne. The mantle is well-known from the ancient Near East as a symbol for the person who is wearing it. The act of transferring one's mantle could then have been thought to symbolize the transference of something more abstract, such as a legal status. This would then be the historical explanation of how the legal function of transferring a legal status came to be attached to the act of transferring the mantle. There is also a clear case of analogy between the

---

[9] See e.g. Geertz (1973:208, n. 19), who defines 'symbol' as "any physical, social, or cultural act or object that serves as the vehicle for a conception". Gorman (1990:22-3) follows Geertz in defining "symbolic action". See also Alonso Schökel (1988:110): "The symbol is the object perceived plus something else that is revealed in it."

[10] For the descriptions of the various parts of the human body in the OT and their symbolic meanings, see Dhorme (1923), who concentrates on how the names of the different parts of the body are used metaphorically, and Oelsner (1960). Gruber (1980) contains much useful information in this area.

[11] For clothing in the OT, see e.g. Hönig (1957), Haulotte (1966), Brongers (1982), and in the ancient Near East in general, see e.g. Weippert (1977).

symbolic act of transferring a mantle and the legal function of transferring a legal status.

The historical explanation of an act is sometimes quite transparent, as in the case discussed above from 1 Sam 18:4. In other cases, however, the relationship between the symbolism related to the performance and the legal function is quite opaque, which is an open invitation to speculation in the search for a historical explanation. One example where this is the case is the act of putting the hand under the thigh of someone else in order to take an oath. It has been suggested that the word *yārēk*, "thigh" is actually a euphemism for the genital organs in the descriptions of this act, namely Gen 24:2, 9 and 47:29. The genital organs would then symbolize either the procreative force, or the offspring which could function as witnesses or pose a threat on the one who takes the oath, or the ancestral spirits who would also pose a threat. The problem is, however, that besides the texts which describe this act there is no sufficient basis upon which to posit either a euphemistic use of *yārēk* or that the genital organs would have symbolized either offspring or ancestral spirits. The historical explanation of the act along these lines is therefore very much open to speculation.

This analysis is not intended to provide a complete inventory of legal symbolic acts in the OT. A selection has therefore been made, which includes the most important acts. This leads to another limitation of this analysis, namely the boundary that has been drawn between cultic and non-cultic law.[12] 'Cultic law' is here used in the sense of priestly rituals and legislations specifically related to the cultural sphere of life in ancient Israel. The acts which have been chosen for analysis are all related to the latter category of non-cultic law. However, this distinction is not meant to imply that the ancient Israelites considered the boundary between cultic and non-cultic law to be as fixed as it has been drawn here.[13] There are several symbolic acts in the OT which are very much legal but within the sphere of cultic law.[14]

The ambition of this analysis has been to understand legal symbolic acts as they are described in the OT. No effort has therefore been made either to prove or disprove the historicity of these specific occurrences of the acts.[15]

---

[12]   See e.g. Reventlow (1963) concerning the scholarly debate concerning what is to be meant by cultic law.

[13]   Cf. Paul (1970:36-40) and Boecker (1984:118-24).

[14]   For example the laying on of hands, testing by giving bitter water to drink in Num 5:11-31 and the act in Deut 21:1-9, which could be considered a border-line case since it is the elders and not the priests who perform the act, see further Wright (1987a).

[15]   See e.g. Malul (1990:73). .

To take one example, when the *gōʾēl*, "kinsman-redeemer" in Ruth 4:8 removes his sandal, he is undoubtedly performing an act which is symbolic as well as legal. However, in the analysis of this act below no attempt is made to investigate whether this particular act actually occurred, a question which is naturally linked to the question of the historicity of the book of Ruth at large. It is not only that such questions of historicity are especially elusive, but they are also of little or no relevance for the understanding of the legal symbolic acts. To return to the kinsman-redeemer in Ruth 4:8, whether he actually performed such an act at a specific point in time is of minor importance. What is of real importance for this analysis is the fact that the act was a legal symbolic act, commonly performed under similar circumstances in ancient Israel.

It is unlikely that legal symbolic acts in the OT are literary creations and therefore do not describe a part of the legal institutions of ancient Israel. It is worth noting that very seldom in the literature dealing with these acts is it suggested that this should be the case. For these reasons it is presumed throughout this analysis that in order to show the proper cultural flavour and appearance of these acts, they have been described by the various biblical authors with their proper legal functions.[16] This is also relevant in relation to the question of whether a legal symbolic act is being reused in a non-legal context. The understanding of an act differs markedly if it was expected to be associated with a legal symbolic act, or if it was meant to be an innovative symbolic act. One example of such a reuse of a legal symbolic act is the so-called 'divine anointing'. The legal symbolic act of royal anointing had the legal function of accomplishing the royal status of an individual, who was thereby elected for this particular purpose. When God is then described as choosing his candidates for the throne, he is said to anoint them, an act which is performed by a prophet, as, e.g., in 1 Sam 10:1 and 16:13, the divine anointing of Saul and David. These anointings are not meant to be legal, however, but rather to emphasize the divine election of the pretenders to the throne. As people normally anointed someone to be king, so also God is described as anointing the ones he has chosen for this position. This reuse of a legal symbolic act provides the divine election with added emphasis through the association with the legal force inherent in the legal symbolic act. In some cases, however, all that is found of a legal symbolic act is how it is reused in a non-legal context. In this case the understanding of the legal symbolic act naturally becomes more difficult

---

[16] See Patrick (1985:193), who has a similar line of argument for legal proceedings: "One would expect authors to depict court transactions with sufficient realism for their readers to recognize them." See also Malul (1990:70).

and hypothetical and opens the way for a more elaborate use of comparative material.

This analysis is not meant to be a comparative study, although comparative material from neighbouring cultures is used to some degree.[17] The use of comparative material is limited to the mere phenomenological aspect of such material, similar to what Malul calls a typological comparison.[18] This typological comparison is different in principle from a historical comparison, which is used to argue for historical connections in some form. This, however, is precisely what a typological comparison is not. Typological comparison is furthermore used in two different ways in this analysis, one illustrative and one explanatory.

Firstly, it has as its purpose to illustrate the OT material by means of extra-biblical material. When a legal symbolic act in the OT is compared with an act from some extra-biblical material in this illustrative way, the purpose is only to show that a similar act is found outside the OT. The similarity between the two acts can then be related to either their performances, their legal functions, or both, but the comparison is not intended to provide the OT act with a legal function. Sometimes the comparison can also serve a contrastive purpose, as when an act from the OT has the same performance as an act from extra-biblical material, although their legal functions differ. At the most, this illustrative manner of using the comparative material functions as a confirmation of what has already been found in the analysis of the legal symbolic act in its own literary context, since this analysis attempts to give prime importance to the literary context in which these acts are described.[19]

Secondly, when it is not possible to discern the legal function of an act on the basis of how it functions within its literary context, the use of comparative material takes on a different form. The purpose is then no longer simply to illustrate what has already been found in the analysis of

---

[17] That this analysis is not meant to be a full-fledged comparative study can be seen from the fact that extra-biblical texts are only referred to in their original languages in so far as it forms a relevant contribution to the argument. This should be an indication to the reader that this analysis is primarily oriented towards the OT by means of contextual analyses of the relevant texts.

[18] Malul (1990:14-9). For the proper use of comparative material, see also Talmon (1978a), Wilson (1980:15-6) and Wright (1987:5-9).

[19] See the sixth principle of Wilson (1980:16): "When applying comparative material to the biblical text, the interpreter must allow the biblical text itself to be the controlling factor in the exegetical process. The comparative material can thus be used only to form a hypothesis which must still be tested against the biblical text. The exegesis of the text itself will then support, disprove, or modify the hypothesis."

the act, but to explain the act by providing it with a legal function. It should be remembered that the comparative material is still used according to the phenomenological or typological approach, which means that no historical relationship is implied by this use of the comparative material. This explanatory use of comparative material becomes particularly relevant when a legal symbolic act has been reused in a non-legal context, as was described above. When the legal function of an act has been achieved in this way, namely by means of a comparison with an extra-biblical act and not by means of an analysis of how it functions in its literary context, the hypothetical nature of the solution will have to be noted.[20] To return to the act of Jonathan in 1 Sam 18:4, it is possible that Jonathan's act is meant simply as an act of love towards David and nothing more. However, there are certain extra-biblical texts which describe a legal symbolic act which is likely to be reused in this text in order to provide Jonathan's decision with an added emphasis. Although the act which Jonathan is said to perform is not intended to have a legal effect, the mere association with a legal symbolic act will nevertheless make his decision appear stronger and more definite.

The attempt to date a legal symbolic act by relating it to the date of the text in which it is described is questionable. A legal symbolic act may be very old as a legal custom[21] within the Israelite culture, while at the same time appear in literary form in a rather late part of the OT.[22] This is the main reason why no attempt has been made in this analysis to relate these legal symbolic acts to a historical description of how the legal institutions developed in ancient Israel.

Similar reservations should also be made for source-critical questions in relation to the texts in this analysis. The diachronic approach in analysing the text of the OT is a subject all its own, and has its place in exegetical studies. However, the traditional approaches to how it should be practised

---

[20] For a similar approach, see Wright (1987:7-9).

[21] 'Custom' is defined by Black (1979:347) in the context of law as follows: "A usage or practice of the people, which, by common adoption and acquiescence, and by long and unvarying habit, has become compulsory, and has acquired the force of a law with respect to the place or subject-matter to which it relates." The term 'customary' is only used here as part of the expression 'customary law'. An act is said to be 'conventional' in this analysis when it depends upon the general consent for its meaning.

[22] See e.g. Mendenhall (1990:96), who makes a similar case with the reuse of the ancient treaty structure in Deuteronomy.

is more than ever a matter of scholarly debate.[23] Since the present analysis focuses on how legal symbolic acts function in the textual worlds presented by the texts, the effort to create a hypothetical text through the use of source-critical methodologies leads to the creation of a hypothetical context for the act, i.e., another textual world, and possibly to a new, hypothetical function for the symbolic act.[24] It has therefore been deemed more appropriate in this analysis to rely on the understanding of whoever constructed the biblical narratives in which these legal symbolic acts are found. Their knowledge of how these acts functioned in their socio-cultural context, is likely to be more reliable than a hypothetical context reconstructed by a modern scholar. Again, this is not to say that various forms of source-criticism are useless. As will be shown below, however, the legal function of a legal symbolic act is not found by merely observing how the act is performed, but by understanding how the act functions in its context. To analyse a text into its possible earlier stages is therefore not a suitable method when the purpose is to understand legal symbolic acts. Therefore, when texts which are usually considered to have a complex history of composition are studied in the analysis, this matter will be noted, although not always interacted with.

1.2 What is a Legal Symbolic Act?

The question 'What is a legal symbolic act?' will be answered by means of a definition, together with the basic criteria which emerge out of that definition. Then these legal symbolic acts will be compared to another group of symbolic acts in the OT, namely those acts performed by the prophets. A second comparison is then made with so-called performatives. These com-

---

[23] See e.g. Berlin (1983:111-29) on the method in general, Whybray (1987:129-31, 221-42) for its relation to the study of the Pentateuch and Longacre (1989:9-12) with some further valuable references.

[24] See e.g. Vorster (1985:60-1), who uses the expression "narrative world", and Ricoeur (1981:112): "Hermeneutics can be defined no longer as an inquiry into the psychological intentions which are hidden beneath the text, but rather as the explication of the being-in-the-world displayed by the text. What is to be interpreted in the text is a proposed world which I could inhabit and in which I could project my ownmost possibilities." A similar case can be made for a "ritual world", see Gorman (1990:15). For the importance of the context in literary interpretation, see e.g. Kittay (1987:106): "When a given sentence has been artificially taken out of context (or rather out of *its* context), the features of the world that we take to be normal, and our usual expectations of our world (in so far as these are relevant to the utterance), serve as an implicit context (the default frame) determining our interpretation - be it literal or metaphorical - and belie the claim to intelligibility of context-free sentences."

parisons will serve to emphasize the distinctively conventional character of legal symbolic acts.

1.2.1 A Definition of 'Legal Symbolic Act'

A legal symbolic act will be defined in the following way in this analysis:

> *A legal symbolic act is a non-verbal act which fulfils a legal function when it is performed under the proper circumstances and when the legal function is different from the physical result of the act.*

Some basic criteria for what should be called a legal symbolic act can be deduced from this definition.

1. The legal symbolic act must be a non-verbal act. When a piece of land changed owner, it was apparently accomplished by calling out the name of the new owner over the field.[25] However, since this act was verbal, it will not be included in this analysis, although it was undoubtedly legal.

A problem that will be encountered in the analysis below is how to distinguish between an expression which describes the performance of a legal symbolic act and an idiomatic expression.[26] The description of an act must therefore be shown to describe not only that the act could be performed, i.e., its performability, but also the actual performance of the act. Anything less will make the conclusion equally less certain.

Something must be said about the choice of the term 'act'. 'Ritual' could be used, if it was clearly defined as referring to secular rituals.[27] However, the common association between 'ritual' and some form of religious context and function[28] makes it rather unsuitable for a specifically legal context and function. The term 'gesture', although well-known and widely used, is limited to physical movements with a less complicated performance. This would cover some of the acts studied here, e.g. raising the hand, but it would not be sufficient as an overall description. The term 'act' has been chosen instead of 'ritual' because of its rather neutral meaning and associations. It is preferred to 'gesture' because it can be used to describe more complex and especially interactive performances, e.g. sharing a meal, grasping the horns of the altar, shaking the hand and anointing the head.

---

[25] See Galling (1956). See e.g. Amos 9:12.

[26] See e.g. Gruber (1980:278-80).

[27] See e.g. Myerhoff (1977:199).

[28] See e.g. the definition of 'ritual' by Turner (1977:183).

2. The act must be performed under the proper circumstances in order to fulfil the requirements for a successful legal symbolic act. It is difficult to provide general characteristics for these circumstances, but they would at least have to include some contextual indications to convey that the act is related to some form of legal proceeding. Such indications could be of various kinds, but the most important indications are technical terminology and phraseology which are well known to occur in legal contexts, the presence of witnesses, the place of the act in the literary structure and the locality of the performance of the act. One example of an act with a rather elusive legal function is the act of sharing a meal, i.e., the covenant meal. However, one decisive factor in this case is the place of the meal in the literary structure. In all the cases where this act is thought to occur according to this analysis, Gen 26:30; 31:46, 54 and 2 Sam 3:20, the meal has a pivotal function in the literary structure. Something seems to happen by means of the meal, which ends the description of an agreement and prepares for the end of the proceedings.

This criterion of proper circumstances is very much particular to each legal symbolic act, since they all have different circumstances. However, when there are more than one occurrence of one and the same legal symbolic act, the indications which are found in the context of one act can be used to understand the other occurrences. The sum of the indications which have been found can then be used to analyse the more doubtful examples of the acts, and even mark out the characteristics which are necessary in order to parse an expression as a description of a particular legal symbolic act.

3. The legal function of the act must be different from the manifest result of the act, i.e., the act must *symbolize* the legal function. In contrast, a punitive act is legal in the sense that it performs a legal function, but its physical enactment is the same as its legal function. A punitive act is therefore not symbolic. What is more, the punitive act is more easily understood than a symbolic act, since it does not involve more than the physical enactment of the act. A symbolic act, in contrast, relates to yet another item which should be understood by the interpreter, if the symbolic act is to function properly. This is usually balanced by the conventional character of symbols, namely that their meanings are commonly agreed upon.[29] This agreement then resides within the socio-cultural context in which the symbol is used. The context therefore limits the range of possible meanings for a symbol. This function of the context is of vital importance in the attempt to understand what a symbol means in a particular instance. On the other

---

[29] See Firth (1973:60).

hand, a symbolic act may be non-conventional, which leaves it up to the performance of the act to communicate the symbolic meaning of the act.

1.2.2 Conventional and Innovative Acts

The particular character of legal symbolic acts can be enhanced by comparing them with another group of symbolic acts in the OT, namely the symbolic acts of the prophets. Fohrer, who has made a well-known study of these acts, seeks to separate the symbolic acts of the prophets from on the one hand, 'magical acts' and on the other, 'profane symbolic acts'.[30] The difference between 'prophetic' and 'profane' is that the profane act lacks any religious meaning, whereas the prophetic act is virtually founded on divine authority. This means that legal symbolic acts would be included in the profane symbolic acts.

What is most important in comparing these prophetic acts with legal symbolic acts is that the prophetic acts are apt to be innovative rather than conventional in the construction of their meanings.[31] This of course suits the situation of the OT prophets, since they were not likely to communicate things that were generally agreed upon. Instead, they used symbolic acts to communicate new and often astonishing information, which then had to be made clear by the performance of the acts. A conventional act, on the other hand, is not meant to be understood simply by discerning how it is performed, as is the case with an innovative act. Instead, the conventional act is supposed to be understood by relating its performance to a particular meaning which is generally agreed to be related to that particular act. An important consequence of this is that a legal symbolic act, being a conventional act, must be performed in strict adherence to how it is agreed upon to be performed, if it will achieve its aim of effecting a certain legal change.

A legal symbolic act is then conventional because its legal function can not be understood simply by understanding how the act is performed. Instead, the meaning of the act must be sought for outside the mere performance of the act, namely in the socio-cultural context where the act is performed and where it receives its status as conventional. However, the legal symbolic acts in the OT are only available for study in literary form. The best way to understand how they functioned in their socio-cultural context is then to understand how they are used in their respective literary

---

[30] Fohrer (1968:104-7).

[31] Alonso Schökel (1988:113) even calls the prophetic acts pantomimes. The relationship between an innovative act and a conventional act can be compared with the relationship between a newly created metaphor and a frozen one.

context.[32] Another way of saying this would be that the acts should be understood in the way they function and are used within the textual worlds in which they are found.

However, earlier studies of these acts have made the mistake of turning to the procedure in their search for the legal function. The search has then lead to the historical explanation of the act, since the historical explanation endeavours to explain how the legal function was originally connected to a particular performance. That, however, is not the proper way to understand the legal function. This can be compared to the mistake of confusing the etymological explanation of a word with what the word means when it is used.[33] The same distinction between history and use should be made regarding legal symbolic acts, which is the main reason why this analysis emphasizes the literary context. In the attempt to understand the legal function it is the use of the act which is important and not its history.

1.2.3 Legal Symbolic Acts and Performatives

Since a legal symbolic act has the ability not only to communicate certain information but also to bring about a certain legal result, it can be compared to a performative sentence. A performative sentence has the ability to accomplish what it describes, when it is stated under the proper circumstances.[34] It is interesting to note that scholars from different areas of study have lately come to similar conclusions regarding the 'performative' nature of certain acts. A review of some of the attempts in this direction will therefore be given here. It should be remembered, however, that the attempt here is not to apply the term 'performative' to legal symbolic acts, since that term should be restricted to the verbal code in order to avoid confusion. The point is rather to illustrate the efficaciousness of these legal symbolic acts by comparing them with performatives.

---

[32] See Gorman (1990:25) for a similar line of argument in relation to the interpretation of OT priestly rituals. He holds that in order to understand the socio-cultural context of the rituals, "close attention to the language used to depict the ritual situation must be a focal point of attention. Language is the means for opening up the possibilities of what the social field of the Priestly ritual might have been. At the same time, however, it can also act as a constraint on what the social field was not." The constraining function of the literary context is of major importance in understanding symbols in general.

[33] See e.g. Lyons (1968:45-50, 407).

[34] See Austin (1975:6-7) and Lyons (1977:725-45). For the more elaborate terminology of locutional, illocutional and perlocutional, see Lyons (1977:730).

Tambiah, working in the area of anthropology, regards rituals as performative acts.[35] He also makes a clear analogy between the performative status of the ritual act and the words which usually accompany the act. This is of importance in relation to those legal symbolic acts in this analysis which are accompanied with what appear to be performative utterances. As when the ritual is an amalgam of word and act, the same might very well apply in those instances where a legal symbolic act is used together with an utterance.[36]

Hillers regards ancient Near Eastern legal acts, or rites as he prefers to call them, as performatives.[37] However, he incorrectly puts an either-or distinction between the symbolic character of the acts on the one hand and their performative character on the other. The reason why Hillers makes this distinction seems to be that according to his terminology, for an act to be 'symbolic' means that the symbolic meanings of the parts that make up the acts are relevant and added together. What he seems to forget is that the act as such has a symbolic meaning.

Allwood, working in the area of linguistics, uses the expression "communicative acts" in order to include both verbal and non-verbal acts.[38] What makes these communicative acts so distinct is their so-called "conventional force". To perform an act with this force, "commits either the individual using it, or the social institution he represents, to a certain set of social consequences."[39] He notes further that "A very special type of conventional force is that which is legally codified. Here, we could talk of legal force."[40] These conventional communicative acts are what Austin called performatives, while Allwood uses the more precise expression "institutionalized performatives" to emphasize the close connection between the act and the social institution.[41] When communicative acts have conventional force and are institutionalized activities, they have to be performed according to the precise conventions which regulate the potential success of the acts. Allwood also describes these acts as "symbolic behaviour that takes place in highly institutionalized ritualistic types of communication such as legal proceedings or religious ceremonies."[42]

---

[35] Tambiah (1985:78-80).

[36] This relationship between verbal and non-verbal forms of communication is taken up by Kruger (1989:54-5) in his study of non-verbal communication in the Ugaritic "Baal epic".

[37] Hillers (1990:359-63).

[38] Allwood (1987:179).

[39] Allwood (1987:122).

[40] Allwood (1987:122).

[41] Allwood (1987:203-4).

[42] Allwood (1987:121).

This illustration makes it even more clear than before that a legal symbolic act will only perform its legal function in so far as it conforms to the legal conventions of the socio-cultural context in which it is used. What legal symbolic acts gain in clarity and unambiguousness by their character as "institutionalized performatives", to use Allwood's expression, they lose by not being able to communicate innovatively. They must adhere to the conventional performance in order to communicate their conventional information. It is only by reusing legal symbolic acts in non-legal contexts that they can be made to communicate something beyond their conventional quantity of information. In doing that, however, they cease to be specifically legal and remain as symbolic acts in general, similar to the prophetic acts described above.

1.3 What Makes a Symbolic Act Legal?

When a symbolic act in the OT is found to be conventional, according to what has been said above, its meaning depends on a common agreement on how it should function. When such a conventional symbolic act is related to the particular socio-cultural sphere of law, the common agreement to which the act refers is some form of law. What, then, does it mean for a conventional symbolic act in the OT to be legal, and on what form of law is such an act based?

In order to explain what it is that makes the symbolic acts of this analysis legal, the concept of 'customary law' will be presented as the form of law on which these acts are based. Customary law is basically the manifestation of certain social norms which are held by people at large within a certain social group. Such norms regulate behaviour in different areas, in this case legal practice. The basis upon which customary law then functions is the overall agreement on these norms. Indeed, the existence of a society which functions on the basis of customary law is dependent on the common adherence to these particular social norms. In what sense a social norm is legal is defined more precisely by Hoebel:

> A social norm is legal if its neglect or infraction is regularly met, in threat or in fact, by the application of physical force by an individual or group possessing the socially recognized privilege of so acting.[43]

When such a legal norm is applied in a particular case, it takes the physical form of a legal custom, e.g. a legal symbolic act. Since the social norm which brings meaning to the custom is legal, it follows that the custom is

---

[43] Hoebel (1954:28).

also of a legal nature.[44] The customary law of the ancient Israelite society can then be defined as the sum of its legal norms, together with their corresponding legal customs. For example, the legal symbolic act of royal anointing in the OT was only legal in so far as it was performed according to the norm which was agreed upon by people governing how someone became king. When the norm was applied, it took the form of a legal custom, namely the anointing of the one who was to be king. Any attempt to make someone king without abiding by this norm and without following the legal custom would have been opposed, if necessary by force. In contrast, if such an attempt had not been met with opposition, royal anointing would not have been legal. However, when the society of ancient Israel became monarchical, a conflict inevitably arose between the conventional norms and the norms behind the monarchical jurisdiction.[45]

Excursus: Customary Law in the OT

Since customary law is of such an importance in understanding the legal background for the legal symbolic acts in the OT, some of the basic characteristics of the customary law of the OT will be presented. The following summary is based on a study by Bellefontaine,[46] who distinguishes customary law from what she calls simple conventions, non-judicial norms and law. The law is then seen as a social control from a centralized authority. Simple conventions, non-judicial norms and customary law would have operated into monarchical times, when state law started to take over as centralization began to take shape. The basic characteristics of customary law as it is found in the OT are as follows:

1. Customary law is local, mainly on the level of the *mišpāḥâ*, the clan. Some legal symbolic acts in this analysis are on the lower level of the *bêt ʾāb*, the family, where the paterfamilias, the male head of the family, held the absolute authority.[47]

2. Customary law is oral. The moment at which it is written down tends to coincide with the point when it ceases to function as customary law. This should be compared with the distinction made below between the origin of

---

[44] See Gorman (1990:18) for a similar line or argument regarding how a particular view of the world order gives rise to a particular system of conduct in the form of rituals.

[45] So e.g. Wilson (1990:197-201). Reviv (1989:92-4) holds that the "traditional law", which is called customary law here, was never replaced by state law, although he notes that the OT does not say much about state law.

[46] Bellefontaine (1987:51-3). Her list has been expanded here in order to suit the study of legal symbolic acts.

[47] See Bellefontaine (1987:49) and Niehr (1987:42-50). For family law in the OT in general, see e.g. Phillips (1973).

the individual laws of the OT law-codes as customary law and the function of the law-codes themselves.

3. Customary law is general but concrete. The general prescription is applied to a particular case where it is interpreted, and then it reverts to its general state. This is unfortunately very difficult, if not impossible to describe from the way customary law is handled in the OT. To know how this application was made we would need access to the form which customary law had before it was applied. However, this is not available.

4. Customary law is sanctioned, which means that it has been given a certain authority to be legitimate and functional. This authority then rests on different levels, depending on the nature and circumstances of the incident. Within the family it was the paterfamilias who had the authority, but if a case went beyond one particular family, the elders of the town would function as judges or witnesses, as in Ruth 4. On the higher level of the šēbeṭ/maṭṭê, the tribe, the connection between the towns was probably rather loose, which made judicial activity between them more difficult. This may be the reason why the OT contains very few examples of jurisdiction at this level. One example, however, is the act of the Levite in Judg 19:29-30 and the following punitive act against the tribe of Benjamin in Judg 20. It was apparently the absence of a common leader that made the execution of judicial authority more difficult on the tribal level.

5. Customary law usually requires some form of 'court' to perform a judicial function. This does not necessarily have to be a particular judge or group of judges. It might just as well be the local public opinion which fulfils this function.[48] This local authority applies the general laws but does not create them, since they merely function under the common approval of certain cultural conventions. However, on the level of the family there would be no need for a public opinion since the paterfamilias had the ultimate authority and thereby fulfilled this function. The customary law which is performed at this level is then called 'family law'. It was only when matters had to be dealt with between families within the same town that the local public or judges had to be resorted to.

So far, law has been considered in the form of customary law. However, the OT also contains several collections of written laws, or codified law.[49] The problem then is how to to correlate the two concepts of codified law and customary law. This can be compared to an ongoing discussion concerning the function of the various legal codes from the ancient Near East. When these law-codes were discovered, they were first thought to have been normative, in the modern sense of the term. However, there later

---

[48] See Hoebel (1954:25). Jackson (1989:197) notes that much of the Book of the Covenant may be described as "self-executing laws", formulated so as to avoid recourse to third-party adjudication.

[49] See e.g. Boecker (1984:116-65).

arose the consensus view that they had been academic exercises and not normative legislations, something which Westbrook has shown convincingly in a recent study.[50] Jackson even holds that their purposes were only didactic, sapiential and monumental.[51]

When this discussion is applied to the law of the OT, however, it should be remembered that it relates to the function of the law-codes as such. It is quite clear from the study of the individual laws, on the other hand, that they have originated as part of customary law.[52] The legal symbolic acts which are described in the OT law-codes and studied here, the act of piercing the ear of the slave in Exod 21:6, together with its parallel in Deut 15:12-17, and the act of removing the sandal in Deut 25:9, should therefore be considered to have been part of customary law. The literary formation of the codes, on the other hand, may very well have a later, scribal origin.[53]

1.4 A Variety of Legal Functions

The purpose of a legal symbolic act is to bring about a certain legal change, i.e., a change whose validity is based upon the compliance with certain legal norms. These acts can also be called efficacious,[54] since they effect a certain legal change, something which has been shown above in the comparison with performative sentences. It would be useful, however, to be able to make a more specific distinction among the various legal functions of the acts in this analysis. An important criteria which can be used to make such a distinction is the possible relationship between the legal symbolic act and a prior agreement. When an act relates back to an agreement, the legal function of the act is to ratify that agreement, i.e., to put the agreement into working order.[55] The nature of a ratifying legal function is then to effectuate a prior agreement. The other main form of legal function is that which does not refer to a prior agreement. This form is naturally

---

[50] Westbrook (1989). Cf. also Westbrook (1985; 1988).

[51] Jackson (1989:186). Similarly also Malul (1990:106).

[52] So Jackson (1989:199), who proposes an early customary origin for the individual laws in the Book of the Covenant. Otto (1988:93, n. 217) also holds that the laws in the Book of the Covenant were derived from practice and not academic exercises.

[53] So e.g. Jackson (1989:199), who holds that the literary structuring of these laws has a scribal, court origin and should be dated later than the individual laws. Otto (1991:175-9) also holds that the formation of the larger structural units of the law arose in a different context, namely in an urban culture and possibly in scribal schools.

[54] For this term, see Patrick (1985:233), who relates it to ratification.

[55] See Black (1979:1135), where 'ratification' is described as "the confirmation of a previous act done either by the party himself or by another; as, confirmation of a voidable act."

broader than the ratifying legal function, since it not only effects the legal change, but also encompasses the content of the legal change. A legal symbolic act with such a function is said in this analysis to 'accomplish' the legal change.

> The legal agreement which is referred to and ratified by means of various legal symbolic acts is usually called *běrît* in the texts which are scrutinized in this analysis. Unfortunately, this is a word which has caused serious problems to OT scholars, not only in relation to its etymology, but also in relation to how it is used in the OT.[56] This has then influenced the discussion as to how *běrît* should be translated. However, this is an area of study which has not been dealt with in this analysis. The word *běrît* is therefore translated here consistently with "covenant", not in any particular legal sense but only as a common way of translating *běrît* into English.[57] When a legal agreement made outside of ancient Israel is referred to, it is called a 'treaty'.

The legal functions of the acts in this analysis are then described on three levels. Firstly, they all effectuate a certain legal change, which is the overall description. The second level is whether a legal function relates to a prior agreement or not, i.e., whether it is a case of ratification or accomplishment. On the third level the legal functions are described in the way they function in each particular case. With the act of lifting the hand in oath-taking as an example, its legal function is, on the first level, to effectuate an oath. On the second level, the legal function is to accomplish the oath, since no prior agreement is referred to. On the third level, Abram's act of lifting the hand in Gen 14:22 accomplishes the oath which he takes in relation to the King of Sodom.

---

[56] See e.g. Kutsch (1973), Weinfeld (1973), Mettinger (1976:301-4), Barr (1977), McCarthy (1981:1-24), Nicholson (1986), Brettler (1989:134) and Høgenhaven (1990).

[57] See e.g. Barr (1977:36) and McCarthy (1981:10). The study of Barr (1977) is an excellent treatment of the word *běrît*, since Barr takes into consideration the important linguistic distinctions of synchronic-diachronic and paradigmatic-syntagmatic in his analysis.

2 Analysis of Legal Symbolic Acts

2.1 Raising the Hand

2.1.1 Introduction

The act of raising the hand occurs in the OT with various functions, such as to take an oath, to display power, often in a hostile sense, to pray and to bless. It is also described with several different expressions, namely *hêrîm yād*, *nāśāʾ yād* and *nûp yād*.[1]

The following analysis will concentrate on the occurrences of the act which have a legal function related to oath-taking. This will involve the two expressions for raising the hand *hêrîm yād* and *nāśāʾ yād*. They are both used with the functions of oath-taking and hostile display of power, but they differ when it comes to prayer and blessing, where only *nāśāʾ* is used. It is therefore not surprising to find that *nāśāʾ* is used in Ezekiel for oath-taking and not *hêrîm*. This will be returned to below in the analysis of the texts from Ezekiel.

2.1.2 Procedure

The procedure of this act is fairly simple, although it is uncertain to what degree the hand was raised. Was only the forearm raised, and if so, was the upper arm straight or bent downwards, or was the whole arm raised, perhaps with a slight bend at the elbow? It appears that no exact description of the act can be made. A likely reason for this is that the procedure could vary somewhat, without affecting the legal function.

It is never stated whether the right or left hand was used. However, considering the higher symbolic status of the right hand in general, it would seem natural that it was used in this act. There are some texts that may show that the right hand was used in several similar legal contexts. In Ps 144:8 and 11 the liar's right hand is *yěmîn šeqer*, a "deceitful right hand".[2] This probably refers to a handshake that once confirmed an agreement which has subsequently been broken. Another alternative, however, would be to take "right hand" as a metonymy for the oath itself. An interesting parallel could then be found in Zech 8:17, which speaks of a *šěbūʿat šeqer*,

---

[1] The expression *nûp yād* has earlier been translated as "wave the hand", but the proper translation should be to "raise the hand", so Milgrom (1983:133, n. 8) and Ackroyd (1982:443).

[2] My translation.

"deceitful oath".[3] Furthermore, in Gen 48:17 Jacob lays the right hand on the head of Ephraim in giving him the blessing. In Isa 62:8 God takes an oath, but since he cannot take it by himself, he takes it by the strength of his right hand. These texts show, then, that it was undoubtedly the right hand that was raised in taking an oath.

Excursus: Deuteronomy 32:40 According to the LXX

An interesting argument in the same direction, i.e., that it was the right hand that was raised, is the LXX reading of Deut 32:40: ὅτι ἀρῶ εἰς τὸν οὐρανὸν τὴν χεῖρά μου καὶ ὀμοῦμαι τῇ δεξιᾷ μου καὶ ἐρῶ Ζῶ ἐγὼ εἰς τὸν αἰῶνα, "Behold I raise up my hand to heaven and I swear with my right hand and I say, I am forever." The middle part, καὶ ὀμοῦμαι τῇ δεξιᾷ μου, "and I swear with my right hand", is not found in the MT. The most probable explanation is that the translator has inserted this phrase in order to explain the act of raising the hand, described in the immediately preceding phrase. The dative τῇ δεξιᾷ could be taken in two ways, either as swearing by the right hand, which would be exceptional since it is never stated with a pure dative in the LXX, but mostly with κατά, as in Isa 62:8, or as describing the means by which the swearing was performed. This instrumental use is found in the LXX in Lev 14:27 (τῷ δεξιῷ); Judg 7:20; 16:29 and Isa 41:10. There is also an example with ἐν in Gen 48:13. This shows that the translator thought of an act as being performed, and with the right hand in particular.

Lust holds that the LXX reading is to be preferred, however. This is due to his thesis that the phrase *nāśā᾽ yād* does not refer to an act that is performed in connection with an oath, but to an act done either in favour of someone or against someone. However, Lust fails to show why the LXX reading is to be preferred, and in particular how the shorter text of the MT came about. The LXX reading of Deut 32:40 will be returned to below under Legal Function, together with a more elaborate refutation of Lust's thesis.

What is significant in the description of the procedure of this act is that only one hand is used. When two hands are raised it is always done in the context of prayer or blessing.[4]

The only example which is explicitly a matter of oath and still describes the use of two hands is Dan 12:7. This exception, however, can be explained by the particular circumstances which will be described below

---

[3] My translation.

[4] See Gruber (1980:32-41). Gruber (1980:32-3) actually claims that the expression *nāśā᾽ yādayim* occurs in Ezek 20:6 and the other relevant passages of that book, which is never the case. It is always the singular of *yād* that is used.

under Legal Function. As a matter of fact, it would seem that it is only against the background of the custom of using one hand that the use of two hands in Dan 12:7 becomes understandable.

2.1.3 Legal Function

2.1.3.1 Introduction

It is no new insight that this act is connected with oath-taking.[5] However, at a closer scrutiny of the relevant texts it will be apparent that the relationship between the act itself and the oath-taking is difficult to ascertain. Usually the act has been considered complementary to the oath-taking,[6] or as part of the oath, or again as synonymous with swearing an oath.[7] This will be discussed in the analysis below.

The texts to be studied are Gen 14:22 where Abram performs this act in an account of his meeting with the king of Sodom, Dan 12:7 where an angel performs a similar act in a vision, and Deut 32:40 where God is described anthropomorphically as raising his hand while taking an oath, which is also found in Exod 6:8; Num 14:30; Ezek 20:5 (2), 6, 15, 23, 28, 42; 36:7; 44:12; 47:14; Ps 106:26 and Neh 9:15.[8]

2.1.3.2 Genesis 14:22

This is the only text where a human is described as performing this act, while otherwise the act is performed by an angel or God. This makes Gen 14:22 the most important occurrence of this act, since the texts which describe the act as performed by an angel or God are apt to have been influenced by their visionary and anthropomorphic character.

To begin with, the literary context will be searched for indications of a legal context, which would then argue for a legal function of the act.

The context is a meeting between Abram, here pictured somewhat like a warrior-leader,[9] and the king of Sodom. Abram has just been described as the saviour of Sodom, and the king of the city presents a plan to satisfy

---

[5] See e.g. Woude (1971:670), Giesen (1981:43) and Ackroyd (1982:439, 453).

[6] So e.g. Westermann (1981:238) and Wenham (1987:318).

[7] So e.g. Horst (1957:379) and Schatz (1972:267).

[8] Römer (1990:504-6) has grouped all cases of the expression *nāśā' yād* with God as subject into four categories; oaths of punishment, oaths in Egypt to declare himself and promise the exodus, oaths concerning the land and, finally, oaths of punishment during the desert wandering. Since this is not directly relevant to the question of legal function, but more to the question of the application of the oath, it will not be elaborated here.

[9] So Muffs (1982:81-2) and Wenham (1987:319).

both parties. According to this plan, Abram can keep the booty as long as the king gets the people back, v. 21. Some kind of agreement between the two parties would then be expected, which could be the proper context of a legal act. However, Abram does not agree with this proposal from the king of Sodom, and the reason seems to be that he does not want to be shown to have received any support from the king, vv. 23-24. In order to strengthen this decision he takes an oath, v. 22, which is then negative in its character.

It is important to note that the undertakings between the two parties concern the booty and the prisoners from the capture of Sodom, which Abram has restored, vv. 11 and 16. It is also interesting that the expression *ʾim-miḥûṭ wĕ͑ad śĕrôk-na͑al*, "neither thread nor sandal-lace"[10] in v. 23 can be shown to be a variant of a rather common ancient Near Eastern formula for expressing totality, or in this case in negated form, absolutely nothing. This expression is often found in legal contexts.[11] It would therefore seem that the context argues for a legal function of the act of raising the hand.

The construction of the oath will now be analysed in order to understand the legal function of the act. The analysis of oaths in relation to the legal symbolic act of raising the hand will be based on the work of Thorion.[12] He has made a thorough investigation of both the various parts which make up the of oaths in the OT, as well as the different ways of constructing oaths.

Excursus: The Constituents of Oaths in the OT

Thorion distinguishes between three parts which can make up an oath or a description of an oath, namely the oath introduction, the oath formula and the oath content.[13] It is not necessary for all three parts to be present for the oath to be complete. The oath content is mandatory, whereas the other two components are not. In fact, it is only rarely that all three are found composing an oath.[14]

---

[10] My translation.

[11] See Speiser (1934) and Muffs (1982). Cf. e.g. PRU IV, 17.340:31.

[12] Thorion (1984). Other technical analyses of the construction of oaths are GKC (471-2), Joüon (1923:503-5), Nyberg (1952:315-6), Leeuwen (1973:34-8) and Waltke & O'Connor (1990:678-80), but they are not as thorough as Thorion's analysis. Lehmann (1969) also studies the oath in the OT, but with a one-sided approach by which he seeks to read blessings and especially curses into the oaths. He also stresses the possibility of dating texts by means of their oath-formulas. Both these methodological principles are highly doubtful.

[13] Thorion (1984:42). His terms are "Schwurvorspruch", "Schwurformel" and "Schwurinhalt".

[14] So Thorion (1984:44).

The oath introduction is that part where it is declared that the oath-taking party is about to take an oath, e.g. *wayyiššābaʿ hammelek*, "The king swore", 1 Kgs 1:29.

The oath formula is the part where the oath-taking party declares the basis upon which his oath rests, e.g. *ḥay-yhwh*, "As the Lord lives", 1 Kgs 1:29. Two uses of the verb *šābaʿ* in the niphal are to be noted. When the verb is in the first person suffix conjugation, it either describes an oath taken in the past, or it functions as part of the oath-taking, and is then an oath formula.[15] This is a distinction that is not quite clear in Thorion's work, and the analysis of Ezek 20:5-6 below, under Legal Function, will depart from Thorion's view in this case.

The oath content is where the oath-taking party declares what is to be upheld by means of the oath. The oath content can be either asyndetic or not. When syndetic, it is introduced by certain introductory words or phrases, such as *ʾim* or *kî* in various combinations. When *ʾim* stands before the verb, e.g. *ʾim-yitkappēr*, 1 Sam 3:14, the verb together with the whole clause is negated, "shall not be expiated".[16]

In applying Thorion's model to Gen 14:22, the part that matches with the expression *hărîmōtî yādî ʾel-yhwh ʾēl ʿelyôn qōnēh šāmayim wāʾāreṣ*, "I raise my hand to the Lord, El Elyon, the creator of heaven and earth",[17] is the oath formula.[18] What follows in vv. 23-24 is then the oath content. It is introduced with *ʾim*, which negates the verb.[19] No oath introduction is used in this text.

---

[15] So Thorion (1984:43).

[16] Concerning the historical explanation of the oath construction, especially the question of a self-imprecatory clause, see GKC (472), Joüon (1923:505), Nyberg (1952:315), Lehmann (1969:86-7), Leeuwen (1973:37) and Waltke & O'Connor (1990:679). GKC, Lehmann, Leeuwen and Nyberg all argue for the rather common view that there was originally a self-imprecatory clause of which only the particle *ʾim*, "if" remains. This *ʾim* then came to mean "surely not" and when negated "surely". Joüon proposes a contamination of different forms as an explanation, and Waltke & O'Connor express doubt as to whether an explanation can be found.

[17] My translation.

[18] So Thorion (1984:44, 48).

[19] The unusual construction with two occurrences of *ʾim*, one at the beginning of v. 23 and one immediately before the verb, is probably due to the irregular word order object-predicate. The first *ʾim* can then be seen as a way of emphasizing that absolutely nothing would be accepted.

The oath formula consists of a description of an act towards God, which could be taken as an appeal for a witness.[20] God himself would then testify to the fact that Abram will keep his promise. Furthermore, it is interesting to note that Abram does not state explicitly that he is swearing an oath. This could be explained by the fact that the utterance in the oath formula is functionally equivalent with another well-known oath formula, namely *nišba'tî*, "I swear" as in 2 Sam 19:8, *byhwh nišba'tî*, "I swear by the Lord".[21] The utterance "I raise my hand", and by implication the act itself, have then gained a wider function, from that of calling for God as a witness to that of providing the basis for the whole oath-taking.

A further argument for the legal character of the act is the use of the suffix conjugation in *hărîmōtî*, "I raise up", for which the term 'instantaneous perfect' could be appropriate.[22] What is emphasized thereby is that the act is performed simultaneously with the utterance of the description of the act. However, as was shown above, the utterance together with the act has gained a further meaning, namely to function as the oath formula. In this function the use of the suffix conjugation in the utterance is more likely to be performative. Since the act is still connected to the utterance, this wider function also applies to the act. The act and the utterance would then refer to the base upon which the oath rests, which lies inherent in the oath formula. The act and the utterance thereby invoke the proper legal code, by means of which they are interpreted as a proper oath. The conclusion is then that the act, together with the utterance, is what actually makes the oath function in a legal sense. In other words, the act and the utterance together accomplish the oath.

A more literary oriented reason for the use of the expression "raise the hand" in the present context is the fact that "hand" is used earlier in the text in v. 20, where Melchizedek, priest of El Elyon, "creator of heaven and earth", says that this El Elyon will command Abram's enemies into his

---

[20] The act is sometimes used for the purpose of calling for someone, cf. Isa 13:2, where the expression *hānîpû yād* is used, and Prov 1:24, where the expression *nāṭîṭî yād* is used, see Ackroyd (1982:440). Falk (1959a:269) holds that the hand was raised as a way of taking the hand of God in entering a covenant, which is unlikely as a historical explanation. Another unlikely historical explanation of the act is proposed by Crown (1963-64:107-8), namely that it originally referred to the implied punishment which was connected with an oath. The act was therefore originally to run a finger across the throat, symbolizing to cut the throat. For this act and the describing expression *napištam lapātum*, "touch the throat" in connection with oaths in the Mari texts, see Hoskisson (1992:203-10). See also Kühne (1986:92-3).

[21] So e.g. Giesen (1981:43).

[22] See Waltke & O'Connor (1990:488).

"hand".[23] Then in v. 22 Abram swears by raising his "hand" towards the Lord El Elyon, "creator of heaven and earth". Abram thereby sides with Melchizedek against the king of Sodom.

The legal function of the act, together with the utterance, is then to accomplish the oath taken by Abram.

2.1.3.3 Daniel 12:7

In this text, Daniel has a vision of an angel who raises both hands towards heaven while taking an oath. The following part of v. 7, *wayyārem yĕmînô ûšĕmōʾlô*, "and he raised his right hand and his left hand",[24] is an oath introduction and not an oath formula, since it describes someone taking an oath in past time. This is then followed by an oath content introduced by *kî*. Since there is no oath formula, the text cannot have been considered as a proper part of an oath-taking procedure. It serves no other purpose than to describe the event, and it does not include a reference to the swearing, which is stated separately. It is, however, certainly the same act as in Gen 14:22 that is referred to, namely the act of raising a hand while taking an oath, although in this text both hands are used.

As in Gen 14:22, the act can be seen in the close context to invoke a witness to the oath that is about to be taken.[25] However, from what has been said regarding the act in Gen 14:22, it would be natural to consider the act, here as well, to function as the oath formula and thereby as the accomplishment of the oath. However, since the text merely describes the event, there is no equivalent of the utterance in Gen 14:22 which would share the function of accomplishing the oath.

That both hands of the angel are used has earlier been explained as a way of adding solemnity to the oath.[26] Another explanation can be found, however, which is due to the particular circumstances surrounding this text. Normally the act with both hands raised was exclusively meant for

---

[23] This of course evokes the source-critical question of vv. 18-20. These verses are considered by most scholars to be a later insertion into the text, e.g. Schatz (1972:82-3) and Westermann (1981:225). Doré (1981:90) considers these verses to be the peak of the narrative, as also Wenham (1987:306-7, 316), who considers the question of an insertion to be an open question, because of how vv. 18-20 are interwoven into the literary structure.

[24] My translation.

[25] So e.g. Goldingay (1989:309).

[26] So e.g. Montgomery (1927:475) and Goldingay (1989:309). According to Sittl (1890:141) this is the case with the act of raising the hand in oath-taking in the Greco-Roman culture.

praying, and then the verb used is not *hêrîm*, "raise" but *nāśāʾ*, "raise" or *pāraś*, "spread".[27] Since this is a vision which describes an angelic being addressing God, the genre has transformed the description of the act into a hybrid form, where both hands are raised in order to accomplish an oath. Such a construction is possible since the act in Dan 12:7 does not occur in a realistic context as the act in Gen 14:22, but in a visionary context, where such conventions can be relaxed.

> There is one extra-Biblical example of both hands being raised in taking an oath, namely in an Aramaic inscription by Panammu I from around 730 BC, on a statue of Hadad.[28] Panammu foresees struggles at the court after his death, and therefore lays down certain rules to regulate these struggles. In l. 28 the accused party is to speak *mt[.]nšh*, "On his oath".[29] Then in l. 29 apparently the same party *[y]śʾ ydyh*, "lifts up his hands" to his ancestral god and takes an oath. This could be a proper description of how the act was performed in this particular context. It is more likely, however, that it is the result of a mingling of two acts, raising one hand in oath-taking and two in prayer.

The legal function of the act is then to accomplish the oath-taking, similar to the function of the act in Gen 14:22.

2.1.3.4 Deuteronomy 32:40

Here God himself is described as taking an oath. The whole of v. 40, *kî-ʾeśśāʾ ʾel-šāmayim yādî weʾāmartî hay ʾānōkî leʿōlām*, "For I raise up my hand to heaven, and say, as I live forever"[30] is an oath formula, which actually consists of two oath formulas, both that he raises the hand and that he swears by himself. The oath introduction is short, only *weʾāmartî*, "and I say", and vv. 41-42 form the oath content.[31]

God raises his hand towards heaven which, when used by humans, can be seen as an appeal to God and his abode. When God himself is said to

---

[27] For examples with *nāśāʾ*, see Lev 9:22; Pss 28:2; 119:48; 134:2; Lam 2:19, and *pāraś*, see Exod 9:29; 1 Kgs 8:22, 38; Ps 44:21. Both verbs alternate between *yād* and *kap* for "hand".

[28] See Gibson (1975), 13:28-29. *KAI* 214:28-29 has a different reading.

[29] Gibson (1975:68-9).

[30] My translation.

[31] The conjunction *ʾim* which introduces the oath content in v. 40 should not be confused with the ordinary *ʾim* which is found in oaths to negate the verb. In this case it is a temporal conjunction, "when I have sharpened", see Waltke & O'Connor (1990:643). Lehmann (1969:83-4), however, takes it as a conditional particle and translates, "may I live forever if I wet my flashing sword" as being spoken by God, which is unlikely.

perform this act, however, this meaning must be redundant and the act, together with the utterance, remain with the function of accomplishing the oath. This is, then, evidence of how the function of calling for witness to the oath-taking has given way to the wider function of accomplishing the oath itself. As far as the second oath formula is concerned, it has been transformed due to the fact that God speaks in first person. He now bases the oath expressly on himself and his longevity, as in Num 14:21 and 28. These changes of the oath formulas are due to what was said earlier concerning Dan 12:7, namely the breakdown of conventions when applied to references that lie beyond the normal range of the conventions.

A literary explanation for the use of the description of this act in v. 40 can be found in analyzing the near context. In v. 39 God says that "no one can deliver from my hand", in v. 40 it is the hand that he uses to accomplish the oath and in v. 41 he describes how his hand will perform the judgement. This emphasizes the strength and power of God, and it might very well have been the reason why the author chose to use two oath formulas.

> Lust holds that the phrase in v. 40 should be interpreted in accordance with these other expressions in the near context where the hand is mentioned.[32] This is most unlikely, however, especially since Lust bases his argument on the longer reading of the LXX which, as has been argued above, is unlikely to be original. The best explanation for the addition of the phrase "And I swear with my right hand" in the LXX is that the translator has not properly understood the wider, legal function of the act in v. 40. Instead, he has attempted to clarify the description of the performance of the act.

The legal function of the act in Deut 32:40 is then similar to the function found in Gen 14:22 and Dan 12:7, namely to accomplish the oath. This also applies to the utterance, in analogy with the utterance in Gen 14:22.

2.1.3.5 Ezekiel 20:5-6 et al.

In Ezekiel there are ten instances where God is the subject of what seems like a description of the act of raising the hand, 20:5 (2), 6, 15, 23, 28, 42; 36:7; 44:12 and 47:14. Ezek 20:5-6 and 36:7 will be studied more thoroughly, while 20:15, 23, 28, 42; 44:12; 47:14, together with Exod 6:8; Num 14:30; Ps 106:26 and Neh 9:15, where the same expression occurs, will be referred to when relevant.

---

[32] Lust (1967:523; 1969:159-60).

When the immediate context of Ezek 20:5-6 is scrutinized, it is interesting to find that in v. 3 an oath is taken by God, and the oath formula is the well-known phrase *ḥay ʾānî*, "As I live". God swears that he will not be questioned, but if the prophet wants to proclaim judgement over the people, he is more than ready to comply. Ezekiel is told to remind the people of the wickedness of their forefathers, which is blatantly contrasted with the goodness of God towards the people in Egypt. This is described in vv. 5-6 in the form of an oath taken by God to make himself known to the people. These verses are structured delicately to reach a climax in v. 6 through the repetition of the phrase "I raised my hand".[33] The overarching theme is stated at the beginning of v. 5a, namely that God chose Israel. This is then elaborated further in v. 5b-c where the same content is substantially repeated twice, in both instances introduced with the phrase "I raised my hand":

5a *běyôm bohŏrî běyiśrāʾēl*
5b *waʾeśśāʾ yādî lězera*[34] *bêt yaʿăqōb*
    waʾiwwādaʿ lāhem běʾereṣ miṣrāyim
5c *waʾeśśāʾ yādî lāhem lěʾmōr ʾănî yhwh ʾĕlōhêkem*
6   *bayyôm hahûʾ nāśāʾtî yādî lāhem lěhôṣîʾām mēʾereṣ miṣrāyim*

5a On the day when I chose Israel,
5b I raised my hand concerning the seed of the house of Jacob,
    I made myself known to them in the land of Egypt.
5c I raised my hand concerning them and said, "I am the Lord your God."
6   On that day I raised my hand concerning them, to bring them out of the land of Egypt.[35]

It is clear that v. 5b-c does not constitute an oath, but anticipate the oath introduction in v. 6, *nāśāʾtî yādî*, "I raised my hand".[36] This distinction is further shown by the use of the waw prefix conjugation in v. 5b-c in contrast to the suffix conjugation in v. 6. Thorion regards v. 6a as an oath formula, but since it is a description of an act taken in the past, this can hardly be the case.[37] In v. 6 there is also a resumption of v. 5a through the

---

[33] Contrast the attempt by Lust (1967:498-9; 1969:106-8) to place v. 6 immediately before v. 10.

[34] The three cases of the preposition *lě*, translated here "concerning", are taken as denoting advantage, see Waltke & O'Connor (1990:207-8).

[35] My translation.

[36] Greenberg (1983:364) notes that v. 5 is preparatory for vv. 6f.

[37] Thorion (1984:44).

expression *bayyôm hahû*, "On that day" and of v. 5b-c by the naming of the object of God's oath. However, that which constitutes v. 6 as an oath in distinction to v. 5 is that the content of the oath is stated in v. 6; God brought the people out of Egypt.

In relation to the act which is described in Ezek 36:7, it is interesting to see how the context surrounding the description of the act is constructed as a play on the similarities between different idioms. In v. 6 the people of Israel are said to *kĕlimmat gôyim nĕśāʾtem*, lit. "raise up the disgrace of the nations". Later in v. 8, the mountains are said to *ûperyĕkem tiśʾû*, lit. "raise up their fruit" for the people. In between these two occurrences the description of the act is found in v. 7, where God takes an oath against the surrounding peoples, *ʾănî nāśāʾtî ʾet-yādî*, "I raise my hand", to the effect that they will be disgraced, *kĕlimmātām yiśśāʾû*, lit. "raise up their disgrace". A similar pun is found in 44:12, where God raises his hand in an oath against the Levites to the effect that they will pay the consequences of their sins, lit. "raise up their sins". It is possible that the expression "I raise my hand" is used in these texts because of the associations that come with the different idiomatic expressions. Since this word-play indicates an awareness of the procedure of the act, the description of the act itself should not be categorized as an idiom.

These texts describe the same act which was found earlier in Gen 14:22; Dan 12:7 and Deut 32:40, and with the same legal function of accomplishing the oath. However, since the act is used anthropomorphically in these texts, some changes have occurred. There is no longer a need for a reference to heaven, to which the raised hand is pointing, since God himself is performing the act.[38] The proper formulation of the oath is lacking, with the proper introduction to the oath content occurring only in Ezek 36:7, *ʾim-lōʾ*. This shows that the phrase has become more of a technical expression for God taking an oath.

Excursus: Why Does God Raise His Hand?

In this technical form, the expression is used interchangeably with the expression *nišbaʿtî*, "I swear", depending on in which tradition God is said to take an oath. One example is Deut 10:11: *ʾet-hāʾāreṣ ʾăšer nišbaʿtî laʾăbōtām lātēt lāhem*, "the land that I swore to their ancestors to give them." This can be compared, e.g., to Ezek 20:28: *ʾel-hāʾāreṣ ʾăšer nāśāʾtî ʾet-yādî lātēt ʾōtāh*

---

[38] See Zimmerli (1969:443), who regards the phrase *nāśāʾ yād lĕ* as originally referring to an act with the function of calling for a third part as a witness.

lāhem, "into the land which I raised my hand to give them".[39] The former expression abounds in Deuteronomy,[40] where the only example of the latter expression is in 32:40, studied above. On the other hand, the latter expression occurs, as was seen above, in Ezekiel, where the former does not.[41] Apparently, the distribution of these two expressions follows the traditional blocks of tradition, i.e., the priestly and the deuteronomic/deuteronomistic.

On the basis of this strict distribution of the two expressions, Lust argues that the reason why the priestly tradition, including Ezekiel, prefers *nāśāʾ yād* and not *nišbaʿ* is that God was not to be described as taking an oath with humans.[42] This is based upon Lust's interpretation of the act, described as *nāśāʾ yād,* as an act which is not connected with oath-taking, but as an act of dealing favourably or unfavourably with someone.[43] This would then stand in sharp contrast to the deuteronomic/deuteronomistic tradition, which had no objections against describing God in such a way. However, as has been shown above, there is a resemblance not only in the act that is described, but also in the whole construction of the oath-taking procedure in Ezek 20:5-6. This cannot point to any other function for the act than oath-taking.[44] Another argument against Lust is Deut 32:40, where he is forced to regard the expanded reading of the LXX as original. Finally, the most important text for regarding the raising of the hand as related to oath-taking, Gen 14:22, receives only two lines in Lust's study.[45]

The LXX reading of Ezek 20:5-6 shows, interestingly enough, the same tendency as in Lust's study, namely to down-play the oath-taking by God. The first occurrence of *ʾeśśāʾ yādî,* "I raised my hand" in v. 5 is read by the LXX as καὶ ἐγνωρίσθην, "and I was known". The second occurrence is translated as καὶ ἀντελαβόμην τῇ χειρί μου, "and I helped with my hand", which is also used for *nāśāʾû yādî,* "I raised my hand" in v. 6. This can

---

[39] My translation. This can be compared with the formulation of the oath in *AP* 14:5, *wymʾty ly ʿlyhm bsty,* "and you swore to me concerning them by the goddess Sati". The major difference is that the oaths in these legal documents from Elephantine are all assertory, i.e., oaths that solemnly declare the existing facts, whereas the oaths studied here from the OT are promissory, i.e., oaths that solemnize a future undertaking of the oath-taking party, see Yaron (1961:32).

[40] Deut 1:35; 10:11; 31:20, 21, 23; 34:4. There are also several examples in third person singular, e.g. 1:8; 6:10; 8:1. It also occurs in Josh 1:6; Judg 2:1 in first person, and in Josh 5:6; 21:43, 44 in third person.

[41] It also occurs in Exod 6:8; Num 14:30; Ps 106:26; Neh 9:15. For a discussion of the relationship between Exod 6:2ff. and Ezek 20, see Weimar (1973:148-9), Blum (1990:236-7) and Römer (1990:505). These scholars all tend to the view that Exod 6:8 is dependent on Ezek 20.

[42] Lust (1967:520-2; 1969:161) and Bettenzoli (1979:201).

[43] Lust (1967:517; 1969:154) and Bettenzoli (1979:201).

[44] So e.g. Zimmerli (1969:443), Weimar (1973:148-9, n. 184) and especially Römer (1990:492-3, esp. n. 7), who gives a detailed refutation of Lust's view.

[45] Lust (1967:519, n. 122; 1969:157, n. 40).

hardly be a misunderstanding on behalf of the translator, since the following examples of *nāśaʾū yād* in 20:15, 23, 28, 42; 44:12 and 47:14 are translated by ἐξαίρω, or αἴρω, "lift up". Whatever the reason for this softening of God's oath-taking is, it should be noted that it is based on the understanding of the act as occurring in the context of oath-taking. Had it been an act of good-will only, there would have been no reason for a different reading.

The legal function of the act of raising the hand which is reflected in these texts is the same as was found earlier, namely to accomplish the oath. However, the act has become less observable in these texts, due to its anthropomorphic use. The description of the act has turned into more of a technical phrase, which, however, should not be considered an idiom.

2.1.4 Historical Explanation

The legal act of raising the hand in taking an oath is based on an act which was used to call for someone, as in Isa 13:2, where the expression *hānîpû yād* is used, and in Prov 1:24, where the expression *nāṭîṭî yādî* is used. The function of this act in the context of oath-taking was originally to invoke God as a witness to the oath-taking. What then appears to have happened is that the act came to be used for the accomplishment of the oath itself.[46]

---

[46] See Dhorme (1923:145).

2.1.5 Summary and Conclusions

1. The procedure of this legal symbolic act is to raise the right hand while taking an oath. The meaning of the act does not seem to be related to any particular position of the raised hand and arm.

2. The legal function of the act of raising the hand in the context of oath-taking is to accomplish the oath. In Gen 14:22 and Deut 32:40 it shares this function with the simultaneous utterance, "I raise my hand".

3. The historical explanation of the act is that an act of calling for someone else came to be used in the context of oath-taking for invoking God as a witness to the oath-taking. This act then gained the further meaning of effectuating the accomplishment of the oath itself.

2.2 Shaking the Hand

2.2.1 Introduction

The texts that contain an expression related to a handshake can be divided in three categories. The first category includes those texts which describe a more general form of agreement, 2 Kgs 10:15; Ezra 10:19 and Ezek 17:18. The second category includes Prov 6:1; 11:15; 17:18; 22:26 and Job 17:3, which describe the handshake in the more specific legal context of an agreement of surety and pledge. The third category, in which the expression used is idiomatic and therefore does not describe the performance of an act, includes 1 Chr 29:24; 2 Chr 30:8 and Lam 5:6. Because of the idiomatic nature of the expression in this third category, these texts will not be relevant to this analysis.[1]

2.2.2 Procedure

The different expressions used for this symbolic act are *nātan yād*, lit. "give a hand" in 2 Kgs 10:15; Ezra 10:19; Ezek 17:18, and *tāqaʿ kap/yād*, lit. "strike a hand" in Prov 6:1; 11:15; 17:18; 22:26 and Job 17:3. The first expression always occurs with *yād*, "hand". The second expression always occurs with *kap*, lit. "palm", except in Job 17:3 where *tāqaʿ yād* is used. Scholars have generally been hesitant to call the symbolic act in Proverbs and Job a handshake. It is therefore usually translated quite literally as "strike a hand".[2] However, the verb *tāqaʿ* is used in the OT with several quite different meanings, e.g. blowing a horn in Josh 6:4 and Judg 3:27. To resort to the meaning of "strike" in these texts seems therefore to be a case where that which is perceived as the basic meaning is resorted to when the relevant meaning is uncertain.

In trying to find the proper reference of the phrase, it should be noted that a related meaning of the expression *tāqaʿ kap* is "to clap hands" in Nah 3:19 and Ps 47:2.[3] It would therefore seem likely that what is involved in the texts from Proverbs and Job is an act where one or perhaps both hands of each of two persons meet. The most natural conclusion would then be that the texts describe a handshake. This is especially the case if the texts

---

[1] Another idiomatic expression which relates very well historically to a handshake is *yād lĕyād*, lit. "hand to hand", in Prov 11:21 and 16:5. It denotes that something will most certainly occur, see McKane (1970:437) and Ackroyd (1982:438).

[2] So e.g. McKane (1970:321, 429, 502) and Ackroyd (1982:438-9).

[3] Another expression which means "to clap hands" is *māḥaʾ yād/kap*, lit. "strike a hand", Isa 55:12; Ezek 25:6; Ps 98:8.

containing *nātan yād*, lit. "give a hand" are taken into consideration. The fact that they have a different expression does not mean that they must refer to a different act, but simply that the two expressions mirror different legal contexts. This is the best explanation of the difference in terminology from a synchronic perspective.

From a historical perspective, however, it should be noted that the two expressions refer to two different parts of the handshake. The expression "give a hand" reflects the stretching out of the hand by both parties. It is therefore natural that the more general word for hand, *yād* has been used, since it does not specifically denote the configuration of the hand. This has then come to stand for the result of the stretching out, namely the handshake itself. The other expression, "strike a hand", however, reflects the moment when the hands clasp each other. It is therefore natural that the word for the palm has been used, namely *kap*, since the act was performed with the meeting of the palms of the hands. This has then come to stand for the whole act of the handshake.

There is a real problem in the texts studied here as to whether they describe the performance of an act, or whether they simply contain an idiomatic expression. The only text where the handshake undoubtedly occurs is 2 Kgs 10:15. The expression in Ezek 17:18 is less likely to be interpreted as an idiom, whereas the expression in Ezra 10:19 is quite problematic. In the texts dealing with surety or pledge the problem is also relevant.

Regarding the expression in Ezra 10:19, *wayyittĕnû yādām lĕhôṣîʾ*, "they gave their hands to bring out",[4] there is one major argument against interpreting it as a description of an act, namely that it is not stated with whom the men shook hands. Instead, the expression "they gave their hands" is followed by the preposition *lĕ*, "to" with an infinitive, which could argue for the fact that the expression means "they submitted to" or something similar. In a clearly idiomatic use as in 2 Chr 30:8, this prepositional construction is also used, *tĕnû-yād lyhwh*, lit. "Give a hand to the Lord".[5] The use of the expression in Ezra 10:19 would then also be idiomatic. However, the construction could be referring to the result of the act, and therefore make use of the prepositional construction. Furthermore, there are three arguments that point to the fact that a symbolic act was meant to have been performed. Firstly, in the context it is said in v. 14 that all those

---

[4] My translation.

[5] In 1 Chr 29:24 a similar construction is used, namely *nātĕnû yād taḥat šĕlōmô*, lit. "They gave a hand under Solomon", which makes the submissive character of the expression quite explicit.

who have taken foreign wives should appear before selected leaders to answer for their behaviour, and to find a way of putting the foreign women aside. This public event would be the natural context for an official symbolic act, such as a handshake. Secondly, in v. 19 the men with foreign wives are said to offer a ram. The official character of their change of heart is strengthened by the sacrifice, and this would argue for the fact that the expression "give their hands" also refers to an official act. Thirdly, the possessive pronoun in *yādām*, "their hands" argues for that the hands are actually referred to. In the instances where an idiomatic use of this expression is clearly to be found, namely 1 Chr 29:24; 2 Chr 30:8 and Lam 5:6, there is no pronoun attached.[6]

Ezek 17:18 is another instance where it is not stated with whom the handshake is performed, in this case with whom King Zedekiah shook hands. The pronoun is used however, "his hand", which argues for a reference to the performance of an act.

Considering the texts from Proverbs, it is stated in Prov 6:1 with whom the handshake was performed, *tāqaʿtā lazzār kappêkā*, "shake your hand with a stranger".[7] This, together with the fact that the pronoun is used, argues for the idea that the expression does refer to an act. However, in Prov 11:15; 17:18 and 22:26 it is not stated with whom the handshake is performed, and the pronoun is not used. On the basis of Prov 6:1, however, these other expressions can be viewed as contracted forms of the formulation in 6:1 and therefore they can be said to refer to an act as well.

In Job 17:3 it is made explicit that the handshake is performed with someone, "Who would shake my hand?"[8] Since the pronoun is used as well, it is likely that the expression refers to the performance of an act.

The conclusion is that a handshake is described in these texts, with the possible exception of Ezra 10:19.

---

[6] A similar case of idiomatic use is probably to be found in 1 Macc 6:58 with a legal function.

[7] My translation. The singular of *kap* is preferred in analogy with the other occurrences of the expression in 17:18; 22:26; Job 17:3. The singular has the external support of several manuscripts and versions, see *BHS*. It could well be a case of plene spelling of the pausal form, see GKC (97).

[8] My translation.

2.2.3 Legal Function

2.2.3.1 Introduction

The texts from Proverbs and Job present some intricate problems regarding the technical function of suretyship, which will be dealt with in order to find out what the proper legal function of the act is. The expression in Job 17:3 stands apart, not only because the other examples come from Proverbs, but because of its problematic construction. The remaining three texts, 2 Kgs 10:15; Ezra 10:19 and Ezek 17:18 all deal with agreements of a more general nature than suretyship, thus using a different terminology. The analysis will begin with the more general agreements in 2 Kgs 10:15; Ezra 10:19 and Ezek 17:18, then turn to the texts from Proverbs, 6:1; 11:15; 17:18; 22:26 and lastly deal with Job 17:3.

2.2.3.2 2 Kings 10:15

In 2 Kgs 10, Jehu continues with his campaign, and in vv. 12-16 two events on his way to Samaria are described. In vv. 12-14 Jehu meets the brothers of Ahaziah and subsequently has them killed. In vv. 15-16 he meets Jehonadab, son of Rechab, and they become allies. The agreement is shown both by means of a question posed by Jehu and answered by Jehonadab, and a request by Jehu for an act, *těnâ ʾet-yādekā*, "give your hand",[9] which is then performed by Jehonadab. This act demonstrates more than just a helping hand from Jehu's side to assist Jehonadab up into the chariot, which a closer analysis of the context will bring out.[10]

Jehu starts with a question in v. 15 which can be seen as a condition for a possible agreement between the two, *hăyēš ʾet-lěbāběkā yāšār kaʾăšer lěbābî ʿim-lěbābekā*, "Is your heart as true to mine as mine is to yours?" This statement is usually regarded as a rather clumsy construction.[11] However, in the light of the fact that this occurs in preparation for a binding agreement, it should not be surprising to find some unusually technical formulations.[12]

Jehonadab subsequently assures his loyalty to Jehu, which leads to a request from Jehu for a confirmation by asking Jehonadab to give him his

---

[9] My translation.

[10] A similar case where entering the chariot of a superior is a sign of agreement is 1 Kgs 20:33.

[11] So e.g. Hobbs (1985:122), but see Cogan & Tadmor (1988:115) for a different view.

[12] Another, similarly unusual expression used to declare loyalty is found in 1 Kgs 22:4 and 2 Kgs 3:7, *kāmônî kāmôkā kěʿammî kěʿammekā kěsûsay kěsûsêkā*, "I am as you are, my people are as your people, my horses are as your horses." (My translation.)

hand. Jehonadab does this, and the immediate consequence of the agreement is that he is brought up into Jehu's chariot[13] to join him in his campaign against Samaria.

As mentioned earlier, the act of giving the hand can be interpreted as an attempt by Jehu to help Jehonadab up into the chariot. It is hard to decide whether this meaning is present or not. Perhaps it is not a question of choosing either the legal function of ratifying an agreement or the helping hand. The meaning of the helping hand would then be supportive to the legal function of ratifying the agreement.

The conclusion is that the handshake ratifies the agreement made between Jehu and Jehonadab. This is also a case where the agreement is made on a personal level. Although the two parties are of different rank, it is difficult to decide whether this has any relevance for the legal function of the act.

2.2.3.3 Ezekiel 17:18

In Ezek 17:1-21 there is a riddle[14] in vv. 1-10 with its solution given in vv. 11-21. The whole thrust of the solution is that King Zedekiah of Judah has, by his behaviour, despised the oath which he has taken, and thereby broken the covenant which he has entered.[15] This is repeated three times in vv. 16, 18 and 19. In v. 15 the breaking of the covenant alone is mentioned. What is described in v. 13 as an oath and a covenant between Zedekiah and the Babylonian king, is in v. 19 said by God to be an oath and a covenant which have been made in relation to him, and then despised and broken.

In v. 18 there is a triad of expressions for the agreement or broken agreement made by Zedekiah, *ûbāzâ ʾālâ lĕhāpēr bĕrît wĕhinnê nātan yādô*, "And he despised the oath and so broke the covenant, even though he had given his hand."[16] In addition to the double expression mentioned above, namely the despised oath and the broken covenant, there is also the expression *nātan yādô*, "he had given his hand". This is probably a reference to a symbolic act on Zedekiah's behalf, referring to his submission as a vassal under his suzerain, the Babylonian king. There is a difference between this expression and the other two in v. 18, in that while the former two describe the broken relationship, *nātan yādô*, "he had given his hand"

---

[13] See Barrick (1982:482-3) for the precise formulation.

[14] For the relevance of this term for *māšāl*, see Brownlee (1986:259).

[15] The combination of "despise an oath" with "break a covenant" in v. 18 is made with the preposition *lĕ* and an infinitive construct, the meaning of which would be epexegetical. See Waltke & O'Connor (1990:608).

[16] My translation.

refers to the point in time when the vassal-suzerain relationship was established. The author achieves this transition very eloquently by using *wĕhinnê*, lit. "and behold", thus changing the scenic description for the reader.[17] The reader is, for a very short time, transported back to the moment when according to 2 Kgs 24:17, the Babylonian king made Jehoiachin's uncle Mattaniah king in Jerusalem and re-named him Zedekiah, cf. Jer 37:1. If it is correct to take this expression as referring to the symbolic act of shaking hands between Zedekiah and the Babylonian king, it means that the symbolic act was not only used between parties of equal status but also between parties of such unequal status as Zedekiah and the Babylonian king. This example is even clearer than the one examined earlier concerning the handshake between Jehu and Jehonadab.

The legal function of the handshake would in this case have been to ratify the vassal-suzerain agreement between the two parties. It is likely that the handshake occurred simultaneously with the oath, since the oath had a similar function.

Excursus: A Diplomatic Handshake

A relief-picture in the central position on the front of a throne-base from Nimrud describes a handshake between two noble parties. The one at the right is Shalmanezer III, King of Assyria and the one at the left is without doubt Marduk-zakir-shumi, King of Babylon.[18] At the back of the throne-base there is an inscription belonging to the picture, which contains what must surely be an explanation of what is illustrated in the picture. Marduk-zakir-shumi's brother, Marduk-bel-usate, had apparently revolted, after which Shalmanezer III stepped in and set things straight. The text reads as follows: "I struck down Marduk-bel-usate with the sword, (and) established Marduk-zakir-shumi on the throne of his father."[19] This would mean that although Marduk-zakir-shumi was the legitimate heir to the Throne of Babylon, he was installed by the power of Shalmanezer III, King of Assyria. It is likely that Shalmanezer III made some form of treaty with Marduk-zakir-shumi after he had struck down the rebellion.[20]

---

[17] See Berlin (1983:91) for this particular use of this phrase.

[18] So e.g. Mallowan (1966:446) and Brinkman (1968:196, n. 1199). Weidner (1966:151) offers a different interpretation, namely that both figures are Shalmanezer III. That one could be Marduk-zakir-shumi is for Weidner out of the question, since such a parity agreement would be both unparalleled and unthinkable under the historical circumstances. However, Weidner has been criticized by Brinkman (1968:196, n. 1199).

[19] Hulin (1963:55-6, 64).

[20] So e.g. Mallowan (1966:445).

The museum of Baghdad 65574. Nimrud, Throne-room of Fort Shalmanezer. The relief is made of yellow limestone, and its height is 20 cm. The figure is from Keel (1984:85), used with permission by the author.

There are two important conclusions that can be drawn from the analysis of this picture. Firstly, the handshake was used in Assyria in the 9th century BC to ratify an agreement. Secondly, the handshake was used to ratify an agreement on the level of international diplomacy, apparently on a parity level.[21]

2.2.3.4 Ezra 10:19

As was concluded above under Procedure, this text contains an expression that could be regarded as idiomatic, although it would seem that an interpretation of the expression as describing an act is somewhat more likely. The analysis of the legal function below naturally presupposes the reference to an act, although the problematic nature of the expression must be kept in mind.

In Ezra 10:1 the people react to the prayer of Ezra, and Shecaniah approaches him to acknowledge the sin of the people in marrying foreign women. In v. 3 he says: "So now let us make a covenant with our God to send away all these wives and their children".[22] In v. 5 Ezra requires the

---

[21] This confirms the opinion of Munn-Rankin (1956:86), that "an international agreement was confirmed by some such formal gesture as clasping or striking hands." Munn-Rankin makes this deduction from an acta contraria, namely to thrust back a hand outstretched in friendship in order to turn down an offer or to terminate an agreement.

[22] This should not be seen as a new covenant but as a renewal of an already existent covenant, so e.g. Fensham (1982:134). See also Clines (1984:126). There is a parallel to this in 2 Kgs 23:1-3.

leaders of the people to swear an oath, thereby binding them to carry through this commitment. This oath is probably connected with the covenant, but not identical with it. In v. 11 Ezra encourages the people to confess their unfaithfulness in marrying foreign women. In v. 19, those who have taken foreign women as wives pledge to put them away. The promise is formulated as *wayyittĕnû yādām*, "they gave their hands".[23] This would then mean that the handshake was a ratification of the agreement made, namely that the foreign wives would be taken away. The text does not state with whom the men shook hands, which, as was said above under Procedure, is an argument in favour of an idiomatic interpretation of the expression.

However, on the basis of the interpretation of the expression as referring to an act, the legal function would be to ratify the agreement between the men and the leaders of the people.

2.2.3.5 Proverbs 6:1

Here is an admonition not to stand as surety for a neighbour, since it may have disastrous consequences.[24] The text says, *bĕnî ʾim-ʿārabtā lĕrēʿekā tāqaʿtā lazzār kappêkā*, "My son, if you have entered surety for a neighbour and shaken your hand with a stranger".[25] In order to understand the legal function of the symbolic act in question, the identity of the *zār*, "stranger" must be disclosed.[26] Is he the same person as *rēaʿ*, "neighbour" or are they two different persons? Scholars have disagreed over this point and no consensus seems to have developed.[27] In favour of the view that two different persons are involved, the argument is generally put forth that "stranger" can hardly be used for the same person as "neighbour". In favour of the view that they are indeed referring to the same person is the parallel construction of the verse. On the assumption that the parallelism is roughly synonymous, "neighbour" will correspond with "stranger". There is also the evidence from the other occurrences of this expression in Proverbs. Prov 11:15 says that *raʿ-yērôaʿ kî-ʿārab zār*, "to enter surety for a stranger will bring trouble", Prov 17:18, *ʿōrēb ʿărubbâ lipnê rēʿēhû*, "he who enters surety for his neighbour" and Prov 20:16, *lĕqaḥ-bigdô kî-ʿārab zār*, "take his

---

23 My translation.

24 Other texts from Proverbs that mention the handshake, 11:15; 17:18; 22:26, are referred to when relevant.

25 My translation.

26 See Snijders (1977:562-3).

27 See McKane (1970:321-2) for a summary.

garment, for he has entered surety for a stranger."[28] In the light of these parallels it is hard to avoid the conclusion that both *zār*, "stranger", and *rēaʿ*, "neighbour" are stereotyped expressions for the same person in these texts.[29] Both terms can be used as a direct object to the verb *ʿārab*, "stand surety for", and therefore it comes as no surprise to find them in a parallelism in Prov 6:1. One deviance from the normal pattern is that the preposition *lĕ*, "to" is used together with both designations. A probable explanation would be that since the preposition was required in the second part of the verse, qualifying with whom the handshake was performed, it was also used in the first part, due to analogy.[30] This would mean that the handshake took place between the guarantor and the one for whom he had entered surety, namely the debtor.

The consequence of the handshake is elaborated on later in v. 2, when the guarantor is spoken to as "snared by the utterance of your lips, caught by the words of your mouth." The word *ʾimrê*, "words" probably refers to an oath, meaning that the guarantor pledges to stand surety in case the debtor fails to pay his debt to the creditor. This oath probably accompanied the handshake and together the two formed a legally binding agreement between the guarantor and the debtor. This is made clear at the end of v. 3, where it is said that by standing surety he has fallen into the hands of his *rēaʿ*, "neighbour", i.e., the debtor. So when the debtor cannot pay, the guarantor is legally answerable to the debtor, not the creditor. Strictly speaking, then, the guarantor is only indirectly involved in a legal relationship with the creditor, in so far as he enters into the place of the debtor. This means that the legal relationship that is at stake here, in analyzing the legal function of the handshake, is the one between the debtor and his guarantor.

Prov 20:16 describes what will happen in case the debtor cannot pay his debt.[31] The guarantor is then bound to pay the debt and if, as in this case, he has no funds of his own, his clothes are taken instead. This is formulated in a different way in the second part of v. 16, where the debtors are called upon to take his garment as a pledge to pay the debt.[32]

---

[28] My translations.

[29] According to Snijders (1977:563) *zār* in Prov 6:1 stands for someone who does not belong to the family, since the family regulated their affairs privately, without official involvement.

[30] So e.g. Plöger (1984:61).

[31] Prov 27:13 is an almost exact doublet of 20:16.

[32] This is the only occurrence where the semantic ranges of *ʿārab*, "to stand surety" and *ḥābal*, "take as pledge" meet. Although the verbs do not overlap, there is a formal overlap in the derivative *ʿērābôn*, "pledge", in Gen 38:17-20. This will be discussed

To summarize, in the legal sphere of surety the handshake between the debtor and his guarantor, together with an oath, had the legal function to ratify an agreement between the two. The purpose of this agreement was twofold; firstly to make the debtor acceptable to the creditor and, secondly, to make the guarantor liable to pay the debt in case the debtor became insolvent.

2.2.3.6 Job 17:3

In Job 17:3 there is an enigmatic expression, *śîmāh-nāʾ ʿorbēnî ʿimmāk mî hûʾ lĕyādî yittāqēaʿ*, translated in the NRSV as "Lay down a pledge for me with yourself; who is there that will give surety for me?" The context is that of a complaint on Job's behalf against his friends. There is no one at his side, so in v. 3 he turns to God in his plight. Unfortunately, there are a number of problems with this text that will have to be dealt with in order to find out the proper legal function of the symbolic act in v. 3.

> The problems are, firstly, the vocalization of *ʿrbny*, whether it is a verbal or a nominal form, secondly, the first person singular pronominal suffix in *ʿrbny*, depending on the first problem, and, thirdly, the meaning of the niphal form *yittāqēaʿ*. According to the MT, *ʿorbēnî* is a qal with a first person singular pronominal suffix, meaning "stand surety for me". This is normally changed into *ʿerbonî*, the noun *ʿērābôn*, "pledge" with a first person singular pronominal suffix.[33] The problem in relation to the verbal form has been what to do with the initial phrase, *śîmāh-nāʾ*, "put" or "place". However, with the change to *ʿerbonî*, the verb takes an accusative. On the basis of the reading *ʿerbonî*, the suffix then becomes a problem. Is Job offering a pledge to God,[34] making the suffix subjective, or is he asking God for a pledge, which makes the suffix objective?[35] In order to answer this question the other half of the verse will have to be taken into consideration. The niphal form, *yittāqēaʿ*, is best taken as a case of niphal tolerativum, meaning "allow his hand to be shaken".[36] Since Job cannot expect anyone of his friends to stand surety for him, the most natural alternative would be to present a pledge of his own. The suffix is therefore subjective.

---

below in connection with Job 17:3 where there is a possible occurrence of *ʿērābôn*, "pledge".

[33] So e.g. Habel (1985:266) and Clines (1989:373).

[34] So e.g. Habel (1985:276) and Clines (1989:394).

[35] So e.g. Rowley (1976:123) and Hartley (1988:268).

[36] So e.g. Clines (1989:373). See also Waltke & O'Connor (1990:389-90).

This text, then, presents another example of what could happen to a debtor. If he cannot find anyone to stand surety for him, he is forced to put up some sort of pledge to the creditor, in Job's case to God. Although this is an illustrative use of the handshake in Job 17:3, it does show how the symbolic act was supposed to function in a proper legal context, namely to ratify an agreement between a debtor and his guarantor.

2.2.4 Historical Explanation

The handshake is nearly universal as a symbol for agreement. Two parties meet and by means of the hand, which usually symbolizes a person's power and authority, an agreement is made. The act appears to have been used when the agreement was to be shown to have been made on a parity level, although in reality this was not always the case. At some time, however, the expression used for the handshake gave rise to an idiom, meaning "to pay homage", which can be found in 1 Chr 29:24; 2 Chr 30:8; Lam 5:6 and possibly Ezra 10:19.

2.2.5 Summary and Conclusions

1. The handshake is clearly described as taking place in 2 Kgs 10:15. It is also highly likely that such is the case in Ezek 17:18; Prov 6:1; 11:15; 17:18; 22:26 and Job 17:3. However, the expression in Ezra 10:19 could be viewed as idiomatic, although it has here been regarded as describing an act. A clearly idiomatic use can be found in 1 Chr 29:24; 2 Chr 30:8 and Lam 5:6.

2. For the relevant expressions, the indications of idiomatic use are the lack of a pronoun attached to "hand", the lack of a reference to whom the handshake was performed with and the use of a prepositional phrase. The expression would then mean "to submit to". In the light of these indications, it remains a problem whether the expression in Ezra 10:19 is idiomatic or not.

3. In the context of legal practice dealing with surety, the formulation used, *tāqaʿ kap/yād*, "strike a hand", is different from the expression used in more general agreements, *nātan yād*, "give a hand". There is no reason, however, to see the two expressions as referring to different acts. The difference in terminology is more likely due to different legal contexts.

4. The handshake was used as a legal symbolic act to ratify a prior agreement.

5. In 2 Kgs 10:15; Ezek 17:18 and probably Ezra 10:19 the handshake is used as a legal symbolic act to ratify agreements on different levels. The level of international diplomacy is found in Ezek 17:18, in Ezra 10:19 it is a case of internal agreements among the people of Judah and in 2 Kgs 10:15 the handshake ratifies an agreement on a personal level.

6. In Prov 6:1; 11:15; 17:18; 22:26 and Job 17:3 the handshake was used in the more technical sense of ratifying an agreement between a debtor and the guarantor. This agreement was binding in so far as the guarantor must pay the debt in the event the debtor was unable to do so. An oath probably accompanied this symbolic act and shared the legal function.

2.3 Putting the Hand Under the Thigh

2.3.1 Introduction

The texts that are to be analysed here are Gen 24:9 and 47:29, the two occurrences of the symbolic act of putting the hand under someone's thigh. Both instances deal with a patriarch, Gen 24:9 with Abraham and 47:29 with Jakob.

2.3.2 Procedure

There are two problems related to the question of the procedure of this act. The first problem is to establish which part of the body the word *yārēk* generally refers to, without taking into consideration the texts under discussion here. The second problem is whether *yārēk* should be regarded as euphemistic for the male genitals.[1] If so, the act would be performed by putting the hand under the other person's genitals.[2]

Does *yārēk* refer to the thigh in general, to the thigh as part of the leg, or the upper part of the thigh, in relation to the loins and the hip? The word *yārēk* is used in the expression *kap-yārēk*, "hip socket" in Gen 32:26 and 33, which is in the same region as the loins and the hip.[3] On the other hand, a distinction is made in Exod 28:42 where the linen breeches of the priests are said to reach from the *motnayim*, "loins", to the *yĕrēkayim*, a dual form. This would argue for the translation "thigh" in distinction to "loin" or "hip".

In the expression "girding the loins", and when something is said to be tied to the loins, e.g. a sword, three different words for "loins" are used:

1. *ḥălāṣayim*, always used figuratively, Isa 5:27; 11:5; 32:11; Job 38:3; 40:7.
2. *motnayim*, used literally, 2 Sam 20:8; 1 Kgs 2:5; Ezek 23:15; Neh 4:12, and figuratively, Jer 1:17; Nah 2:2; Prov 31:17.
3. *yārēk*, always used literally, Judg 3:16; Ps 45:4.

---

[1] For the use of *yārēk*, see Oelsner (1960:327-9) and Hamp (1977).

[2] E.g. Speiser (1964:178), Freedman (1976:4), Westermann (1981:471), Malul (1985:198) and Smith (1990:468-9). *KB* (405) says regarding *yārēk* in these texts, "Gegend d. Schwurs where the hand of the swearing is placed", whereas in *HALAT* (419) this has become "gegend d. Geschlechtsteile b. Schwur".

[3] Smith (1990:466-9) argues that *kap-yārēk* is euphemistic for the genitals, which is unlikely. Smith strangely enough translates *taḥat* in the description of the act as "upon", a meaning definitely alien to the Hebrew preposition.

It would appear from the variations of these expressions that these three terms were regarded as quite similar, to the point of being synonymous. There is another expression which makes use of two of these three terms, namely "come forth from the loins". It occurs with *ḥălāṣayim* in Gen 35:11; 1 Kgs 8:19; 2 Chr 6:9, and with *yārēk* in Gen 46:26; Exod 1:5 and Judg 8:30. This expression clearly refers to the origin of the procreative force, which is the area surrounding the genital organs. It is therefore rather common to regard the use of *yārēk* in this expression as a euphemism for the genital organs.[4] This is indeed possible, although it does not appear to be compulsory, judging by its use. In Num 5:21, 22 and 27 the *yārēk* of a woman is said to *nāpal*, "fall away", which probably refers to a miscarriage. The word *yārēk* then refers to that part of the body where the procreative forces are thought to be located, and by the use of metonymy this part of the body then refers further to the foetus. The conclusion from this word-study is that *yārēk* should be translated in general as "thigh", although it needs to be specified that in most instances it is the upper part of the thigh that is referred to, namely the area surrounding the genital organs.[5] This area is sometimes referred to as the seat of the procreative force of an individual.

The second problem is whether *yārēk*, "thigh" is used euphemistically for the genital organs in the texts under discussion here, namely Gen 24:9 and 47:29.[6] As has been shown above, this is quite possible, since *yārēk* is sometimes used to refer to the seat of the procreative forces, which is then naturally related to the genital organs. However, in the descriptions of the act in Gen 24:2, 9 and 47:29, the hand is expressly said to be put under the thigh, *śîm yād taḥat yerek*, which is quite understandable in its literal sense. It does not say that the thigh was touched or grasped, which would immediately make the euphemistic meaning relevant. It would therefore be safer to regard the description as referring to the actual procedure, where the hand was placed under the other person's thigh, probably the upper part. The act could then itself be meant to function euphemistically for the act of touching the genitals.

There are no hints that the act is performed in front of witnesses. On the contrary, it seems to have been a family matter, and as such an example of family law, a sub-category of customary law. The oath probably involved an utterance which was spoken simultaneously with the performance of the act. This will be taken up further under Legal Function below.

---

[4]   So e.g. Malul (1985:194, n. 9, 198).

[5]   So also e.g. *HALAT* (419) and Dhorme (1923:154).

[6]   So e.g. Ullendorff (1979:445) and Westermann (1981:471).

Until recently there was no known parallel from the ancient Near East to this act. However, Malul has drawn attention to an old Babylonian letter from Kisurra in south Mesopotamia.[7] The addressee appears to have required an oath by the envoy, accompanied by a gesture, "Let your envoy grasp my testicles and my penis, and then I will give (it) to you."[8] However, the parallel is only relevant on the level of performance, and on the basis of the euphemistic use of *yārēk* for the genitals in Gen 24:2, 9 and 47:29.[9]

2.3.3 Legal Function

2.3.3.1 Genesis 24:9

The scene where the servant performs a symbolic act runs from v. 1 to v. 9. In v. 10 a new scene begins, which concerns the journey which the servant is about to make. Verses 1-9 serve the purpose of explaining why Isaac cannot follow along with the servant in order to find a wife. The answer the text gives is that the land has been given to Abraham and his seed, and therefore they should not leave it.

In v. 2 Abraham asks the servant to *śîm-nāʾ yādĕkā taḥat yĕrēkî*, "Put your hand under my thigh", although the act itself is not said to be performed until in v. 9, *wayyāśem hāʿebed ʾet-yādô taḥat yerek ʾabrāhām ʾădōnāyw*, "So the servant put his hand under the thigh of Abraham his master". In between these two expressions there is a passage which focuses on oath-taking, which will lead to the legal function of the symbolic act. In v. 3 Abraham tells the servant that *wĕʾašbîʿăkā*, "I will make you swear", in vv. 7-8 he explains that God *nišbaʿ-lî*, "swore to me" and how the servant can be released *miššĕbuʿātî*, "from this oath of mine". In v. 9b the servant is said to take the oath requested in v. 2, *wayyiššābaʿ*, "and (he) swore". Therefore it seems a reasonable conclusion that the symbolic act and the oath-taking are intimately connected in this text.

A closer look at v. 3 provides the analysis with some important clues as to the legal function of the act. The initial *wĕ* is best taken as causal, which would explain the request for the act in v. 2 as Abraham's intention to make his servant take an oath. The act would then be an integral part of the oath-taking. However, there appears to be more involved in the oath-taking

---

[7] Malul (1987). The text has been published by Kienast (1978:157).

[8] Malul (1987:491).

[9] In relation to his analysis of this text, Malul (1987:492) appears rather over-confident in claiming that *yārēk*, "thigh" is used for "seed" or "posterity" in biblical Hebrew. Besides the two texts which are under discussion here, there is only the figurative use in Num 5:21, 22 and 27, where "thigh" is used metonymically for "foetus".

than simply the act, since v. 3 describes how the oath should be sworn by the God of the heavens and the earth. This probably refers to a statement that was given by the servant simultaneously with the performance of the act. It is then the act together with the statement that make up the oath-taking.

Since, however, an oath could be made by means a statement alone, the question should be put as to why the act is performed as well? There are no clear indications in the text as to why the act is used. However, a case can be made for regarding the oath-taking to have been made by means of the act and the statement, as a way of making the oath particularly strong and binding.

Why, then, would this oath need to be strengthened? Since Abraham is described as old and near his death, v. 1, he is unable to control the acts of the servant. The distance between Abraham and his servant also calls for a strong bond between them, to make sure the servant fulfils his promise. Intermarriage with the Canaanites is also a deep concern. The seriousness of the matter would therefore call for an unusually strong oath on behalf of the servant.

This means that the symbolic act of putting the hand under the thigh in Gen 24:9 has the legal function of accomplishing the oath which the servant takes. The act shares this function with a statement which is taken by the servant at the same time as he performs the act. It is a particularly strong and binding form of oath-taking, which was needed because of the particular circumstances.

2.3.3.2 Genesis 47:29

In this, the second occurrence of the symbolic act of putting the hand under the thigh, there are some similarities to Gen 24:9 as well as some differences. The requests for the act in Gen 24:2 and 47:29 are similarly formulated, *śîm-nāʾ yādĕkā taḥat yĕrēkî*, "put your hand under my thigh". As in Gen 24:2, the act is also requested in 47:29 by an aging patriarch, namely Jacob, but now it is to be performed by his son, Joseph. The oath concerns Jacob's burial, which is obviously beyond his ability to control and which makes him totally dependent upon Joseph to keep the oath. The reason why the act is used in this text to perform the oath-taking is the same as it was for the act in Gen 24:9, namely to satisfy the patriarch's need for a particularly strong and binding oath. A major difference in relation to Gen 24:9 is that Jacob is not concerned for the continuance of his family but for his final resting place, i.e., to be buried with his forefathers and not in Egypt.

When Jacob asks Joseph in v. 29d to *śîm-nāʾ yādĕkā taḥat yĕrēkî*, "put your hand under my thigh", no connection is made with an oath. In v. 31a-b, where Jacob asks Joseph to swear an oath, which he does, there is analogously no connection with the symbolic act. Between vv. 29d and 31a there appears Jacob's description of the content of the oath, which he has requested from Joseph. Here, as in 24:9, the symbolic act is then intimately connected with the oath, to the extent that the two appear to be functionally equivalent. The oath, requested and performed in v. 31, therefore implies the performance of the symbolic act. This leads to the conclusion that the act and the oath are substantially the same. There is no reference to a statement being made in relation to the act, although Jacob's request in v. 31 could imply such a statement. This must, however, be regarded as uncertain.

The same legal function would then apply for the act here in 47:29 as in 24:9, namely to accomplish the particularly strong and binding oath which Joseph takes in relation to his father.

2.3.4 Historical Explanation

As was said above under Procedure, *yārēk*, "thigh" is usually regarded as a euphemism for the genitals in Gen 24:2, 9 and 47:29. However, it was found to be more likely that the hand is meant to be put under the thigh and not in relation to the genitals. It would then be the act itself which would associate euphemistically to the genitals, on the basis of the symbolic relationship between the thigh and the genitals. Beyond this, however, we are left to speculate as to how the procedure of the act was connected to the legal function.

The thigh, as a euphemism for the genitals, is often regarded as a symbol for the offspring.[10] By touching the symbol for the offspring, the person performing the act would invoke a future punishment from the offspring, which would take place if he did not keep to the oath. Or he could be referring to the offspring as a symbolic witness to the oath. Yet another alternative is to understand the act as referring to the ancestral spirits, who would threaten to punish the performer in case he did not fulfil the oath.[11]

---

[10] So e.g. Malul (1985:194-5, esp. n. 10).

[11] So Malul (1985:198). According to Malul, however, this is not only a historical explanation but part of the intention behind the act in Gen 24:9 and 47:29. The reason why Malul emphasizes the historical explanation seems to be that such an assumption becomes a link between the ancestral spirits related to the symbolic act itself and the expression *paḥad yiṣḥāq* in Gen 31:42 and 53, usually translated "Fear of Isaac", which

The reason why this becomes so speculative is that there is no available material to guide the historical explanation in either of these directions. The euphemistic use of *yārēk* for the genitals is disputed, as was shown above, and there are no indications that the thigh symbolizes descendants or even ancestral spirits.

If we concentrate more on the act of touching the thigh with the hand, there are two interesting cases in Jer 31:19 and Ezek 21:17. The prophets strike their own thighs in a symbolic act of remorse and perhaps even submission.[12] When this is then performed by touching the thigh of someone else, it could symbolize the submission of the performer under the other person's strength and authority. That would agree very well with the legal function of the act as accomplishing the oath in a particularly strong way, in order to ensure the aging patriarch that the oath will indeed be accomplished. The submission would then be the connecting link, historically speaking, between the performance of the act and its legal function. This explanation does not necessarily argue against the symbolic meaning of the thigh as offspring and the various interpretations which have been generated on that basis, since the question would still have to be asked why the thigh in particular was struck. Indeed, the symbolic meaning of the thigh as offspring may well provide the reason why it came to symbolize strength in the first place. However, the historical explanation for the act, which has been presented here, does question whether it was the symbolic meanings of the thigh as genitals and offspring which were relevant in the formation of the legal symbolic act.

---

in Malul's opinion reflects the same symbolic act, based upon the meaning of *paḥad* as "thigh".

[12] This symbolic act is also found in extra-biblical material, e.g. in The Descent of Ishtar, where Ereshkigal demonstrates her disappointment by smiting her thigh and biting her finger, see *ANET* (108). For this comparison, see Lipiński (1970) and Gruber (1980:380-4).

2.3.5 Summary and Conclusions

1. The performance of this act did not mean that the hand touched the genitals. Instead, it was performed according to the expression of the act, namely by placing the hand under the thigh of someone else. If euphemism was involved, it was the act itself that was used euphemistically and not the word "thigh" in the description of the act.

2. The act was performed in the intimate legal sphere of the family, which meant that it was not connected with any form of official legal sanction. It should therefore be considered as a case of family law, a sub-category of customary law.

3. The legal function of the symbolic act was to accomplish the oath. A statement which declared the oath-taking could accompany the act and share its legal function, as was the case in Gen 24:2, 9, but it does not appear to have been compulsory, as it is not mentioned in connection with the act in Gen 47:29.

4. The historical explanation of the act should probably be based on the symbolic act of striking one's thigh as an act of remorse and submission. When a person then touches the thigh of someone else, he would symbolize his submission to that person's strength and authority. It is possible that the symbolic meaning of strength for the thigh is based on the fact that "thigh" could refer euphemistically to the genitals, and that it thereby came to symbolize the offspring.

2.4 Walking Through a Divided Animal

2.4.1 Introduction

Gen 15:17 and Jer 34:18-19 each describes an example of what is perhaps the most problematic legal symbolic act in the OT. Since Gen 15 and Jer 34 deal with the subject of covenant, and in particular this is true of Gen 15, which describes the covenant between Abram and God, they have been subjected to intense study. A short summary of the present status of scholarly activity regarding these texts will be given here, and then a new attempt will be made at understanding the legal function of this symbolic act.[1]

In addition to legal function, there are two other major questions that have puzzled scholars in the past regarding the act in these texts.

1. Should the act be interpreted as self-imprecatory, i.e., as invoking a fate similar to the cutting up of the animals upon the covenant party who performs the act?

2. Is the preparatory act a sacrifice? The preparatory act of dividing the animal or animals is often included by scholars with the act of walking between the parts. This question mainly concerns the act in Gen 15, since its preparation has more of a sacrificial character than the act in Jer 34.

---

[1] See Hasel (1981; 1984:365-6) for a more complete review. There are some unlikely views that should be mentioned here, however. Henninger (1953:352-3) holds that the act was a mystical-sacramental rite, through which the performer identified with certain properties of the victims. This view has not gained much support, but see Caqout (1962:61) for a similar view. Hofmann & Vorbichler (1981:145-6) qualifies the view of Henninger on the basis of Herodotus II.139. The act would then be rejuvenating, through the power of the blood of the slaughtered animals, likely to have been touched by the party who passed through the animals. Since it is God who performs the act in Gen 15 and not Abram, they are forced to conclude that a scribe has misunderstood the act. Wenham (1987:331-3) distinguishes himself by interpreting the different animals in Gen 15 as representing the nation of Israel. God's walk between them is then a reference to his walk with the people. Wenham draws heavily on the fact that the animals used are normal sacrificial animals. This act would then confirm the covenant between Abram and God. The main problem with this interpretation is that in spite of the close formal parallel to the symbolic act in Jer 34, there is no connection whatsoever to the meaning of it. This makes Wenham's interpretation seem unlikely. Eilberg-Schwartz (1990:168-9) sees the cutting up of the animals as symbolizing the split between Abram on the one hand and his father and brothers on the other, as caused by the divine promise to him. He finds support for this in the Nuer culture in Africa, where the cutting up of an object may end kinship relations. There is, however, no explanation of the passing through the divided animals, which means that the parallel is not even phenomenologically relevant. For comparing the Nuer culture with the OT, see e.g. Fiensy (1987).

In trying to answer these questions, scholars have usually referred to certain examples of what appear to be similar legal symbolic acts from the ancient Near Eastern context. Since these acts are referred to quite often in the literature, and have had extensive influence on earlier interpretations of the biblical texts, a brief overview of these texts will be given here. The purpose is primarily to weigh the relevance of these parallels in their relation to the act in Gen 15 and Jer 34.

Excursus: Some Alleged Parallels

1. This is a treaty from Mari, ARM 2.37, 18th century BC. The making of a treaty is described in the following way in ll. 6-7: "Puis pour tuer l'ânon (d'alliance) entre les Ḫanéens et (les gens d') Idamaraz, ... ". The official did not accept the puppy and the goat that were presented to him in order to perform the treaty act, l. 8, but requested a donkey, which he thought would be satisfying to his lord, l. 11. He then says in ll. 13-14: "J'ai etabli la concorde entre les Ḫanéens et (les gens d')Idamaraz." The expression *ḫayaram qatālum*, "kill a donkey" is functionally equivalent in this text with the expression "make a treaty". This means that the killing of a donkey performed the legal function of ratifying a treaty.[2] There is no trace of either self-imprecation or sacrifice.

2. In a rather recently discovered letter from old Babylonian Rimah, Zimri-Lim of Mari writes to Hatnu-rapi of Karana, quoting from a letter he has received from him:[3]

> I here shall lead out the kings my allies (*lit.* brothers) who enjoy good relations with me; let us kill donkey foals (*i.e.* make treaties of alliance); let us put the oath by the life of the gods between us.

Zimri-lim replies in ll. 38-40: "May donkey foals and the oath by the life of the gods be set between us". The same conclusion can be drawn from this example as from the act in ARM 2.37, namely that the killing of a donkey ratifies the treaty. What is interesting in this example is that the act is accompanied by the taking of an oath. There is, however, no trace of either self-imprecation or sacrifice, although the oath could point in the direction of the former.

3. This is part of a treaty between Abba-AN and Iarimlim from the 17th century BC:

---

[2] See e.g. Noth (1957:144-5), Held (1970:33), McCarthy (1981:91) and similarly Tadmor (1982:134-5).

[3] Dalley (1976), 1:10-12. See also Greenfield (1986:393).

> Abba-AN is under oath to Yarimlim, and[4] also he cut the neck
> of a lamb. (He swore:) "I shall never take back what I gave
> thee."[5]

The act and promissory oath of Abba-AN function to solemnize his gifts to
Iarimlim.[6] The gifts in turn function as compensations for obedience. The
symbolic act is therefore not immediately connected with the making of the
treaty, but with the surety of the gift.[7] No self-imprecation is mentioned
explicitly, and no trace can be found of a sacrificial character to the act.

4. The following is part of a vassal treaty between Ashurnirari VI of
Assyria and Mati'ilu of Arpad from the 8th century BC:

> This spring lamb has been brought from its fold not for sacrifice,
> not for a banquet, not for a purchase, ... not to be slaughtered for
> [...]: it has been brought to sanction the treaty between
> Ashurnirari and Mati'ilu. ... This head is not the head of a lamb,
> it is the head of Mati'ilu, it is the head of his sons, his officials,
> and the people of his land. If Mati'ilu sins against this treaty, so
> may, just as the head of this spring lamb is torn off, and its
> knuckle placed in its mouth, [...], the head of Mati'ilu be torn
> off, and his sons [...].[8]

In this text the legal function of the act of killing the animal is made very
clear, namely "to sanction the treaty".[9] The symbolic meaning of the act is
to associate the fate of Mati'ilu with that of the animal. This identification
can be said to constitute the treaty-curse relevant in the case of a broken
treaty. However, the act does not seem to function as a treaty ratification,
and it is explicitly said that the lamb is not brought forth as a sacrifice.

5. In the Sefire Treaty I.A:39-40 from the 7th century BC, we note the
following phrase: "[Just as] this calf is cut up, so shall Mati'el be cut up,
and his nobles shall be cut up."[10] This is part of several curses that will fall
on Mati'el and his family, in case they do not abide by the treaty. Two
reservations need to be made, however. Firstly, the context is that of wax
figures, which makes it likely that this is done to a calf made of wax.[11]

---

[4] The oath and the act are to be kept distinct, due to the connective *ù*, so e.g. McCarthy
(1981:93). Cf. *GAG* (170-1). For the text see Wiseman (1958:126), ll. 39-42.

[5] McCarthy (1981:307). Wiseman's translation (1958:129), "(Let me so die) if I take
back that which I gave thee!" tends to read too much into the oath formulation.

[6] As noted by Wiseman (1958:124).

[7] So Hasel (1981:65), although he notes that the act can be a ratification of the treaty.

[8] *ANET* (532).

[9] An interesting parallel to this description can be found in Livy I.XXIV, where a ceremonial combat was to take place between the armies of Rome and Albany. Before the
combat, the respective kings made a treaty, accompanied with imprecatory oaths on
both sides, based on the slaughter of a pig.

[10] Gibson (1975:32-3).

[11] So Gibson (1975:42). Hasel (1981:67) appears to be open to the possibility.

Secondly, the act is not given any function related to the making of the treaty, but is wholly a part of the curses. There is also no trace of the act being considered sacrificial.

6. Among the curses of the vassal treaty of Esarhaddon from the 7th century BC, there is the following example, ll. 547-54:

> Just as this ewe is cut open and the flesh of its young placed in its mouth, so may he (Shamash?) make you eat in your hunger the flesh of your brothers, your sons, and your daughters. Just as (these) yearlings and spring lambs, male and female, are cut open and their entrails are rolled around their feet, so may the entrails of your sons and daughters be rolled around your feet.[12]

It is possible that these curses were acted out, and perhaps simultaneously read aloud.[13] They would, however, still be a part of the curses and not of the oaths, taken earlier in the treaties. The acts would not ratify the treaty[14] and they would not be sacrificial.

Weinfeld, Petersen and Hasel, who have tried to integrate most of these texts with the descriptions of the acts in Gen 15 and Jer 34, agree that these parallels can be divided in two categories.[15] This would include an early, second millennium phase involving examples 1-3, and a late, first millennium phase, involving examples 4-6. Gen 15 would thus belong to the early phase and Jer 34 to the later.[16] However, these scholars differ on the important points of sacrificial character and self-imprecation.

According to Weinfeld, the act in Gen 15 should be interpreted as a covenant of grant, binding the suzerain to the oath which is taken.[17] The act in Jer 34, on the other hand, should be seen as a vassal treaty, in which the vassal takes upon himself to fulfil his obligations. Weinfeld also notes the sacrificial character of the act in Gen 15, in contrast to the act in Jer 34 and holds both to be self-imprecations. Petersen considers the act in Gen 15 as

---

[12] *ANET* (539).

[13] So Frankena (1965:139).

[14] So Hasel (1981:66-7).

[15] Kutsch (1973:44; 45-6, n. 28), however, does not differentiate between these examples, since he finds them all to be self-imprecatory or imprecatory. This applies to the act in Gen 15 and Jer 34 as well according to Kutsch. Tadmor (1982:136) sees a continuity in the practice of what he calls the sacrificial killing of an animal in treaty making, from the early eighteenth to the 6th century BC. Of the examples described above, Tadmor includes 1-4.

[16] McCarthy (1981:93-4, 149-53) also divides them into two categories, but he is more hesitant towards the sharp boundary between them. He notes that the differences may very well be due to the chronological lacuna which exist between the two groups (1981:153).

[17] Weinfeld (1970:199).

a sacrificial practice in order to establish a covenant.[18] He differs from Weinfeld, however, in that he prefers not to see the act in Gen 15 as a self-imprecation, as opposed to the act in Jer 34.[19] Hasel shares the view of Petersen in rejecting the interpretation of the act in Gen 15 as a self-imprecation.[20] He considers it a "covenant ratification sacrifice", and distinguishes between a "sacrificial preparatio" and a subsequent "divine ratificatio".[21] In contrast to Petersen and Weinfeld, however, Hasel holds it possible that the act in Jer 34 is self-imprecatory, although he considers the text too uncertain to reach a conclusion.[22]

Loewenstamm deals with the questions of self-imprecation and sacrifice by means of traditio-historical analysis. He postulates that the act in Gen 15 was originally a self-imprecation, and that it involved only the slaughter of a heifer, v. 9. Later on this self-imprecatory act was expanded into a description of a sacrifice.[23]

Still, it remains to be said that none of the parallels described above portray the same act as in Gen 15 and Jer 34. None of them presents either a divided animal or someone partaking in the covenant by walking through the parts.[24] The fact that the act in Gen 15 and Jer 34 may have the same legal function as some of these acts is another matter. It would seem, however, that the question of similar legal function has often been confused with the question of similar performance. There are actually some Hittite texts which describe an act where animals are split into halves, and one text even mentions the act of passing through the parts:

> If the troops have been beaten by the enemy they perform a ritual 'behind' the river, as follows: they 'cut through' a man, a goat, a puppy, and a little pig; they place half on this side and half on that side, and in front of them they make a gate of ..... wood and stretch a ..... over it, and in front of the gate they light fires on this side and on that, and the troops walk right through, and when they come to the river they sprinkle water over them.[25]

---

[18] Petersen (1977:15).

[19] Petersen (1977:7-9).

[20] Hasel (1981:68-70). He does not refer to Petersen's study.

[21] Hasel (1981:70; 1984:366).

[22] Hasel (1981:63).

[23] Loewenstamm (1968:506), followed by Westermann (1981:267).

[24] Ha (1989:73) holds this view regarding the act in Gen 15, and his conclusion is that the only relevant parallel is the act in Jer 34. See also Greenfield (1986:392-5).

[25] The translation is from Gurney (1954:151). The text is KUB XVII.28.IV:45-55. Cf. also Masson (1950:5-6). A similar act of purification, practised by the Macedonian

However, this text is not in any way related to the making of a treaty. Instead, the act is used as a rite of purification in connection with the regrouping of an army after it has suffered a defeat.[26] It is therefore an act with a performance that is similar to the biblical act, but with quite a different function.[27]

The conclusion from this overview of extra-biblical examples is that the act in Gen 15 and Jer 34 should be studied on its own, without necessarily being compared with acts that are similar only in performance or legal function. The closest parallel to the example of the act in Gen 15 remains the example in Jer 34 and vice versa.

2.4.2 Procedure

We will begin by studying Jer 34 and then follow up with Gen 15, as this latter text has caused more discussion among scholars.

In Jer 34 a covenant between Zedekiah and his people is described, first in third person, vv. 8-11, and then in the form of an oracle from God in vv. 12-22.[28] The oracle consists of a description of the circumstances surrounding the covenant, similar to vv. 8-11, and a judgement in vv. 17-22. The people were to set free all their Hebrew slaves, vv. 8-10 and 13-14. Apparently this covenant was connected with a symbolic act, vv. 18-19.

---

army in 182 BC, is recorded by Livy XL.6.1-2, see Nilsson (1906:404-6) and Eitrem (1947:36-8).

[26] So Masson (1950:18). He gives examples of this act from not only Hittite texts but also from ancient Greece and Macedonia, as well as from modern times. He concludes: "Dans tous les textes qui ont été versés au débat, il est seulement question de *purification*: nulle idée de *pacte* ne se décèle dans les rituels hittites ou macédoniens, non plus que dans les usages modernes." Gurney (1954:151) also sees the act as a purification of the army. He also notes its similarity to the act in Gen 15. For further discussion of the examples of the act from ancient Greece and Macedonia, see Nilsson (1906:404-6), Eitrem (1947) who also compares with the act in Gen 15 and Jer 34, and Hofmann & Vorbichler (1981). There is an interesting example of an act of passing through a slaughtered animal in Plato *Laws* VI.753.D, where the act is clearly of a legal nature. When certain officials are to be selected through a third round of voting, those who vote are to pass between the slaughtered animals, διὰ τομίων πορευόμενος, as they do so. It was a way of making the voting more solemn, apparently by making the voters take an oath as they performed their task. See Eitrem (1947:38-9) for further study of this text.

[27] So e.g. McCarty (1981:95) and Hasel (1981:74, n. 34).

[28] The origin of this story is debated. Weippert (1973:191, 228-9) holds that it does not come from a deuteronomistic redactor, but that it has its origin close to Jeremiah, and Holladay (1989:238) agrees with her conclusion. Thiel (1981:39) argues that vv. 8-22 has been thoroughly reworked in a deuteronomistic redaction, and Carroll (1986:649) considers the story to be "a Deuteronomistically shaped sermon".

The covenant was followed, but only for a short while, after which time the people took back their slaves, vv. 11 and 16. This forms the background for the judgement oracle in vv. 17-22. There is, however, a problem with the description of the symbolic act. It is not until vv. 18-19, when the judgement is pronounced by God, that something is said about the procedure of this act. In vv. 8-11, where the covenant is described in third person, nothing is mentioned about the act. It would seem, from reading the oracle in vv. 17-22, that knowledge of the act is presupposed and then further elaborated upon.

What is learned from v. 18 is that a calf is cut in two, and the leaders of the people pass between its parts. In v. 19 it is said that all the people passed between the parts, but this is likely to be a hyperbole, since the leaders can be said to have represented the people. The covenant that was made concerned the king and the people of Jerusalem, v. 8.[29] Nothing is said as to whether both parties walked between the parts. Since this covenant between a king and his people is best described in terms of a vassal relationship with the burden of holding to the covenant stipulations laying on the vassal, i.e., the people, it is probable that only the lesser party of the covenant walked between the parts.

If the act in Jer 34 is compared with the act in Gen 15, there is an obvious similarity, but also some significant differences. Abram is told in Gen 15:9 by God to cut certain animals in two, which resembles Jer 34:18-19. The animals in Gen 15:9 are different, however. They include a heifer, a she-goat and a ram, all three years old, together with a turtledove and a pigeon. The birds are not cut up, v. 10.[30] Abram then lays the parts opposite each other, v. 10. In v. 17, God is symbolized by a smoking oven and a flaming torch, which pass through the divided animals.[31] Abram, on the other hand, does not walk between the parts, but falls into a deep sleep, v. 12.[32] This means that in both instances of this symbolic act, only one

---

[29] Ha (1989:74) holds that the covenant was unilateral between the leaders of the people as the superior party and the slaves to be liberated as the subjects of the covenant. This is nowhere stated in the text, which explicitly states that Zedekiah made a covenant with the people of Jerusalem, v. 8. It would seem that Ha needs a close correspondence between the act in Jer 34 and the act in Gen 15, where God, as the superior party of the covenant, walks through the divided animals. Ha can then postulate a literary relationship between the two texts, but at the expense of neglecting the actual statement in Jer 34:8.

[30] For an attempt to explain this, see Begg (1987:9-11).

[31] It might be called a theophany, so Jeremias (1977:207-8). Cf. e.g. Exod 13:21; 14:24; 19:18; 20:18; 24:17; Isa 31:9.

[32] See McAlpine (1987:158-9, 205-6) for this motif.

party walks between the parts of the animals. In Gen 15:17, however, it is the superior party of the covenant who walks between the parts, as opposed to the act in Jer 34:18-19, where it is the subordinate party. This could be explained by viewing the covenant in Jer 34 as obligatory, and the one in Gen 15 as promissory. Both, however, would be describing a non-parity relationship.[33]

2.4.3 Legal Function

2.4.3.1 Jeremiah 34:18-19

There is an interesting wordplay in Jer 34:18. The leaders are said to have transgressed the covenant, and they "did not keep the terms of the covenant which they had made before me; the calf which they cut in two and walked between its parts."[34] However, before this discussion is taken any further, some alternative interpretations must be taken into consideration.

Excursus: Is Jeremiah 34:18 in Need of Repair?

The construction of v. 18 has long been considered in need of repair. The most popular change of the text has been to read *kāʿēgel*, "as the calf" instead of the MT, *hāʿēgel*, "the calf".[35] The verb at the beginning, *wĕnātatû*, "I will make" is said to govern this construction as a second accusative, meaning "I will make them like the calf". Several scholars keep the MT but still consider it a second accusative.[36] The distance between the predicate and the second object, however, makes this construction rather unusual. It should also be noted that the verb *nātan*, "make" never occurs with this meaning of making someone like something else without the preposition *kĕ* in front of the second object.[37]

Keil explained the absence of *kĕ* as being due to added emphasis on the second object, although he did not provide any other examples.[38] This way of reading *hāʿēgel*, whether or not it means that the MT should be modified, involves a common misunderstanding, however. As Kapelrud notes, the use

---

[33] See Mettinger (1976:303) for this terminology.

[34] My translation.

[35] So e.g. Volz (1922:316), Rudolph (1968:224), Thiel (1981:41), Miller (1984:611-2), Carroll (1986:644-6) and Sarna (1989:114-5). This has also worked itself into the critical apparatus of *BHS*.

[36] So e.g. Keil (1873:87), Schedl (1982:249-50) and recently Holladay (1989:242), with a rather extensive discussion.

[37] The example given by Holladay (1989:242), Isa 3:4, is not relevant since the meaning is there to make someone *into* something else.

[38] Keil (1873:86-7). He also noted that the article on the second object is rather uncommon, although it does sometimes occur, e.g. in 2 Sam 3:27.

of *ha'egel* as a second accusative would not mean that God will make the transgressors "as" the calf, but "instead of" the calf, or even "into" the calf.[39] He argues that the symbolic act, which was originally without any self-imprecatory function, is used secondarily by the prophet as a threat.[40] However, it is hard to understand fully how the difference between these two interpretations would emerge on the part of the reader. Kapelrud shows this himself when he interprets the phrase as with *kĕ*, "as", later on in his article.[41] As to the function of the act, Kapelrud agrees with Hasel that the symbolic act functioned as a covenant ratification. Bright proposes another alternative, namely to put "the calf" after "they cut" in order to avoid the cumbersome construction,[42] although without any external support. Driver prefers to revocalize *lĕpānăy*, "in front of me", into *lipnê*. The preposition *lipnê* usually means "in front of", but here Driver proposes the rather unusual meaning "like", which would produce the translation, "like the calf which they cut".[43] This is supported by the vocalization apparently followed by Aquila, ἐνώπιον τοῦ μοσχοῦ, "in front of the calf". This would, however, seem uncalled for in light of the occurrence of almost the same phrase in v. 15, *wattikrĕtû bĕrît lĕpānay*, "you made a covenant before me".

The LXX[44] has in part the same construction as the MT, τὴν διαθήκην μου, ἣν ἐποίησαν κατὰ πρόσωπόν μου, τὸν μόσχον ὃν ἐποίησαν, "my covenant, which they made before me, the calf which they made". It leaves out, however, the walking through the parts in vv. 18 and 19, and adds in v. 18, ἐργάζεσθαι αὐτῷ, "to serve it" instead.[45] This could mean that the translator either did not understand the act of walking through the parts or found it unsuitable. What is presented instead in v. 18 is an allusion to the incident of the golden calf in Exod 32.[46] Another plausible explanation to this strange reading of the LXX is that it is based on a damaged text.[47]

It would seem that hitherto scholars have been unable to come to grips with the text without emending it.

---

[39] Kapelrud (1982:138-9).

[40] Kapelrud (1982:140). He calls this a "new and for the people astonishing interpretation of the ancient well-known rite".

[41] Kapelrud (1982:140).

[42] Bright (1965:220). This was also suggested by Condamin (1936:254). It is followed by e.g. Thompson (1980:609, n. 7).

[43] Driver (1937-8:121-2).

[44] Jer 34 in the MT corresponds to Jer 41 in the LXX.

[45] See Stulman (1985:99, 103-4) for the relationship between the MT and the LXX, and the possible Hebrew Vorlage to the LXX.

[46] So e.g. Janzen (1973:105).

[47] So Janzen (1973:105), who considers the reading of the LXX as an attempt to make a damaged text understandable. He is correct in showing that the LXX does not give a free reading, but has close similarities with the form of the MT, although the meaning is different.

The wordplay in Jer 34:18, referred to above, is on the word *kārĕtû*, "cut" or "make" in connection with *bĕrît*, "covenant". The author seems to be well aware of both the literal meaning of the word, used in the second instance, and the idiomatic use in the first.[48] The purpose, however, is more than stylistic. The author is putting the making of the covenant alongside and parallel to the act of dividing the calf in two. This can be shown by a structural diagram of Jer 34:18-20a:

18a	*wĕnātatû ʾet-hāʾănāšîm hāʿōbĕrîm ʾet-bĕrîû*	
18b	[*ʾăšer lōʾ-hēqîmû ʾet-dibrê habbĕrît ăšer kārĕtû lĕpānāy*	
18c		*hāʿēgel ăšer kārĕtû lišnayim*
18d		*wayyaʿabrû bên bĕtārāyw*
19a	*śārê yĕhûdâ*	
19b	*wĕśārê yĕrûšālayim hassārisîm*	
19c	*wĕhakkōhănîm*	
19d	*wĕkōl ʿam hāʾāreṣ*	
19e		*hāʿōbĕrîm bên bitrê hāʿēgel*]
20a	*wĕnātatû ʾōtām bĕyad ʾōybêhem ...*	

The relative pronoun *ăšer*, "which", in 18bβ is repeated in 18c to serve the parallel between the making of the covenant and the cutting up of the calf. The same purpose is served by the repetition of *kārĕtû*, "cut" in 18c.[49] The word *hāʿēgel*, "calf" in 18c is used in apposition to *bĕrît*, "covenant", in congruence with the double meaning of *kārat*, "cut". There is also a word-play on the verb *ʿābar*, which in 18a means "transgress (the covenant)" and in 18d and 19e "walk through (the parts)".[50] The author has put the cutting of the calf, *hāʿēgel ăšer kārĕtû*, in apposition to the making ("cutting") of the covenant, *habbĕrît ăšer kārĕtû*.[51] This appositional construction emphasizes

---

[48] Barr (1977:27) claims that "the original ritual value of kārat when combined with bᵉrīt continued to be known in the culture, and this is realized in the famous passage Jer 34:18." However, this is not necessarily the case. Simply because the author uses the same verb with two different meanings does not mean that one meaning can be added to the other. It is more likely that the author of Jer 34:18 has created a word-play on the literal meaning of "cut". The conclusion is that the author did not necessarily have any knowledge of a "ritual value" for kārat. He simply noted, probably with a certain amount of amusement, that the same word could be used in both expressions.

[49] Thiel (1981:41) notes the word-play, but ends up with a chiastic arrangement, *ʿābar–kārat–kārat–ʿābar*, since he considers the first relative clause in v. 18 to be a deutero-nomistic expansion.

[50] My translations.

[51] So Barthélemy (1986:711), with an extensive discussion of different views. See Keil (1873:86) for this view in older scholarship.

the fact that a covenant has indeed been entered into by means of walking through the divided animal. The means by which the covenant was entered into is put in apposition to the result, which could be a case of specifying apposition.[52] It is achieved by slowing down the pace of the narrative and sustaining the tension made explicit at the beginning of v. 18, where it was made clear that the covenant had indeed been broken. Since the logical progression from 18a is left somewhat in the air until 20a, where it is resumed, this difficult construction could well be described as an anacoluthon.[53] The extent of this has been illustrated in the diagram above by means of square brackets. An example of how the thread has been lost is the elaborated version of 18d in 19a-e. The conclusion is, therefore, that the act of walking through the divided animal was considered to be the actual covenant ratification.

The punishment for breaking the covenant is stated in vv. 20-22. The only possible connection between the fate of the calf and the punishment said to await the people is found in v. 20, where the corpses of the people are to be "food for the birds of the air and the wild animals of the earth." One could imagine that the divided animal would be a suitable illustration, but v. 20 explains that the immediate cause of this fate will be the enemies attacking the land and Jerusalem. There is, therefore, no connection between the fate of the calf and the future fate of the people as to the specific way the punishment was to be performed. However, it is clear from vv. 20-22 that the breaking of the covenant had severe consequences.

It is common among exegetes to talk about a so-called imprecation, or self-imprecation, in regard to this text.[54] Since, as was shown above, scholars usually read "I will make ... as the calf" in v. 18, this is usually considered to be explicit in the text.[55] The point would be that the party who walks between the divided parts of the animal takes upon himself a curse, meaning that if he breaks the covenant he will suffer like the animal. As has been shown above, however, there is nothing to substantiate this in the text of Jer 34:18. The only thing that can be said for sure is that it is presupposed that breaking the covenant brings severe punishment. The

---

[52] See Andersen (1974:47-9).

[53] So apparently Barthélemy (1986:711), "Cela nous engage à comprendre les vss 18 et 19 comme une longue phrase qui se perd dans les sables." For further examples of anacoluthon in the OT, see GKC (505-6) and Nyberg (1952:305).

[54] So e.g. Hillers (1964:26), who considers the oracle to be related to treaty curses, Thompson (1980:613), McCarthy (1981:94), Carroll (1986:645-6) and Sarna (1989:114-5).

[55] So e.g. Snijders (1958:272), Lohfink (1967:106), McCarthy (1981:94 and Tadmor (1982:136).

legal function of dividing a calf and walking through the parts is, according to Jer 34:18, to ratify a covenant that has been made. There is no evidence from the text to imply a self-imprecatory sense of the act.

There is also nothing that would indicate a sacrificial nature of the preparatory act of cutting up of the calf, Jer 34:18. To consider the mere dividing of an animal as necessarily a sacrifice only serves to make the concept of sacrifice more difficult to understand, and does not aid in understanding the act in Jer 34:18-19.

2.4.3.2 Genesis 15:17

Gen 15:7-21 seems to be constructed chiastically, which is of importance in understanding the symbolic act which is described. The whole scene begins with the statement of God in v. 7. Then the plot is created by means of Abram's question in v. 8, which prepares the ground for the symbolic act to come. Abram has doubts as to the question of "possess", which is the literary hinge between vv. 7 and 8. Then comes the description of the symbolic act and its preparation in vv. 9-11 and 17, placed around a statement by God in vv. 12-16.[56] The whole scene is enclosed by returning to a quiet pace in vv. 18a-21, which is the equivalent of v. 7, namely the promise of the land.[57] This means that Abram's question as to how he can know that he will possess the land in v. 8, is answered in two ways. Firstly, by the spoken promise in v. 13, extending the promise to Abram's offspring, and secondly by the symbolic act which assures him that God will stand by his promise. This promise was made to Abram personally in v. 7, but in v. 18 it is the offspring that will possess the land. This is probably intentional, since it is Abram who is involved in the actual making of the covenant.

Verses 17-18 form the climax of the whole scene. God performs the symbolic act in v. 17, and this is followed immediately in v. 18 by a

---

[56] Verses 13-16 is usually considered to be from a different source than its present context, but Lohfink (1967:40, 44) has shown that these verses were created specifically for their present location. Hoftijzer (1956:54) considers these verses to be an original part of the chapter.

[57] So e.g. Westermann (1981:272). Gen 15 has not escaped the traditional source-critical analysis. For a summary of different views, see Westermann (1981:253-5) and Ha (1989:30-8). Ha (1989:215-6) believes that Gen 15 was created by a single author in the exilic period, and that it can not be associated with either deuteronomistic, priestly or prophetic circles. Anbar (1982:54-5), on the other hand, considers the chapter a conflation of two deuteronomistic narratives, perhaps from exilic times. Abela (1986:14) has studied the chapter from a synchronic point of view, to investigate what is usually said to be evidences of different sources. See also Van Seters (1975:263) who stresses the chapter as a unity, and Wenham (1987:326).

description of the legal function of the act: "On that day the Lord made a covenant with Abram". This is introduced by means of the phrase *bayyôm hāhû*, "on that day", which refers adverbially to a particular day in the past.[58] More precisely, it concludes the foregoing action, marks out the point of the story and explains the previous act.[59]

This means that in Gen 15:17, as well as in Jer 34:18-19, the symbolic act of walking through the parts of the divided animal or animals has the legal function of ratifying a covenant. However, as soon as this is said, it must be remembered that God is involved in the act, which means that the act does not have the same proper legal context as was found with the act in Jer 34:18-19. The act in Gen 15:17 is therefore an example of a reuse of a legal symbolic act in a non-legal context. There are several contextual indications that point in this direction. There are no witnesses to the act, which normally would have been required. Above all, however, it would seem that this reuse of the legal symbolic act has influenced the performance of the act itself, namely the choice of the animals which are divided. These animals were ordinary sacrificial animals, and were probably chosen for that very reason. Through this similarity with sacrifices, the divine presence is indicated and emphasized, as it is also by the passing of the oven and the flame. It does not say in v. 17 whether the divided parts are meant to be consumed by the fire, but if so it would be another influence which the part played by God has had on the performance of the act. However, the act in Gen 15:17 is described with a legal function, although the context is altered by the fact that God plays a part in the making of the covenant.

Again, the view that this symbolic act must be the expression of a self-imprecation is widespread among scholars,[60] although the consensus is not as complete as it was in the case with the act in Jer 34:18-19. The text, however, gives no credence to such an interpretation. The only way to interpret the act in Gen 15 as self-imprecatory is to analyze the parts of the act and not the function of the act as such. This is usually done in close comparison with the extra-Biblical acts presented above, and Jer 34:18-19. However, there is no way of knowing for sure that the act in Gen 15:17 was meant to be interpreted according to its procedure, in the sense that to walk through the parts would refer to the risk of sharing the fate of the

---

[58] So Sæbø (1982:570).

[59] See Waltke & O'Connor (1990:313-4) and in particular DeVries (1975:73-4). DeVries (1975:57-136) has a thorough analysis of the phrase as it refers to the past.

[60] So e.g. Clements (1967:20, n. 22; 34, n. 45), Weinfeld (1970:196-8), Westermann (1981:267), Tadmor (1982:136) and Sarna (1989:114-5).

animals. The only conclusion to be drawn concerning the function of the symbolic act in Gen 15:17 is that it ratifies a covenant.[61]

As a matter of fact, to view of the act in Gen 15 as self-imprecatory creates more problems than it solves, since God would, on those premises, take upon himself a curse. This observation has met with different solutions from those who would like to keep the act self-imprecatory, but with little success.[62] The simplest solution to the problem of how God could be placed in a situation which would necessitate a self-imprecation, is that no self-imprecation was intended with the use of the act in Gen 15.

That God is the active one here in Gen 15:17 may be explained by comparing this covenant with the so-called land-grants.[63] In these cases the king, or someone similar, promises that the gift of land will be valid for all time. The donor is thus binding himself to certain agreements, as opposed to the vassal form where the vassal had to comply with certain regulations made by the suzerain. Since the whole affair in Gen 15 is about land and how Abram can be sure that he will possess it, the form of land-grant would suit well, and the covenant would then be of a promissory type.

As to the question whether the preparatory act in Gen 15:10 is a sacrifice, much the same argument as was used against the sacrificial nature of the preparatory act in Jer 34:18 would apply here as well. There simply is no connection to what is usually described as sacrifice.[64]

To conclude, the legal function of the symbolic act in Gen 15:17 is to ratify the covenant which has been made between God and Abram.

Excursus: Judges 19:29 and 1 Samuel 11:7.

There are two texts in the OT that could be relevant to the non-biblical parallels described above, namely Judg 19:29-30 and 1 Sam 11:7. Judg

---

[61] Petersen (1977:7-9) agrees with the conclusion that the act in Gen 15 is not self-imprecatory, but he maintains that the act in Jer 34 is. Hasel (1981:63-4) also argues that the act in Gen 15 can not be self-imprecatory, while leaving the question open regarding the act in Jer 34. Wenham (1982:136) also denies the self-imprecatory nature of the act in Gen 15.

[62] Clements (1967:34) considers it remarkable that God could play this role in this curse ritual. His solutions are that either the curse had been transferred from Abram to God, or that the curse had weakened into a solemn oath. Westermann (1981:267) tries to solve this by arguing that the act had become a fixed formula, which did not produce any further reflections. See also Snijders (1958:272-3).

[63] So Weinfeld (1970:199). For an overview of the relevant terminology, see Mettinger (1976:302-3).

[64] Snijders (1958:271, n. 23) tries to salvage the sacrificial character by describing the act as sacrificial in a wider sense, but this only creates more problems, since such a confusing concept also needs to be defined, which Snijders does not do.

19:29-30 tells how a certain Levite performs a symbolic act by cutting up his concubine and sending the parts across the different borders into all the areas of Israel.[65] The text emphasizes that all the people heard and attended to the summons, 20:1 and 8. This can hardly be said to follow from the authority of the Levite.

In 1 Sam 11:7, Saul performs a similar symbolic act when he cuts up his pair of oxen and sends the parts to all the tribes in the land. It is explicitly stated that the aim is to gather the people to a military campaign. If they do not obey, their oxen will be treated as Saul treated his, v. 7. There is a similar emphasis in this text as in Judg 20:1 and 8, namely the fact that all the people responded, v. 7. However, these texts have met with different interpretations.

Concerning the act in Judg 19:29, it is possible that all Israel responded because they felt the event too outrageous to be passed by silently.[66] That would mean that the symbolic act was a dramatic visualization aimed at awakening the horror of all Israel.[67] Noth saw this as an example of how the members of the so-called amphictyonic league were requested to honour the agreement made in the constituting treaty.[68] It has also been suggested that the difference between the act in Judg 19:29 and the act in 1 Sam 11:7 is that the act in Judg 19:29 required the negotiations in 20:1-11 in order to set the military act in motion, whereas in 1 Sam 11:7 Saul's authority was enough.[69]

1 Sam 11 has been compared to the stories about the major judges.[70] An argument in favour of this is that the Spirit of God is said to have come over Saul, who before this was farming his land, v. 5. His subsequent anger is also in line with this. Some scholars maintain that in contrast to the Levite in Judg 19, Saul had behind him a sufficient authority by which he summoned the people to the struggle.[71]

A Mari text that is often brought into this discussion is ARM 2.48. It describes how a military commander is having difficulties in summoning a

---

[65] I prefer to take *gĕbûl* in v. 29 as "border". The meaning would then be that the Levite sent the different parts across the borders to the various tribes. The expression in 1 Sam 11:7, *wayšallaḥ bĕkol-gĕbûl yiśrā'ēl*, "and he sent (her) throughout the borders of Israel" is very similar to the expression in Judg 19:29, *wayĕšallĕhehā bĕkōl gĕbûl yiśrā'ēl*, "and he sent it throughout the borders of Israel." (My translations.)

[66] See Soggin (1981:289), who finds this to be the only needed explanation.

[67] So Jüngling (1981:239), with further literature.

[68] Noth (1930:100-5). See also Polzin (1969:239). For a criticism of this hypothesis, see e.g. de Vaux (1978:695-715). De Vaux (1961:215-6) considers the act to be a way of calling the people to arms. The response was up to each group, making its own decision.

[69] So Stoebe (1973:227).

[70] So Alt (1966:194-6) and Klein (1983:107).

[71] So e.g. Jüngling (1981:238-9) and Gordon (1986:124).

people called Haneans to battle.[72] He is writing for his lord's permission to cut off the head of a prisoner and send it among the Haneans, telling them by means of this symbolic act what might happen to them if they do not obey. This text is hardly anything but an attempt to frighten the people to perform a certain duty. It has no bearing on the act in Judg 19:29, but as far as 1 Sam 11:7 is concerned, the case may be different.

These texts, Judg 19:29 and 1 Sam 11:7, are examples of an extended use of curses, or threats. They do not occur in the context of covenant making, although Judg 19:29 is hard to understand without some form of prior agreement among the tribes. Saul, as well as the commander in ARM 2.48, is appealing not to a prior agreement but to his own strength, making it possible for him to execute his threat.

2.4.4 Historical Explanation

An attempt to explain this act historically immediately invites to speculation, since there are so few symbolic meanings that can be used in the attempt. However, there are some indications that will be followed here.

To make a covenant is generally regarded as associated with the killing of an animal. It is probably correct to understand the historical explanation of the technical expression *kārat běrît*, lit. "cut a covenant", as a development where the animal which was cut up has been replaced with the goal of the act, namely the ratification of the *běrît*, "covenant".

It has been found above that there are no indications that either of the occurrences of the act in Gen 15:17 and Jer 34:18-19 was self-imprecatory. However, it may well be that the aspect of self-imprecation played a part in the formation of the act.

---

[72] See Wallis (1952:58), who is of the opinion that the Haneans stood in a legal relationship to the king of Mari, making it possible for the king to put forth such demands.

2.4.5 Summary and Conclusions

1. It is clear from the descriptions of the procedure of the act in Jer 34 and Gen 15 that only one party of the covenant walks through the parts. This is best explained by regarding both covenants as of a non-parity nature.

2. In Gen 15 it is the superior party, God, who walks through the parts and in Jer 34 it is the subordinate party, the people. This is best explained by regarding the covenant in Gen 15 as a promissory covenant and the one in Jer 34 as obligatory. The covenant in Gen 15 could well be compared with the ancient Near Eastern royal land-grants, whereas the one in Jer 34 is best compared with vassal treaties.

3. The parallels from the ancient Near East, usually brought forth in analyzing these symbolic acts, are of little or no real value, since they do not describe the same act as in Gen 15 and Jer 34. The only comparison which is relevant for both performance and legal function remains between these two biblical texts.

4. Both in Gen 15 and Jer 34 the legal symbolic act of walking through a divided animal, or animals, has been found to have the legal function of ratifying a covenant that has been made. The main reason is that in both texts the act has been found to be identified with the abstract, technical expression for making a covenant in the OT, *kārat běrît*. The act was therefore a legal symbolic act whereby a covenant was ratified. The act in Gen 15 stands out by the fact that it is a reuse of the legal symbolic act in a non-legal context, although it is clearly emphasized as having a legal function. This change of context is due to the fact that God plays a part in the making of the covenant.

5. There is no need to consider either the act in Gen 15 or the act in Jer 34 as self-imprecatory. That a self-imprecatory interpretation has been so common among scholars is to be attributed to the following factors; firstly, excessive comparison with examples of animal slaughter from the ancient Near East, sometimes functioning as self-imprecatory, secondly, a faulty reading of Jer 34:18, thirdly, the attempt to extract the function of the act from its procedure and, fourthly, the failure to distinguish between the historical explanation of the act and its use.

6. There is no need to consider the act as sacrificial, either in Gen 15 or in Jer 34. No clues exist in the contexts that would lead in such a direction. The mere slaughtering of animals is all too general an act to be considered as sacrificial.

7. The acts in Judg 19:29 and 1 Sam 11:7 are not relevant in relation to the act in Gen 15 and Jer 34. Neither of them can be shown to have any legal function. It is likely that the act in Judg 19:29 functions as a horrifying example and the act in 1 Sam 11:7 as a threat.

8. The historical explanation of this act leaves much in the dark, thus opening the path to speculation. It is clear, however, that killing an animal was connected with the making of a covenant, which can be seen from the etymology of the expression *kārat běrît*, "cut a covenant". It is possible that the aspect of self-imprecation had a part to play in the formation of this act, but that is as far as a historical explanation can proceed without undue speculation.

2.5 Sharing a Meal

2.5.1 Introduction

The texts to be studied here are Gen 26:30; 31:46, 54 and 2 Sam 3:20. These are the texts that most certainly describe a meal with a legal function, to be called a covenant meal in the following. However, other texts have often been claimed as describing this particular legal symbolic act, such as Exod 18:12;[1] 24:11;[2] Josh 9:14;[3] 1 Kgs 1:25 and Obad 7.[4] The allusions in these texts are all too weak for a firm conclusion to be reached, however. In Josh 9:14 the point of tasting the food seems to be to insure that the men had been traveling for a long time. No meal is therefore described in Josh 9:14. In Exod 18:12 the meal functions as a sacrificial meal, without any indications of a legal function.[5] The proper understanding of the meal in Exod 24:11 still appears to be missing.[6]

2.5.2 Procedure.

The procedure for this legal symbolic act is basically that of an ordinary meal, although the circumstances differ among the relevant texts. The meals in Gen 26:30 and 2 Sam 3:20 very much resemble ordinary meals. The meal described in Gen 31:46, 54 is similar to the one in Gen 26:30, except that it occurs in a sacrificial context, v. 54. In 2 Sam 3:20 there is a description of King David's royal banquet for Abner and his men, which is a rather different context from the one found in the other examples. Never-

---

[1] So e.g. Brekelmans (1954:219), Fensham (1964a:54), Cody (1968:165) and Sarna (1991:99). Mettinger (1988:27) regards this view as tempting. De Moor (1990:148-9) holds that Exod 18 refers to a treaty, although he does not mention the presence of a covenant meal. The attempt by Avishur (1988) to show the treaty character of Exod 18:1-12, together with the meal as a covenant meal, is not convincing.

[2] So e.g. Vriezen (1972:113-4, 119), Childs (1974:501-2), de Vaux (1978:446-7) and McCarthy (1981:265-9).

[3] So e.g. Fensham (1964:123).

[4] For further examples of possible instances, see McCree (1926).

[5] So e.g. Childs (1974:329), who holds it possible that v. 12 once described a covenant, but in the form it now has, it is the natural consequence of Jethro's response to the exodus. See also Durham (1987:241, 244-5). Indeed, Cody (1968:158) has to infer that there once was a "covenant-making scene", which has been omitted or displaced at a later stage, to substantiate his view that the meal actually was a covenant meal.

[6] For different views, see e.g. Ruprecht (1980:150-1), Hossfeld (1982:199), Nicholson (1986:173) and de Moor (1990:226-7).

theless, these meals all share the common characteristics of what is to be considered a covenant meal, as will be shown below under Legal Function.

2.5.3 Legal Function.

As was stated above, the covenant meal is similar to an ordinary meal, to the extent that it can be said to be an ordinary meal that has gained a further function. This makes the covenant meal rather unique among the legal symbolic acts in this study, since these acts are normally used solely in their legal function. This, together with the fact that nothing is said explicitly concerning the legal function of the meal, makes it hard to clearly understand the legal function of the act. It therefore depends on the contextual analysis to show that the meals in these instances are indeed used in a way that goes beyond the function of an ordinary meal, namely as legal acts. This will require that the analysis of the relevant texts below be especially sensitive to the respective literary contexts.

2.5.3.1 Genesis 26:30

In order to understand the legal function of the meal in Gen 26:30, several allusions to the making of a covenant between the two parties, Abimelech and Isaac, must first be noted.

Abimelech wishes to make a covenant with Isaac, v. 28. This plea consists of two parts which are both request formulas, "let there be an oath between you and us" and "let us make a covenant with you". The word *ʾālâ*, oath" and the expression *kārat bĕrît*, "make a covenant" are both used in legal contexts in a technical sense. Later in v. 31 the oath is taken, *wayyiššābĕ⁽û ʾîš lĕʾāḥîw*, "They took an oath with one another."[7] Abimelech also assures Isaac in v. 29 that he has done nothing but *ṭôb*, "good" on his behalf. "Good" is a technical term used in legal contexts for fulfilling covenant obligations.[8] The word *šālôm*, "peace" is similarly well known for its technical function in legal contexts.[9] In this context it describes the state of fulfilled stipulations. It occurs twice in this text, vv. 29 and 31, as part of the phrase *šillaḥ bĕšālôm*, "send away in peace". In v. 29 the following statement of Abimelech, "(we) have sent you away in peace" stands in parallelism with the prior statement, "(we) have done to you nothing but

---

[7] My translation.

[8] So e.g. McCarthy (1981:171), Kalluveettil (1982:45), Bovati (1986:144) and Höver-Johag (1982:332-3).

[9] See e.g. Kalluveettil (1982:34-42). See also Munn-Rankin (1956:85-6) for a similar use in ancient Oriental diplomacy.

good". These two phrases then serve to strengthen the point which Abimelech is trying to make, namely that the relationship between Isaac and himself meets the requirements for a covenant between them.

In v. 30 there is a short description of the meal that Isaac prepares for Abimelech and his men. The expression *wayyōʾkělû wayyištû*, "they ate and drank", functions as a hendiadys for having a meal. This meal has a pivotal position in the narrative, since it ends the description of the day of the arrival of Abimelech, and then afterwards in v. 31 a new day breaks with Isaac and Abimelech taking oaths and then parting. There is no explicit mention of how the covenant between Isaac and Abimelech was accomplished, in contrast to the oath which is explicitly taken in v. 31. This leaves the meal in v. 30 to fulfil this function. It would then have a further meaning than that of an ordinary meal, since a particular legal function would be performed by means of the meal.

> The expression "they ate and drank" finds an interesting parallel in a legal document from Mari, ARM 8.85:5'. After the legal agreement has been described, it says in the final line, "il aura mangé". A more extensive expression is found in ARM 8.13:11'-12', a legal document concerning the sale of land: "They ate the ram, drank the cup, and anointed themselves with oil."[10] In these two legal contexts the meal, which occurs at the end, is likely to be interpreted as a ratification of the agreement that has been made. If this is true, then the climax of the description of a legal agreement comes at the end and in a very abrupt way. Nevertheless, the agreement would seem to be in working order, once this act is performed. If this is compared with Gen 26:30, something similar is found. The mentioning of the meal is short and abrupt and ends the transaction, but once the meal is completed, the covenant is apparently ratified.[11]

The pivotal position of the phrase, followed by a geographical dislocation,[12] the fact that the context contains terminology that is well known from covenant-making, the lack of any other explicit means of ratification of the covenant and the mere mentioning of the meal, all serve to strengthen the conclusion that this meal ratifies the covenant which has been made between Isaac and Abimelech. Early the next day they both swear an oath, which probably confirms the newly made covenant.

---

[10] The translation is from Malul (1988:346). Malul (1988:349-50) identifies the word *karrum* in the text from Mari with old Akkadian *kerrum*, "ram".

[11] For further examples from the ancient Near East of meals with a legal function, see Mettinger (1976:220).

[12] See Brekelmans (1954:223), who notes that the conclusion of a covenant often receives this consequence in Genesis.

2.5.3.2 *Genesis 31:46, 54*

This is a description of the occasion when Laban and Jacob made a covenant. Earlier in vv. 36-42, Jacob accused Laban of cheating him. In vv. 43-44 Laban answers by inviting Jacob to make a covenant with him, v. 44a, "Come now, let us make a covenant, you and I". This functions as a superscription to what follows in vv. 44b-54. Indeed, already in v. 44b Laban makes a declaration concerning the function of the covenant, namely that it is to be a "witness" between them.

> Westermann finds this incomprehensible since, firstly, *běrît* cannot be the subject of *wěhāyâ* because it is feminine and, secondly, *běrît* cannot be a witness to itself.[13] The syntactical construction may, however, be a case of constructio ad sensum, of which another example can be found in Gen 39:5, *wayhî birkat*.[14] The reason for this grammatical clash between genders is probably that *běrît* is semantically orientated towards *ʿēd*, "witness", which is masculine. The actual reference of *ʿēd* is later said in vv. 48 and 52 to be the *gal*, "heap", which is also masculine. As to the second problem, it can be said that through metonymy *běrît* is given the figurative meaning of something that is associated with the covenant and which is described immediately afterwards in v. 45, namely the pillar.

Before the analysis of this text is taken any further, however, it should be noted that the events described in the text are not strictly chronological.[15] In vv. 46 and 54 there are descriptions of a meal, and it is hardly possible to regard this as being two different meals. Verses 44-46 should therefore be considered a summary in relation to that which follows. In vv. 44-46 it is said that the covenant will be a witness between the two parties, v. 44b, that Jacob builds a pillar, v. 45, that he and his family build a heap of stones, v. 46, and that they share a meal on the heap, v. 46.

In vv. 47-54 there is then found a more detailed description of what has already been described briefly in v. 44b-46. The voice also changes from third person to Laban in first person in v. 48. In vv. 48-53a Laban refers back to the pillar and the heap of stones in vv. 45-46 and describes their function, namely to be witnesses to the covenant between the two parties.[16]

---

13 Westermann (1981:608).

14 See GKC (465-6) and Waltke & O'Connor (1990:109).

15 For a valuable treatment of this rhetorical process, see Martin (1969).

16 So Daube (1947:63-4, n. 5) and Jackson (1989:189-90). Jackson relates this use of raising an uninscribed stone monument to the inscribed Kudurru-stones from the ancient Near East, which served to mark out boundaries. Graesser (1972:37-9) also

God is also said by Laban in vv. 49 and 53 to be watchman and judge between them.

In vv. 53b-54 Jacob comes to the forefront of the narrative again, and a more detailed description of his function in the covenant-making with Laban is presented than was given in summary form in vv. 44-46. In v. 53b Jacob swears an oath and in v. 54 he offers a sacrifice, after which he invites his family to a meal.[17] The most natural conclusion is that they eat of the sacrificial meat. Concerning the oath which Jacob is said to take in v. 53b, it should be noted that in contrast to Gen 26:31, it seems to be taken before the meal and not after. However, since the text has already been found not to be strictly chronological, this may indeed be the reason for the particular placement of the oath in relation to the meal as well.

In Gen 32:1 the transaction is complete and Laban leaves. This means that the meal has here in v. 54, as in Gen 26:30, a pivotal placement in the literary structure. If v. 54 is viewed in the larger context of the covenant-making, the meal would seem to ratify the covenant between Laban and Jacob. This is strengthened by the use of terminology in the context which is well known from covenant-making, the lack of any other explicit means of ratifying the covenant and the mere fact that the meal is mentioned.

2.5.3.3 2 Samuel 3:20

This is the story of King David's banquet for Abner and his men. In v. 12 Abner sends a message to David, *kortâ běrîtěkā ʾittî*, "Make your covenant with me". In the event that David does this, Abner promises to stand by his side. In v. 13 David agrees to this, *ṭôb ʾănî ʾekrōt ʾittěkā běrît*, "Good; I will make a covenant with you." The use of *ṭôb*, "good", again used in the context of covenant-making, means that David accepts this pledge.[18] Then, in vv. 13-16, David's terms are described and fulfilled. In vv. 17-19 Abner shows himself to be serious in regard to standing by David. Then, when Abner and his men come to David in v. 20, David arranges a *mišteh*, lit. "meal" for them. When Abner then asks David for permission to leave in

---

points out that these pillars served a legal function in marking out the legal relationship between the covenant parties.

[17] See Westermann (1981:610), who notes that the family must have included Laban and his followers.

[18] Incidentally, Abner describes the reaction of "Israel and the whole house of Benjamin", namely that they thought an agreement with David would be *ṭôb*, "good". This is also used in a technical sense, since in v. 21 Abner explains that he is trying to make them establish a treaty with David. Their consent is thus described as "good". So also e.g. Kalluveettil (1982:47).

v. 21, it is stated three times that Abner left *bĕšalôm*, "in peace", vv. 21, 22 and 23.[19] The use of *šalôm*, "peace", in the context of covenant-making has been noted earlier in regard to the meal in Gen 26:30. The covenant between David and Abner then appears to have been accomplished, but there is no explicit reference to the fact that the agreement has been made. It is therefore interesting to note that here, as in Gen 26:30 and 31:54, the the meal has a pivotal position in the literary structure. Once the meal has taken place, the covenant appears to be in working order, and the parties which concluded the covenant can depart from each other, v. 21. The four indications of the legal function of the meals in Gen 26:30 and 31:46, 54 can thus be found here as well.[20] These indications are, firstly, the pivotal position of the meal in the literary structure, followed by a geographical dislocation, secondly, the use of terminology within the context otherwise well known from covenant-making, thirdly, the lack of any other explicit means of ratifying the covenant and, fourthly, the mere fact that the meal is mentioned. These indications lead to the conclusion that the meal in 2 Sam 3:20 ratifies the covenant between David and Abner.[21]

2.5.4 Historical Explanation

The covenant meal functioned simultaneously as an ordinary meal. To share the fellowship at the table of someone's family would have been tantamount to being accepted into that fellowship. No enmity could abide between two parties who had eaten together. With this background, one could well understand why the meal came to function as a way of ratifying an agreement. It was a clear way of displaying the mutual acceptance and agreement between the parties.[22]

---

[19] The LXX mentions it further in v. 24. Gordon (1986:219) believes that this could be a hint at a covenantal agreement between David and Abner. McCarter (1984:117) notices that the author also uses this expression in the wider sense of clearing David of any possible involvement in the murder of Abner.

[20] The absence of oaths is probably due to the fact that it is not a covenant on a parity level, but between a superior or 'suzerain', David, and his servant or 'vassal', Abner.

[21] So also Kalluveettil (1982:12-3). McCarthy (1982:79) calls it "a possible covenant rite". Smend (1977:456), however, denies any such meaning to the meal in this text.

[22] See further McCarthy (1964:185) and Malul (1988:376-8).

2.5.5 Summary and Conclusions

1. The performance of the covenant meal is that of an ordinary meal, which may occur in a sacrificial context.

2. There are four decisive arguments for a legal function of the meals in Gen 26:30; 31:46, 54 and 2 Sam 3:20. Firstly, the meals have a pivotal placement in the literary structure, always followed by a geographical dislocation. Secondly, these contexts contain technical terminology which is well known from covenant-making. Thirdly, no other, more explicit means of ratification or conclusion of the covenants are mentioned. Fourthly, the simple fact that the meals are mentioned at all argues strongly in favour of the view that they have a wider function, although this argument does not necessarily point specifically towards a legal function.

3. The legal function of the covenant meal is to ratify a covenant that has been made earlier between two parties.

4. The covenant meal is not a symbolic meal in the sense that it only functions in its legal, symbolic sense, since it remains an ordinary meal as well.

5. The historical explanation of the covenant meal is quite simple. It is based on the function of the meal to bring a stranger into the family circle through participating in the meal. This suited the legal function of ratifying a covenant well, since a covenant meant agreement between the parties, the termination of enmities and the establishment of peace.

2.6 Piercing the Ear of the Slave

2.6.1 Introduction

This legal act presents some very particular problems, most of which are in the area of procedure. Much has been written concerning the meaning of the expressions ʿebed ʿibrî, "Hebrew slave", waʿăbādô lĕʿōlām, "serve him forever", ḥopšî ḥinnām, "totally free" and ʾel-hāʾĕlōhîm, "to God" in Exod 21:2-6.[1] Some of these questions go beyond the limits of this analysis, but at the same time they may shed some light on the analysis of the legal function of the act. Therefore, the analysis below will include some short discussions of the present situation within scholarship on these issues, including some suggestions as to where the solutions might be found.

There is also the question of the relationship between the description of the act in Exod 21:6 and the similar description in Deut 15:17. This, however, will be touched upon only in so far as it affects the interpretation of the act. Something will also need to be said regarding the related law in Lev 25:39-46 and the description of the incident in Jer 34:8-16.

A problem directly related to the question of the legal function is whether the slave was a debt slave, i.e., a free Israelite who had been forced to sell himself into slavery, or what might be called a proper slave.

2.6.2 Procedure

Since there is so much concerning the procedure of this act that appears to be unclear, it would seem suitable to begin with what is certain. Exod 21:2-6 will be used as the basic text, and the differences in relation to Deut 15:12-18 will be analysed in so far as they are relevant.

The law concerns a slave that has been purchased and bound for a period of up to six years, v. 2a, after which time the law prescribes that the slave should be set free, v. 2b. Then there are more detailed regulations regarding whether the slave was married or not when he entered slavery, whether he has any children, and if wife and children should be set free as well, vv. 3-4. These questions do not immediately relate to the issue of the legal act. In vv. 5-6, however, another regulation is given, which appears to present a counter-case[2] to the earlier law in vv. 2-4. It concerns the case when the slave prefers to remain in slavery even after the six years have elapsed. He is then said in v. 5 to make the following statement: ʾāhabtî ʾet-ădōnî ʾet-ištî

---

[1] My translations.

[2] So e.g. Schwienhorst-Schönberger (1990:303-4).

wĕʾet-bānāy lōʾ ʾēṣēʾ ḥopšî, "I love my master, my wife, and my children; I will not go out a free person". The owner then brings the slave *ʾel-hāʾĕlōhîm wĕhiggîšô ʾel-haddelet ʾô ʾel-hammĕzûzā*, "to God, and he shall bring him to the door or the doorpost", the meaning of which is debated.[3] Then *wĕrāṣaʿ ʾădōnāyw ʾet-ʾoznô bammarṣēaʿ*, "his master shall pierce his ear with an awl". The result is that the slave will *waʿăbādô lĕʿōlām*, "serve him forever".[4]

One of the questions concerns the meaning of the expression in v. 2, *ʿebed ʿibrî*, usually translated "Hebrew slave". The question concerns the term *ʿibrî*, whether it is to be taken as an ethnic term, i.e., as "Hebrew" or as a sociological term, somehow related to the name of the well-known phenomenon of the *ḥapiru*.[5] Much effort has been spent by scholars arguing that *ʿibrî* is evidence of an earlier pre-Israelite use of the lawtext, the most popular view being that it is a remnant of Canaanite law.[6] However, an analysis of all the occurrences of *ʿibrî* in the OT shows that it is always an ethnic term, denoting an Israelite.[7] There may very well have been a historical development of the term, but that does not necessarily affect the present text.[8] The term *ʿibrî* should therefore be taken in an ethnic sense.[9]

The most discussed problem in Exod 21:2-6, however, is the question of the meaning of *ʾel-hāʾĕlōhîm* in v. 6. The two basic alternatives are that it refers either to the owner's house-gods, so-called teraphim,[10] or God, which would stand for the local sanctuary.[11] This is further complicated

---

[3] My translation.

[4] My translation.

[5] The literature concerning this question is vast. For some recent treatments of the question of comparing "Hebrew" with *ḥapiru*, see Loretz (1984) and Na'aman (1986).

[6] So e.g. Lemche (1979:2), "legislation most likely originating in the Canaanite world has been adopted in the Old Testament and, as preserved in Ex 21, 2ff., in a nearly unchanged form." This is a somewhat strange view methodologically speaking, since no Canaanite lawtext has yet been found, so e.g. Sonsino (1980:19). For a more balanced view, see de Vaux (1961:146), Cardellini (1981:250-1) and Phillips (1984:54-5, 59). Thompson (1968:82-3) makes use of a similar, balanced line of argument when he criticizes the view that the law of levirate in Deut 25 would be of Canaanite origin.

[7] So e.g. Riesener (1979:115-21) and Sarna (1991:265-6).

[8] For a convincing explanation of such a development, see Na'man (1986).

[9] So e.g. Phillips (1984:55, 61), Loretz (1984:150), Freedman & Willoughby (1986:1055) and Schwienhorst-Schönberger (1990:306-7). The same line of reasoning would apply to the meaning of the term *ḥopšî*, which has been used as well to reflect a sociological term, *ḥupšu*, see e.g. Lemche (1975:139-40) and Lohfink (1982:125-6).

[10] So e.g. Gordon (1935:139-40), Draffkorn (1957:217), Gaster (1969:403), Paul (1970:50), Weinfeld (1972:233) and Phillips (1984:51).

[11] So e.g. Falk (1959:88), Fensham (1959:161), Loretz (1984:149), Vannoy (1974:240), Childs (1974:469), Blenkinsopp (1983:86-7), Otto (1988:36) and

because of the expression that comes immediately afterwards, "and he shall bring him to the door or the doorpost", which to some scholars appears to be a later addition.[12] These two difficulties are intertwined in such a way that the answer to one is most often used as an argument relating to the other, and vice versa. An attempt must be made, however, to analyze them separately.

The expression *ʾel-hāʾĕlōhîm*, "to God/gods" is often supposed to have referred to an originally Canaanite legal custom of piercing the ear of the slave in the presence of the house-gods, or teraphim, belonging to the slave's owner. However, when this law later became a part of the Israelite legal heritage, such a perspective soon became unthinkable and the expression began to be read as "God" instead.[13] However, to verify such a development is complicated, to say the least. It is one thing to argue that it could have been read as referring to house-gods in a non-Israelite context, but it is quite another to explain that it was in fact read so, and why. The text we are dealing with leads us to posit the implied reader to be an Israelite, and therefore we must read the expression as "to God".

The problem with the expression "and he shall bring him to the door or the doorpost" is, as was stated above, related to the interpretation of the expression *ʾel-hāʾĕlōhîm*. If it was once used to refer to house-gods, then the later expression could hardly have served any other function than to explain the procedure of the act, whether or not it was original or added later. We are then back to the problem how such a view could have found its way into an Israelite law-code. If, on the other hand, the expression *ʾel-hāʾĕlōhîm* originally referred to God, there are three possible interpretations of the expression "and he shall bring him to the door or the doorpost":

1. The expression is original and explains the procedure.[14]
2. The expression is original and describes a subsequent act.[15]
3. The expression was added at a later stage, in order to alter the interpretation from that of the local sanctuary to that of the door of the owner.[16]

Schwienhorst-Schönberger (1990:308).

[12] So e.g. Cardellini (1981:248), Loretz (1984:143-4) and Schwienhorst-Schönberger (1990:308).

[13] So e.g. Draffkorn (1957:218).

[14] So e.g. Fensham (1959:160), Durham (1987:321), Otto (1988:36, 88, n. 134) and Sarna (1991:120).

[15] So Patrick (1985:70-1). Vannoy (1974:229) considers it plausible.

[16] So Loretz (1984:145-6) and Schwienhorst-Schönberger (1990:308).

The second alternative leaves the expression "to God" without any explanation of what was to be done at the sanctuary. Some propose that an oath would have been taken,[17] but this must remain uncertain. According to the third alternative, the addition would have been made, as it was done in Deut 15:17, by a deuteronomistic redactor who could not accept local sanctuaries in light of his attempt to describe a centralized cult.[18] The problem with this alternative is what is to be done with the expression "to God". It could be interpreted in accordance with Deut 6:9, which could have been a way for the centralizing tendency in Deuteronomy to fill the gap after the local sanctuaries.[19] It was then not meant to contradict the earlier law but merely to transfer the procedure from the local sanctuary to wherever the name of God was meant to be put, e.g. at the city gate or perhaps at the entrance to the owner's house. However, it is uncertain whether this is anything more than a theoretical construction. On the whole, this interpretation seems somewhat strained.[20] If the deuteronomists wanted to correct Exod 21:6 into the likeness of Deut 15:17, and harmonize both with Deut 6:9, it is strange that in Deut 6:9 we have only "doorposts", in Deut 15:17 only "door" and in Exod 21:6 both terms. This diversity speaks against an intentional adaptation of the laws to Deut 6:9. Another problem with this interpretation is that there is a difference between piercing the ear of a slave against a door or doorpost, and writing on a door or doorpost. It also demands that the deuteronomists would have regarded the writing on the doorposts as sharing the same reference as "God" in Exod 21:6. But why was the expression "to God" then not retained in Deut 15:17?

These problems make it more probable to understand the expression "and he shall bring him to the door or the doorpost" as an explicative expression, defining more exactly the place of the symbolic act. The subordinate clause begins in v. 5 with *weʾim*, "but if" and a case of the prefix conjugation. It is followed in v. 6 by the main clause, containing four cases of apodosis waw.[21] The second example of *wehiggîšô*, "and he will bring him", would then introduce an explicative clause in relation to the former

---

[17] So e.g. Patrick (1985:70).

[18] So Schwienhorst-Schönberger (1990:308).

[19] Cf. Keel (1981:183-92) for Deut 6:9, and Loretz (1984:145) and Schwienhorst-Schönberger (1990:308) for its application to Exod 21:6. For criticism of this view, see Otto (1988:35-6) and Osumi (1991:162-4).

[20] So e.g. Otto (1988:88, n. 125, 130), who refers to Phillips (1984) for arguments against making Exod 21:2-6 dependent on Deut 15:12-18.

[21] See Waltke & O'Connor (1990:526).

example.[22] It might be that the explicative function, in contrast to the consequential function of *wĕrāṣaʿ*, "and then he shall pierce" and *waʿăbādô*, "and then he will serve him", is explicitly marked out by the repetition of *wĕhiggîšô*, in order to make it clear that it explains the former clause.[23] The first alternative above is then to be preferred.

> It is interesting that when the word *mĕzûzâ*, "doorpost" is in the singular, as in Ex 21:6, it seems to refer only to a doorpost of a sanctuary, 1 Sam 1:9; Ezek 41:21; 43:8; 45:19; 46:2,[24] with Isa 57:8 as a possible exception. The plural is used for the doorposts of a sanctuary, Exod 12:7, 22, 23; 1 Kgs 6:31, 33; 7:5; Prov 8:34, a dwelling house, Deut 6:9; 11:20, and a city gate, Judg 16:3. This argues for that a sanctuary is meant in Ex. 21:6.

The parallel law-text in Deut 15:12-18 has already been referred to. In this text it is not stated that the owner should take the slave "to God", and it contains only a slight reference to the door, when it is said in v. 17 that the owner should take an awl and *wĕnātattâ bĕʾoznô ûbaddelet*, "thrust it through his earlobe into the door". This leaves us completely in the dark as to which door is being referred to. The description of the procedure of the act in Deut 15:17 must be considered an abbreviated version of the one in Exod 21:5-6. One possible reason has been stated above, namely the need for a consistent description of a centralized cult which would demand the erasure of the expression "to God".[25] The act is then considered to have been transformed into a wholly secular act, being performed at the owner's house. Another possible reason could be that the reference to the door was so clear that it did not need a further description. However, since the description is so vague, it must be considered an open question as to which door is referred to in Deut 15:17.

So far, no similar procedure for making someone a permanent slave has been found outside the OT. There are, however, some acts that might appear similar. According to the Middle Assyrian Laws § 44, a legitimate punishment to be performed by the owner on his slaves is that "he may mutilate his ears by piercing (them)."[26] The law of Hammurapi § 282 states that when a slave does not recognize his status as slave, "his master shall prove him to be his slave and cut off his ear."[27] However, these acts are

---

[22] See Waltke & O'Connor (1990:652-3).

[23] My translations.

[24] So Otto (1988:36).

[25] So e.g. Weinfeld (1972:233) and Mayes (1979:252)

[26] *ANET* (184).

[27] *ANET* (177).

punitive acts without any symbolic value. There are, therefore, no extra-
biblical parallels to this act that can be of any direct guidance in the interpretation.

According to Exod 21:6, the owner of the slave pierces the ear of the
slave, apparently against the door or the doorpost mentioned immediately
before. He is said to use a *marṣēaʿ*, "awl", in order to *rāṣaʿ*, "pierce", the ear
of the slave. The paranomastic construction is unmistakable, and might
have served as a device to facilitate the transmission of the law in oral
form. The verb is a hapax legoumena in the OT,[28] and the noun occurs only
here and in the parallel in Deut 15:17, where the verb used is *nātan*, "give",
apparently to simplify the description. Deut 15:17 explains more clearly
the procedure of the act by saying, "then you shall take an awl and thrust it
through his earlobe into the door". Unfortunately, the possible nuances that
originally accompanied these terms are now lost, and we are left with the
rough facts of the act of piercing and something used to perform the act.
The LXX has apparently been in the same situation, since it translates both
rāṣaʿ in Exod 21:6, *nātan* in Deut 15:17 and the more usual term for piercing or perforating, namely *nāqab* in Job 40:24, 26 and Hag 1:6, with
τρυπάω, "pierce through".

It is unclear whether this piercing might have had some practical purpose. One likely possibility would be in order to pass a cord or ring
through the hole in the ear, thus marking the slave. This was prescribed in
the Middle Assyrian Laws § 40 as a punishment for a man who had seen a
veiled harlot and let her go, "they shall pierce his ears, thread (them) with a
cord, (and) tie (it) at his back".[29] A similar line of reasoning would be to
compare the piercing of the ear with the custom of wearing ear-rings. This
custom was well-known in the OT,[30] and it might be a more relevant background to the act, since it was not a matter of punishment. Nothing is said
in Exod 21:6 and Deut 15:17 about the use of the perforated ear, which
might indicate that it was meant as a simple mark in itself. The practice of
marking slaves with some kind of tattoo was also used in the ancient Near
East.[31] It was then a matter of displaying both that the individual was a
slave and sometimes also to whom the slave belonged. There is one
example in an Aramaic legal document, containing a testamentary manumission, "his handmaiden, upon whose hand is a mark, on the right, thus;

---

[28]   See *HALAT* (1198).
[29]   *ANET* (183).
[30]   Cf. Gen 35:4; Exod 32:2; Ezek 16:12.
[31]   See e.g. *BMAP* 5:3; 8:5-9, and Segal (1983), 3:1-2; 5:8; 9:2; 10a:5; 97a:1; 164a:1.

'(belonging) to Meshullam".[32] It might also be the case that the intended use of the mark was so evident that it did not have to be spelled out.

The act of piercing the ear of the slave who has decided to remain a slave on a permanent basis in Exod 21:5-6 is rather unclear in its performance. The best alternative, however, is that the slave was brought to the local sanctuary, where the ear was pierced against the door or doorpost by his owner.

2.6.3 Legal Function

It appears obvious from the text that the legal function of the act is to make the slave a permanent slave. However, there are some problems that, when solved, will help to elucidate various details regarding this transference from the state of liberated slave to that of slave forever, as is stated in Exod 21:6. One such problem is what form of slavery the text is actually dealing with. Has the slave been bought for money, which might imply that he was a slave prior to the purchase, or has he been forced to go into slavery because of inability to pay his debts, which naturally implies that he was a free Israelite before he became a debt slave?

The common practice of debt slavery was found in ancient Israel.[33] It is described in Lev 25:39-46, where it is stated that an Israelite, who could not pay his debts, could sell himself and even his family as temporary slaves. The law is careful to differentiate between the Israelite who is forced into slavery, called "brother", v. 39, and slaves who are not Israelites, but come from neighbouring areas, vv. 44-46. The Israelite who has sold himself is said not to be forced to perform the ordinary work of slaves, v. 39. This is also described in narrative form in Jer 34, where the same distinction is made in vv. 9 and 14. There it is stated that the slaves that are to be set free are the Hebrew slaves, also called Judahites in v. 9, thus excluding the non-Hebrew slaves. However, in the earlier Covenant code in Exodus, no explicit discrimination between Hebrew and non-Hebrew slaves can be found. The probable reason for this is that this law-code, like most ancient Near Eastern law-codes, is not meant to be exhaustive, but is more interested in special cases and deviations from the proper way of dealing with law, such as the case in 21:5-6.[34] The handling

---

[32] *BMAP* 5:3. See also Gen 4:15; Isa 44:5; 49:16; Ezek 9:4.

[33] See de Vaux (1961:82-3) and Jackson (1988:91).

[34] Cf. Westbrook (1988:4-5): "And indeed, comprehensive treatment in the modern sense may not have been the aim of the codes, since they assume in the reader a thorough knowledge of the common law. Often where two codes contain the same case, one will omit some detail which the modern reader would have thought necessary."

of non-Hebrew slaves was probably considered such an unproblematic area
that it did not need to be included in the law-code. This is not very much
different from what was discussed in regard to Lev 25, since it is only in
passing that we learn of the non-Hebrew slaves, and in Jer 34 the non-
Hebrew slaves are only mentioned implicitly. In Deut 15:12-18, however,
it is made quite explicit that it is a matter of a Hebrew man and woman
who are forced into debt slavery. There were thus two kinds of slaves in
ancient Israel, Israelites who had been forced into debt slavery and slaves
from foreign people. The two categories had quite different conditions. In
Exod 21:2-6 it must also be a matter of debt slavery to start with, since it is
stated explicitly that the law only applies to a Hebrew slave and that it is a
temporary slavery. This form of slavery needs a particular legal symbolic
act to be transformed into the hybrid form of an Israelite enslaved *lĕ'ōlām*,
"forever", Ex 21:6 and similarly Deut 15:17. This was otherwise the
normal circumstances for non-Israelite slaves, who were the property of the
Israelites *lĕ'ōlām*, "forever", Lev 25:46.[35]

The law in Exod 21:2 starts with *kî tiqneh 'ebed 'ibrî*, "When You buy a
male Hebrew slave". The use of the verb *qānâ*, "buy" has been claimed to
imply that the slave must have been bought for money.[36] There is also the
matter of the logic of the statement, namely that if a slave is said to be
bought, then he must surely have been a slave before the purchase. It
cannot be held, however, that *qānâ* must imply that money was paid, since
the verb could be used, e.g., in the sense of obtaining a bride in Ruth
4:10.[37] Since the other texts dealing with debt slavery seem to say that the
persons in debt have sold themselves, Lev 25:39; Deut 15:12 and Jer
34:14, the same might very well be the case with the use of *qānâ*,[38] but
from the point of view of the owner. It is possible that this more elaborate
use of *qānâ* in the early law of Exod 21:2 became all too obscure with time,
and was subsequently replaced in common usage with the less ambiguous
niphal form of *mākar*, "sell". The fact that the text of Exod 21:2 states that
a slave was bought does not necessarily mean that the person was a slave
before the so-called purchase. It should most likely be considered as a case
of prolepsis, where the status to which the person is transferred is used by
the author to describe him even before he became a slave.[39]

---

[35]My translation.

[36] So Cardellini (1981:246).

[37] So e.g. Falk (1967:241-3), who notes a similar use of the antonym of *qānâ*, namely
mākar, "sell". See also Weiss (1964) and Lang (1981:487, n. 6).

[38] So Schwienhorst-Schönberger (1990:310, n. 28).

[39] So e.g. Lemche (1975:135).

It would seem from the description of the act in Exod 21:5-6 that the legal procedure is a matter of family law, a sub-category of customary law.[40] What argues for this is the absence of any reference to local jurisdiction. However, it may not be as simple as that. Since it is a matter of making an exception to the law in vv. 2-4, it was apparently felt important to regulate this possibility of sidestepping the law without breaking it.[41] The point of the legislation in vv. 2-4 is that there should be a limited duration of slavery for a Hebrew slave. He should be set free after six years, but there was a possibility for him to remain a slave. In this case, the owner would need to be sure that if the slave changed his mind in the future, the owner would not be charged with breaking the law. If the slave was to be brought to the local sanctuary, as was concluded above, the legal symbolic act can no longer be considered a case of family law, since the act was obviously meant to be performed publicly.[42] It is apparent, therefore, that although the actual entering into debt slavery, as well as the ceasing of it, may be said to have belonged to family law, the exception did not. It needed to be made public, not only by being performed at a public place such as the local sanctuary, but also by making the slave wear a mark. This mark would perpetually make it clear that it was his own decision and not the illegitimate behaviour of his owner that prevented his manumission.

When we come to the question of the legal function of the act of piercing the ear of the slave, it would seem that the owner transfers the slave from the category of debt slavery to that of slavery with an unlimited duration. It is precisely this transference which calls for the official status of the procedure, as explained above.

There seems, however, to be more legal functioning in the text than has been sufficiently recognized until now. The slave makes his decision explicit by his statement in Exod 21:5, "I love my master, my wife, and my children; I will not go out a free person", which serves the function of invalidating the law of his manumission after six years.[43] This statement functions as a performative utterance, whereby the slave achieves the intended result of invalidating the law. This is, then, the first step in the legal proceedings, and it makes way for the second, the transference of the

---

[40] So Phillips (1973:357; 1984:51).

[41] So Phillips (1984:51). See also Jackson (1988:94).

[42] This was recognized quite early, when the expression "to God" was interpreted in *Tg. Onqelos* as *dyny*, "judges", see Gordon (1935:139). The LXX interprets the expression as πρὸς τὸ κριτήριον τοῦ θεοῦ, "to the tribunal of God".

[43] The version in Deut 15:16 is substantially the same.

status of the slave. The legally binding statement made by the slave is thereby a necessary prerequisite for the subsequent act of the owner.

The legal act of piercing the ear of the slave, as described in Exod 21:6, performs the legal function of accomplishing the transference of the slave from the legal state of debt slave into that of perpetual slavery, without a limited duration for his slavery. Because of its status as an exception to the law of manumission, it needs to be performed publicly at the local sanctuary. The mandatory requisite of the act is that it is preceded by a legally binding statement by the slave, whereby he renounces his right to manumission. For the act in Deut 15:17 the legal function remains the same, although the procedure may not be restricted to the local sanctuary.

2.6.4 Historical Explanation

The legal symbolic act of piercing the ear of the slave in Exod 21:6 and Deut 15:17 is based on the well-known fact that the ear symbolizes hearing and, in a further sense, obedience.[44] However, it has mostly gone unnoticed that some evidence can also be brought forward regarding the act of piercing. It was used in the context of crocodile hunting, as is clear from Job 40:24 and 26. God asks Job rhetorically if he thinks he can catch the Leviathan by piercing its nose and then put a cord through it, v. 24, or by piercing its cheek with a hook, v. 26. In v. 28 God asks Job, quite ironically, if he actually believes that the Leviathan would surrender and make an agreement with him, and if Job would be able to take him as an ʿebed ʿôlām, "eternal slave". This is similar to what is described in Exod 21:6 and Deut 15:17. It is quite possible that what is used in these texts from Job to describe the subjugation of the Leviathan is something similar to the legal act in Exod 21:6 and Deut 15:17.

The historical explanation of the legal act is then that the ear, as a symbol for the obedience of the slave, was pierced, which symbolized the submission to the owner. That the hole in the ear was then used to carry some form of tag is quite probable. However, had that been the sole reason for the act, it would probably have been made explicit.

Excursus: Driving in the Nail: A Connection?

A rather distant but still intriguing comparison could be made between this act and the act of driving in the nail, found in Mesopotamian legal material.[45] According to Malul, the act of driving in a nail in a house or a

---

[44]   See Dhorme (1923:89-90) and Liedke (1971:96).
[45]   See Malul (1987a:19).

public place was used in different legal contexts as a way of communicating a certain legal change.

Still a further comparison could be made with the Roman custom of driving in nails at temples at the end of the year as a chronological measure. It was also thought that misfortunes could be atoned for when this act was performed by a public leader. The custom was considered to have come from the Etruscans to the Romans.[46] Considering the well-known contacts between the Etruscans and the ancient Near East,[47] it would not seem inconceivable to consider the possibility of a relation between these different customs. It is to be noted that in both the Babylonian and the Roman contexts the acts are used to make something public and at a public house or sanctuary. This is something they share with the act in Exod 21:6 and possibly Deut 15:17.

---

[46] The literary source is Livy VII.3. See also Fowler (1899:234-5), Hanell (1946:125-41, esp. 138-40), Eisenhut (1964) and Groß (1964).

[47] An example of this would be the Phoenician Pyrgi inscription, which was made together with two similar inscriptions in Etruscan, see Gibson (1982:151-9).

2.6.5 Summary and Conclusions

1. The piercing of the ear of the slave was, according to Exod 21:6, probably performed at the door or doorpost of the local sanctuary. The problems involved, however, make it difficult to reach a firm conclusion.

2. The legal proceedings began with a performative statement by the slave, whereby he disavowed his right to manumission after six years of slavery. This opened the way for the owner to perform his legal act.

3. The legal function of the act of piercing the ear of the slave is that the owner thereby officially proclaims and accomplishes the transference of the legal status of the Hebrew slave, from that of being a debt-slave for a limited duration of time, to that of being a slave of the owner forever.

4. The act had to be made public since it was an exception to the general rule of the law. It created a hybrid form of slavery which normally did not exist in Israel, namely a Hebrew who was slave without a limited duration.

5. The historical explanation of the act is that the ear, as a symbol for the obedience of the slave, was pierced, which symbolized the submission of the slave to his owner.

2.7 Anointing the Head with Oil

2.7.1 Introduction

The legal symbolic act of anointing will be studied here primarily as it occurs in relation to the making of kings. This particular use of anointing will be called 'royal anointing'. As will be shown below, this royal anointing is sometimes reused in a non-legal context. This form of anointing will more properly be called 'divine anointing', since it serves to emphasize the divine election of a pretender to the throne.

The examples of anointing that will be studied are as follows; the anointing by the trees in Jotham's fable in Judg 9:8, 15, the anointings of Saul and David by Samuel in 1 Sam 10:1 and 16:13, the anointings of David as king over Judah and Israel in 2 Sam 2:4 and 5:3, a short comment concerning the anointing of Absalom in 2 Sam 19:11, the anointing of Solomon in 1 Kgs 1:39, the anointings by Elijah in 1 Kgs 19:15-16 and 2 Kgs 9:3, 6, the anointing of Joash in 2 Kgs 11:12 and the anointing of Jehoahaz in 2 Kgs 23:30. The parallel texts in Chronicles will be noted when they are relevant. Some other texts will be studied because they relate to royal anointing, namely Pss 45:8; 89:21 and 105:15. The texts which will be studied regarding priestly anointing are Exod 28:41; 29:7 and Lev 8:12. Although priestly anointing is part of cultic law, there are some interesting parallels between priestly and royal anointing.

Excursus: Earlier Views on Anointing in the OT

In order to grasp the lack of a scholarly consensus regarding royal anointing and particularly its legal function, it will be helpful to give a short description of the different views available. Mettinger, after a lengthy review of different scholarly positions, presents the following alternatives;[1]

1. The sacral interpretation. According to this view the anointing brings about a special relation between God and the king.[2]

2. The secular interpretation. According to this view it was a matter between the people through its representatives and the king.[3]

3. The mediating position. According to this view the sacral and secular aspects were both originally connected with anointing, only to be separated at a later stage.[4]

---

[1] Mettinger (1976:185-8).

[2] So Weinel (1898:54), North (1932:17), Noth (1950:177), Lys (1954:39), Halpern (1981:13-4) and Campbell (1986:51-2, n. 75; 116-7).

[3] So Kutsch (1963:71-2).

[4] So Schmidt (1970:187-8).

According to Mettinger, there was a development from the secular to the sacral.[5] To begin with, the people performed the anointing through their representatives, achieving a contractual relation between the performer and the anointed one. The performer pledged himself to the anointed one in this contractual relation. The change of the subject of the act from the elders of the people to a priest, later thought to act by divine authority, illustrates the development from the secular to the sacral.

Weisman has tried to show that the two alternatives, the secular, which he calls the "public" ceremony, and the sacral, which he calls the "prophetic" ceremony, both existed separately.[6] According to Weisman there was no development from the prophetic to the public. Rather, the prophetic pattern was transferred from the context of anointing as a mythical and ritual motif in the divine nomination of kings in the art of ancient Mesopotamia. The dual anointings would correspond to the two stages in the ancient Near Eastern marriage custom, of which the first, namely the betrothal, had no legally binding force. The legal force rested exclusively with other acts. This would then mean that the first "prophetic" anointing served to designate the king while only the second "public" anointing could proceed with any legal force.

According to Halpern, on the other hand, anointing was originally an anointing to the office of *nāgîd*.[7] He includes both of Weisman's categories in anointing as *nāgîd*.[8] Originally its purpose was not to inaugurate the king in his royal office, but to designate the one chosen by God, and to legitimate the claim of the aspirant to the throne. When the title *nāgîd* became obsolete after the division of the kingdom, however, the expression "anoint to be king" was created. Halpern regards the designation as *nāgîd* to have been originally a sacral designation, which eventually turned into a royal designation. One example of this would be 1 Kgs 1:35, where David says that he has appointed Solomon to be *nāgîd*.[9] This means that according to Halpern, Solomon did not actually become king by means of the anointing performed in 1 Kgs 1:39, but was only designated for the throne.

Since the scholarly positions are so disparate, there is need for a fresh treatment of royal anointing, particularly in relation to its legal function.

---

[5] Mettinger (1976:230-1).

[6] Weisman (1976:385-7).

[7] Halpern (1981:13-5).

[8] Halpern (1981:127).

[9] Halpern (1981:10): "This suggest [sic] that, at an early point, divine designation gave way to royal, at least pragmatically speaking, excluding the prophet or priest from policy formulation and relegating them to a rubber-stamp role." Halpern appears to hold to the opposite view of Mettinger.

2.7.2 Procedure

In some of the texts which mention anointing, there is in addition a description, although short, of the act itself. In 1 Sam 10:1 and 16:13 Samuel anoints Saul and David respectively, in 1 Kgs 1:39 the priest Zadok anoints Solomon, and in 2 Kgs 9:6 an unnamed disciple of Elisha anoints Jehu. When these texts are compared, some interesting results appear. The verb *yāṣaq*, "pour out" is used with the noun *pak*, "vial" and the verb *māšaḥ*, "anoint" with *qeren*, "horn".[10] The expression with *yāṣaq* is also different due to its designation *ʿal-rôš*, "on the head".[11] This shows that *yāṣaq* is not as technical as *māšaḥ* which includes this designation in its semantic range.[12] The verb *māšaḥ* is therefore synonymous with *yāṣaq* *ʿal-rôš*, "pour on the head". In the texts where *yāṣaq ʿal-rôʾš* occurs, namely 1 Sam 10:1 and 2 Kgs 9:1, 3, *māšaḥ* follows immediately afterwards with God as subject, presumably in order to give an interpretation of the act. It should also be noted that in all cases where the act of royal anointing occurs, the verb *lāqaḥ*, "take" is used to initiate the act.

The only occurrence of the place from which the oil used at the anointing was taken is found in 1 Kgs 1:39. The priest Zadok is said to take the horn with oil "from the tent", thus making it explicit that it is a sacral act and therefore performed by a priest, using a sacral oil. This is furthermore the only text which describes who actually performed the royal anointing with an intended legal function. Although this is a rather slender basis to form a conclusion upon, it would seem natural to regard a priest as the normal agent of the act. This point will be returned to below under Legal Function.

The priestly anointing uses a similar terminology, as in Exod 29:7: *wĕlāqaḥtā ʾet-šemen hammišḥâ wĕyāṣaqtā ʿal-rôʾšô ûmāšaḥtā ʾōtô*, "You shall take the anointing oil, and pour it on his head and anoint him." Here *lāqaḥ* occurs at the beginning, *yāṣaq* is used, together with the designation *ʿal-rôʾš* and immediately afterwards comes the explanatory use of *māšaḥ*. The description of the priestly anointing is therefore almost the same as the description of the royal anointing.

---

[10] Noted by Mettinger (1976:206), who argues that this points in the direction of a connection between 1 Kgs 1:39 and 1 Sam 16:13, the latter providing a precedent for the former. See also Edelman (1991:51-2) for the distinction vial-horn.

[11] In 2 Kgs 9:6 *ʾel* is found instead of the expected *ʿal*, which is used earlier in v. 3. Although it is common to emend the text, it may not be necessary, since the two prepositions are known to overlap, see Waltke & O'Connor (1990:216).

[12] This explains why *yāṣaq* and not *māšaḥ* was used in Gen 28:18 when a masseba is anointed.

The anointing was thus conducted by emptying a container of oil over the head of the person to be anointed. As far as the texts relate, it was a priest who performed the royal anointing.

2.7.3 Legal Function

Excursus: Anointing Outside the OT

Anointing was used throughout the ancient Near East in many different contexts and with different functions. This analysis will not include a thorough investigation of all these different uses, since it can be found elsewhere.[13] In private life anointing was used for cosmetic as well as for hygienic purposes.[14] It was also believed to have healing powers. If the legal sphere is focused upon, it was used in the manumission of slaves,[15] to confirm betrothals[16] and purchases,[17] to install vassals[18], substitutionary kings and probably also real kings.[19] This analysis will concentrate on the uses which are relevant in light of the OT.

Ugarit No clear references have appeared so far concerning the use of anointing with a legal function at Ugarit. There are some texts, however, although disputable because of their fragmentary state, which could point in the direction that a royal anointing was known at Ugarit.

KTU 1.2.IV:30-40 apparently concerns the enthronement of Baal.[20] In l. 32 is found *bᶜlm.yml[k ...]*, "May Ba'lu be king!", in ll. 37-38, *št *[...] b rišh.[...]*, "put [...] on his head [...]"[21] and finally in l. 39, *mš[...]*, which might very well be a case of *mšḫ*, "anoint". Although the text is in a very poor condition, the cumulative effect of these considerations makes it at least possible that the act of royal anointing was known in Ugarit.[22]

Egypt The king of Alashiya excuses himself in a letter to the new Pharaoh, *EA* 34, for not sending the proper gifts. Among the gifts he has sent, oil occurs in l. 50-51, with the explicit purpose of "zum Ausgießen auf deinen [Kop]f". It is problematic, however, whether it refers to an anointing

---

[13] See e.g. Kutsch (1963), Veenhof (1966), Mettinger (1976:212-24) and Pardee (1977:14-9).

[14] See Kutsch (1963:4).

[15] See Kutsch (1963:16-8) and Mettinger (1976:221-2).

[16] See Malul (1988:161-79).

[17] See Kutsch (1963:18-9) and Mettinger (1976:216-7).

[18] See Kutsch (1963:34-5) and Mettinger (1976:209).

[19] See Kutsch (1963:36-52) and Mettinger (1976:209-10).

[20] See *ARTU* (43).

[21] The following restoration is suggested by *ARTU* (42): "Put [...] [the crown] on his head", although the restoration is regarded as uncertain, *ARTU* (42, n. 192).

[22] Korpel (1990:281-2) considers this interpretation of *KTU* 1.2.IV:39 possible, although she notes the damaged state of the text.

in relation to the new Pharaoh's accession to the throne, or to a token of friendship with a cosmetic purpose.[23] Another letter, *EA* 51:6-7, tells of how the Pharaoh dealt with Taku king of Nuḫašše , following Moran's translation:

> [*No*]*t*[*e*] (que) lorsque Manaḫpiya, le roi d'Égypte, ton ancêtre, établit [T]a[ku], mon ancêtre, comme roi dans Nuḫašše, il mit de l'huile sur sa tête ....[24]

Moran's translation is to be preferred because he makes explicit the explicative relationship between the phrases "establish as king" and "put oil on his head". This is of some importance, since it is a direct indication of the legal function of the anointing. The subject of the verb "anoint" is the Pharaoh himself. Although it is possible in principle that this expresses the agent of the act, it would have been highly unlikely for the Pharaoh to have performed such an act. Instead, it more likely displays the authoritative and legitimating suzerain behind the installation of Taku into vassalhood.

Hatti Some Hittite texts describe the anointing of a substitutionary king. It is therefore probable that anointing was also a part of the regular king-making, although the Hittite texts are silent on this point.[25] It is especially interesting to note the expression used to describe the act of anointing a substitutionary king, "Dann salbt man den Gefangenen mit dem Feinöl des Königtums".[26] It is especially the verb "salbt" which is interesting, since it is in the third person plural without an explicit subject. A case of anointing as part of king-making is found in a highly fragmentary text: "... Dut]ḫaliịa, Bruder [...] ihn Dutḫaliịa [..., un]d ihn salbten sie zur Königsherrschaft".[27] Yet another text, although fragmentary, speaks about the anointing of a pretender to the throne, probably conducted by the king.[28] The purpose of the act is described in l. 55´, "zur Königsherrschaft salbt", where the king, mentioned in line 54´, is probably the subject. It would appear that the Hittites practised royal anointing, although it is not certain to what extent. It is also interesting that the anointing could be described with an implicit plural as subject. This plural subject would then refer to the authoritative cause behind the anointing and not the agent of the act.

Conclusion According to the texts studied above, the royal anointing was probably known among the Hittites and possibly also at Ugarit. In Egypt anointing was used to install Canaanite vassal kings into their office,

---

[23] See Mettinger (1976:215): "The oil is a token of peace and goodwill that can be developed into a formal contract." For a similar view, see Weinfeld (1988:348). Kutsch (1963:68) interprets the gift in a less technical manner and Pardee (1977:18) considers it an ordinary gift.

[24] Moran (1987:221).

[25] See Kümmel (1967:28).

[26] Kümmel (1967:10-1). The text is KUB XXIV.5+IX.13, obv. 19´.

[27] Kümmel (1967:43). The text is KUB XXXVI.119:3´-5´.

[28] Kümmel (1967:44). The text is KBo XVI.25, obv. 54´-55´.

which makes it probable that it was at least known, if not also practised, in Canaan. Both the Hittite texts and the Amarna letters showed examples of a particular form of expression for the anointing, in the Hittite texts with an implicit subject in third person plural, and in an Amarna letter with Pharaoh as subject. In this form the subject of the verb "anoint" refers to the authority behind the act, which provides it with the necessary legal legitimation. The subject of the verb then is not so much the agent as the cause, which means that the verb functions causatively. This will be returned to below in the analysis of the Biblical texts.

2.7.3.1 Judges 9:8, 15

Judg 9 tells of how Abimelech became king of Shechem and the opposition he met from his brother Jotham. According to v. 6, and implicitly v. 20, it was the inhabitants of Millo and *kol-ba'ălê*, "all the leaders"[29] of Shechem who installed the king. The transaction between the leaders of Shechem and the inhabitants of Millo on the one hand and Abimelech on the other is an agreement of a legal nature. There are several indications of this in the text. In v. 2 the word *ṭôb*, "good" is used, which is common in contexts of legal agreements.[30] In v. 2 there is also the statement made by Abimelech, "I am your bone and your flesh." This expresses not only identification but also loyalty, as Brueggemann has tried to show.[31] The leaders reciprocate this invitation by Abimelech by calling him their *'āḥ*, "brother" in v. 3, a term also known for its legal use.[32] The stage is thus set for Abimelech to become king, since he and the leaders have reached this agreement. It is interesting how the text emphasizes that the two cities support the king-making of Abimelech by making the large groups of leaders and citizens the explicit subjects of the act. This must imply that they are stressed not as the immediate agents of an act, but more as the authoritative body which chooses and makes someone king. Thus, when the expression *wayyamlîkû 'et-'ăbîmelek lĕmelek*, "and they ... made Abimelech king" is used in v. 6 and similarly in v. 16, the subject has the more technical function of legitimating the act of king-making.

---

[29] My translation.

[30] See Höver-Johag (1982:332), who notes that *ṭôb*, "good" occurs especially together with the verb *dābar*, "speak", as it does here in Judg 9:2.

[31] Brueggemann (1970:536-7). This phrase occurs in another text where anointing and king-making is concerned, namely 2 Sam 5:1-3, to be studied below.

[32] See Munn-Rankin (1956:76-9), Kalluveettil (1982:205) and Weinfeld (1988:345).

In the fable told by Jotham in vv. 8-15 there is a difference in terminology concerning the king-making.[33] The authoritative body, here the trees, is not described as having the intention to *himlîkû lĕmelek*, "make PN king" but to *limšōaḥ ʿălêhem melek*, "anoint PN king over themselves" in v. 8 and similarly in v. 15, *ʾim beʾĕmet ʾattem mōšĕḥîm ʾōtî lĕmelek ʿălêkem*, "If in good faith you are anointing me king over you". This means that while the fable uses the phrase "anoint PN king" for making someone king, the narrative frame of the fable uses the more abstract phrase "make PN king". The reason for this shift in expression is surely due to the difference of genre. The fable is more apt to use concrete language whereas the narrative frame uses more abstract language.[34]

It is especially interesting that in the fable the trees as a collective body desire to anoint a king over themselves. This means that the verb *māšaḥ*, "anoint" is used in a causative sense, although it is formally in the qal stem in vv. 8 and 15. This explains how the subject of "anoint" can be plural, since it is the cause of the anointing that is referred to and not the agent of the actual anointing.[35]

The legal function of the anointing would be to accomplish the status of king for someone. If Abimelech was meant to be anointed, it followed upon an agreement that was made between the leaders of Shechem and the people of Millo on the one hand, and Abimelech on the other. It has to be left an open matter, however, whether he was actually meant to be anointed. It is possible, but the text does not explicitly say so.

2.7.3.2 1 Samuel 10:1

In 1 Sam 8:6, 19-20 the people ask Samuel for a king and in v. 22 God himself orders Samuel to give the people what they want. Later, in 9:16 and 10:1, Saul is described as anointed to *nāgîd*, "ruler" over the people, a term that has caused some debate.[36] According to v. 16 this is the result of the people's request. What appears strange in the larger context is that in 9:1-10:15 the noun *melek*, "king" and the verb *himlîk*, "to make a king" are consistently avoided, although they would suit admirably in this context.[37]

---

[33] For some recent and useful analyses of Jotham's fable from somewhat different angles, see Jobling (1986:68-87), de Moor (1990:182-97) and Becker (1990:190-9).

[34] Soggin (1981:174) holds that the fable's use is to be understood as talking of royalty in general, whereas the surrounding context is specifically dealing with Abimelech. This is, less likely, however.

[35] See e.g. Minokami (1989:160).

[36] See e.g. Mettinger (1976:151-84) and Brettler (1989:33-5).

[37] See Gordon (1986:114-5). For the use of these two terms, see Carlson (1964:52-5).

Also, in 9:17 the verb *ʿaṣar* is considered by most scholars to mean "rule", which is quite unusual.[38] Then in 10:16 the drama is revealed to some degree for the reader, when Samuel is said to have spoken to Saul earlier about the *mĕlûkâ*, "kingship". This is probably a reference to the private conversation that Samuel and Saul had on the roof according to 9:25, or it might refer to what Samuel said in connection with the anointing in 10:1.[39] This would then imply that they had talked about Saul becoming king, and then perhaps the anointing had something to do with this as well. Why, then, is this not made explicit at the anointing in 10:1? The reason seems to be that the narrator wants to stress that it is the people who want a king, not God. He only supplies them with the best candidate possible, as Samuel says in 10:24. It is the people who acclaim Saul in 10:24 and make him king in 11:15. God only makes Saul a *nāgîd*, not a king. The anointing of Saul to *nāgîd* is presented as his election by God as the pretender to the throne, whom the people soon make their king. The election and installation of him as king, however, are the responsibilities of the people, not God. This distinction is fundamental for the understanding of 9:1-10:15.

In 12:3, Samuel describes Saul as God's anointed, which probably refers to the anointing earlier in 10:1. The distinction, so sharply drawn earlier, is then no longer useful, since Saul is in effect king. The distinction was only valid in so far as it made clear God's limited engagement in choosing a pretender to the throne and not a king. Now that the distinction has been made clear, however, it is no longer useful to uphold it. Instead, the narrator has Samuel say in 12:13 that God has indeed appointed a king for the people. Later, in 1 Sam 15:1 it is said that God has anointed Saul to be king, and in v. 17 that Samuel has anointed him similarly. The transitory stage of Saul as *nāgîd* is no longer necessary since the point has already been made.

The pace of the narrative slows down in 10:1 through a careful description of details, such as Samuel taking the container of oil, how he pours it

---

[38] McCarter (1980:179) explains it as a semantic extension from the ordinary meaning of "restrain" to "muster", meaning that "Saul is to be the one who will muster the weak and scattered forces of Israel in a strong army of defense." Gordon (1986:115) understands the unusual choice as the result of the unwillingness on the part of the narrator to use the verb "be king". On the other hand, a good case has been made for translating the verb with its usual meaning "restrain" by Polzin (1989:94) and Eslinger (1985:309-10): "An alternative reading for which the normal sense of '*aṣar* is quite sufficient, appears when Yahweh's sarcasm is appreciated." In the light of the restrictions laid down in 1 Sam 8, this seems probable, although Gordon's point is relevant.

[39] Eslinger (1985:335-6) argues convincingly that the relative *ʾăšer* in 1 Sam 10:16 does not refer to the noun *mĕlûkâ* but to the preceding phrase *lōʾ-higgîd lô*, "he did not tell him", meaning "... as Samuel had said."

over the head of Saul and that he kisses him. This slower tempo signals a climax in the narrative, which is the anointing.[40] Another heightening factor is the accompanying utterance by Samuel in v. 1, *hălô° kî-mĕšăḥăkă yhwh ʿal-naḥălătô lĕnăgîd*, "The Lord has anointed you to be *năgîd* over his heritage."[41] This serves to ensure the reader that this is an anointing as *năgîd* and not as king. That God is behind this anointing permeates the whole context. In addition to the fact that it is stated explicitly in v. 1, the asses lost become the asses found in v. 2 by divine intervention, and in 10:6-7, 9-13 the Spirit of God is said to take control over Saul.

Saul's silence and passivity in relation to what happens are significant, and remind of the passivity of Solomon in 1 Kgs 1 when he is anointed. This passivity serves to show the willingness of the individual and the fact that the initiative does not lie with the persons engaged, but with God. This means that the anointing of Saul in 10:1 is not a proper royal anointing with an intended legal function, but instead a theologically motivated act, which serves to emphasize the divine election. Since the common way of making someone king was to anoint him, God is also described as choosing his candidate for the kingship by anointing. This theological use of royal anointing serves to stress the election of Saul as pretender to the throne, but it has no legal function. This theologically motivated form of royal anointing, without a proper legal function, will be called 'divine anointing'. Divine anointing is then a reuse of the proper legal symbolic act of royal anointing in a non-legal context. The legal function by which Saul becomes king is therefore not found with his anointing in 10:1, but in 10:24-25a and in the renewal of his kingship in 11:15. It is possible that these texts imply that the people had Saul anointed, but it must remain uncertain.

The conclusion is therefore that Saul was not, as far as the texts say, anointed to be king in the sense that the anointing legally made him king. The anointing described in 1 Sam 10:1 is a way of describing the divine election of Saul as the pretender to the throne, a case of divine anointing.

2.7.3.3 1 Samuel 16:13

Here Samuel anoints David to be king after Saul. In 16:1 the theme occurs, namely that God has already chosen someone to succeed Saul, and Samuel

---

[40] See Bar-Efrat (1989:161) for the function of delaying the narrative pace.

[41] My translation. The LXX has a substantially longer reading, which for the most part reiterates what is found in the MT. According to McCarter (1980:171) the shorter reading of the MT is due to haplography.

is supposed to anoint him. This anointing therefore concerns the election of kings.[42] Samuel finally anoints David in v. 13, *wayyiqqaḥ šĕmû²ēl ²et-qeren haššemen wayyimšaḥ ²ōtô*, "Then Samuel took the horn of oil, and anointed him". Immediately thereafter the Spirit of God descended on David, as it did on Saul in 1 Sam 10:10.

It is obvious that the text does not intend to describe the anointing of David as an anointing with any legal function. It is more like the anointing of Saul in 1 Sam 10:1, where his divine election was the principal function of the anointing. It is God who has chosen the king after Saul and no one else. It is not even emphasized what David has been anointed to, since the point is primarily that he is indeed anointed, i.e., chosen by God.[43] This anointing is referred to later on in 2 Sam 12:7, where it says that God has anointed David to be king over Israel.[44] David is later anointed twice as king in 2 Sam 2:4 and 5:3, with a clear legal function in both cases. These cases of anointing will be studied below.

It is thus the same theological use of anointing which occurred in 1 Sam 10:1 that is used here in 1 Sam 16:13 to express the divine election of the next king, who is also a rival to the throne. Therefore, this anointing has no legal function, but is another case of divine anointing.

2.7.3.4 2 Samuel 2:4

This is a short description of how David became king over Judah in Hebron. The cause and authority behind the anointing is, according to v. 4, the *²anšê yĕhûdâ*, "men of Judah".[45] There is a problem as to who these men are. They could very well be the elders of Judah, who are mentioned in 1 Sam 30:26,[46] but why then are they not called elders here? It could be that the very wide expression "men of Judah" implies that it was the whole of Judah that made David their king. This is strengthened by the similar phrase in v. 7, *wĕgam-²ōtî mašĕḥû bêt-yĕhûdâ lĕmelek ʿălêhem*, "the house of Judah has anointed me king over them", where the subject is the house of

---

[42] The verb *rā²â*, "see" is here used in the elaborate sense of "discover" or perhaps even "choose". So e.g. Mettinger (1976:112), Eslinger (1985:473-4) and Polzin (1989:157). Polzin translates it as "provide".

[43] See e.g. Mettinger (1976:207).

[44] So e.g. Mettinger (1976:204). In 2 Sam 3:39 David calls himself *mašûaḥ melek*, "anointed king", which is more likely a reference to the anointing in 2 Sam 2:4, so e.g. McCarter (1984:120).

[45] My translation.

[46] So e.g. Mettinger (1976:198), Kutsch (1979:79), McCarter (1984:84) and Reviv (1989:83).

Judah, i.e., the people of Judah. The "men of Judah" in v. 4 should therefore be identified with the elders of the people in v. 7.[47]

The usual expression for anointing is then used for the act in v. 4: *wayyimšěḥû-šām ʾet-dāwid lěmelek ʿal-bêt yěhûdâ*, "they anointed David king over the house of Judah." This causative use of the verb *māšaḥ*, "anoint" has been discussed earlier in relation to Judg 9 and will not be repeated here.

It is interesting to note that there is no emphasis whatsoever in this text on who actually performed the anointing, as was the case as well in Judg 9. It could be that it was so clear who actually anointed David that it did not need to be mentioned. This would only be true, however, if it also was of no major importance who actually performed the anointing. It could have been a priest, a prophet or someone else; it simply did not matter for the description to be sufficient.[48] The important point to be made was apparently who stood behind the act and thereby confirmed its legitimacy, namely the elders as the leaders of the people. The act is then legitimated through a civil legitimation,[49] without any sacral emphasis.[50]

This description, although short, reveals that David received the status of king over Judah by means of his anointing. The legal function of the anointing was to accomplish this status as king for David.

2.7.3.5 2 Samuel 5:3

In 2 Sam 5:1-3, David the king of Judah is again made king, this time over the northern tribes. After the description of how he became king over Judah in 2:4 comes a lengthy description of how leaders of the North are

---

[47] See Ishida (1977:65-6) and Anderson (1989:24) on the problem of what actually constituted the Judah over which David became king.

[48] Mettinger (1976:208) and Kutsch (1979:79-80) consider the anointing to have been performed by the people through their elders, whereas Noth (1950:177) considered a priest to be the likely agent. Schoors (1977:94) holds that the prophet performed the royal anointing, although he does not mention the texts from 2 Sam 2 and 5. He holds that in 1 Kgs 1:39, where a priest performs the anointing, and in 2 Kgs 11:12, where a priest is often considered to perform the anointing, the text has been tampered with. This view, however, is highly unlikely, creating more problems than it solves.

[49] 'Civil legitimation' is used here for the people's legitimation of the king, mostly through their representatives. 'Sacral legitimation' is here used when God legitimates someone, as is the case in the so-called divine anointings, e.g. 1 Sam 10:1; 16:13.

[50] So e.g. Fokkelman (1990:29), who considers the sacral to be implied from the anointing of David in 1 Sam 16:13, leaving the anointing in 2 Sam 2:4 to be an anointing within the limits of military and political pretensions.

eliminated, Abner in 3:27 and king Ishbaal in 4:6-7. The elders of the North then ask David to become their king.[51]

The major difference between 2:4 and 5:1-3 is that 5:1-3 mentions a covenant between David and the elders of the northern tribes. There has been some discussion as to whether a similar covenant is implicit in 2:4 or not. There is also the question of the relationship between the covenant and the anointing of David in 5:1-3. Are they connected in making up an agreement between the elders of the North and their king?

> 2 Sam 5:1-3 has been thought to describe two separate events, one in vv. 1-2, displaying a pan-Israelite ideal, and a second in v. 3, where the anointing occurs.[52] Most scholars, however, have regarded vv. 1-3 as consisting of two accounts of the same event, the one in vv. 1-2 usually being regarded as later than the one in v. 3.[53] The reasons given by McCarter are that v. 3a repeats v.1a, that the Israelites view themselves anachronistically as the "bone and flesh" of David, and the relationship between the promise in v. 2 and 2 Sam 7, which makes vv. 1-2 a deuteronomistic expansion.[54] Mettinger, on the other hand, considers vv. 1-2 as part of the so-called History of David's Rise' and v. 3 as the original tradition of David's investiture.[55] His arguments are that v. 3a repeats v. 1a and that whereas v. 1 says "tribes", v. 3 has "elders".
>
> However, this is not necessarily so. Repetition is increasingly becoming recognized as a vital literary technique.[56] A particular form of repetition is resumptive repetition, where the thread of the argument is picked up by means of repeating the beginning of a narrative, the two similar occurrences thus framing a certain part of the narrative.[57] Gunn is of the opinion that it might well be a deliberate rhetorical device in this case.[58]

To begin with, a fundamental difference between 2:4 and 5:1-3 should be noted. In 5:1-3 the elders of Israel meet with the king of Judah, quite a

---

[51] The parallel text in 1 Chr 11:1-3 is substantially the same.

[52] So e.g. Reviv (1989:84-5).

[53] So e.g. Mettinger (1976:114-5) and McCarter (1984:131).

[54] McCarter (1984:131).

[55] Mettinger (1976:114-5).

[56] See e.g. Alter (1981:88-113), Berlin (1983:136), Sternberg (1985:414-5) and Bar-Efrat (1989:116-7).

[57] See e.g. Talmon (1978), Berlin (1983:126), Long (1987) and Bar-Efrat (1989:215-6).

[58] Gunn (1978:71). So also Anderson (1989:75). Brettler (1989:128) considers it possible that it is a matter of a so-called "double reading", which would make vv. 1-3 a unity. See also Fokkelman (1990:137), who considers vv. 1 and 3 to be complementary and therefore referring to the same subjects and the same event.

different figure than the leader whom the elders of Judah approached in 2 Sam 2:4. This may at least in part explain the need for a more formal agreement between the two parties, since what the northern elders ask for is in reality what has been called a 'personal union' between the North and the South, with David as their king.[59] This unique set of circumstances indicates that a similar agreement as the one made in 5:1-3 is not necessarily implicit in 2:4.[60]

> Several scholars hold that such a covenant is implicit in 2:4, e.g. Alt, Mettinger and Ishida, although Ishida notes the passive role which must have been played by the people.[61] Soggin believes that the elders of Judah were not in the position of being able to choose whether they should make David king or not, since David had already occupied the southern parts of Judah.[62] They only recognized him as king de facto. Tadmor argues with some force that the reason for a covenant between the king and the people in 2 Sam 5:1-3 and 2 Kgs 11:17, is that both texts describe the beginning of a new dynasty.[63] When there was a normal case of monarchical transition, no such covenant renewal was necessary.

It could also be the case that the royal covenant between the king and the people had become so standardized that it was regarded as merely another part of the ceremony of king-making.[64] However, the question of a royal covenant made at the coronation goes beyond this analysis. It will be relevant only in so far as it directly concerns the legal function of the anointing.

In v. 3 it is emphasized that the elders came to the "king" in Hebron, that the "king" made a covenant with them and that they anointed him "king". The reader is clearly supposed to view David as playing the role of the suzerain who is approached by a presumptive vassal, seeking his protection. The price the elders would have to pay, as they show themselves well aware of in vv. 1-2, is their subordination to David as king, hence their anointing of him to be their king. In v. 1 they use a phrase which has occurred earlier in Judg 9:2: ʿaṣmĕkā ûbĕśorkā ʾănāḥĕnû, "we are your bone and flesh." The attempt by the elders to identify David with themselves serves to strengthen the bond that already exists between them. This might

---

[59] So Alt (1953:45).

[60] See Fokkelman (1990:142).

[61] Alt (1953:41), Mettinger (1976:141-2) and Ishida (1977:68).

[62] Soggin (1984:44).

[63] Tadmor (1982a:253).

[64] As suggested by Brettler (1989:134).

also be a more technical way of asking for a covenantal relationship with David. Although this reciprocal relation between the covenant and the anointing lacks explicit proof, it seems highly reasonable in light of the terminology, the reasons being that the elders are seeking a new king and David is trying to extend the boundaries of his realm.

The expression used in v. 3 to describe the anointing is the normal one which has been analyzed earlier, namely *māšĕḥû lĕmelek*, "anoint PN king". As was seen earlier, this is a causative use of the verb "anoint". The elders, as the plural subject in v. 3, are not thought of as actually performing the anointing, but rather as the legitimate authority behind the installation of David as their king. The elders decide the matter, but who actually performs the anointing is apparently as unimportant to the narrator as it was in 2:4.

It should be asked whether the anointing has a sacral character or not in this text. Since it is not said who actually performed the anointing, it is open to speculation whether it was performed by a priest or not. In v. 2 there is a reference to David being elected by God to be his *nāgîd*, which is certainly an allusion to a more sacral character of the king-making as a whole. According to v. 3, the covenant has been concluded *lipnê yhwh*, "before the Lord", which probably implies that it took place in front of a sanctuary. This would also imply the presence of cultic functionaries, one of whom could very well have performed the anointing. In v. 12, David interprets his anointing as king as a clear sign of God's dealings with him. Taking the evidence as a whole, it appears that although the sacral character of the anointing of David in 5:3 is not overly emphasized, since it is after all the covenant that is said to have been concluded "before the Lord" and not the anointing, there could nevertheless have been a sacral setting for both covenant and anointing. In 2:4, however, there is no allusion to a sacral setting for the anointing. Since 2:4 does not mention a covenant between the elders of Judah and David either, the absence of both these factors from 2:4 cannot be accidental. Instead, the conclusion must be that the sacral aspect is brought forth in 5:1-3 primarily in relation to the covenant between the king and the people and not so much in relation to the anointing. This does not necessarily mean that the anointing did not have a sacral character, but all that can be said is that the narrator did not find it necessary to elaborate on this aspect of the anointings in 2:4 and 5:3.

By means of his anointing, David became king over the northern tribes. The legal function of the anointing was then to accomplish this royal status. It would also seem likely that this anointing functioned as the submission of the elders to David as their king, and as such it might have been their response to David's covenant with them.

2.7.3.6 2 Samuel 19:11

Here the people of the tribes of Israel are said to regret that they took sides with Absalom in his rebellion against David. They refer to when they made him their king, *wĕʾabšālôm ʾăšer māšaḥnû ʿālênû*, "Absalom, whom we anointed over us". Prior to this, there is no mention of an anointing of Absalom.

In 2 Sam 15:1-12, however, there are clear indications that Absalom not only aspires to be king, but that he is indeed proclaimed as such. In 15:10 Absalom sends a message to the tribes of Israel, telling them to acknowledge him as king: *waʾămartem mālak ʾabšālôm bĕḥebrôn*, "then shout: Absalom has become king at Hebron!" No anointing is mentioned, however. It is nevertheless stated that the acknowledgment should be made when they hear the sound of the trumpet, v. 10a. The trumpet-sound and the acclamation are both related to the king-making ceremonies found in 1 Kgs 1 and 2 Kgs 11. Furthermore, the fact that Hebron is emphasized as the locality for this ceremony brings to mind 2 Sam 2:4 and 5:1-3, where David was anointed king over Judah and Israel. In 15:11 Absalom invites a large number of people from Jerusalem to a banquet, similar to that which was found in the case of Saul in 1 Sam 9:12-13, 19, 22-24, David in 1 Sam 16:3, 5, 11 and Adonijah in 1 Kgs 1:9, 41. All these indications point to the fact that Absalom was indeed made king, although it is noteworthy that an anointing of Absalom is not mentioned in 15:1-12. It undoubtedly took place, however, as indicated in 19:11.

In 19:11 the people of Israel are said to have anointed Absalom over themselves, leaving out the usual *lĕmelek*, "as king" from the standard expression *māšĕḥû lĕmelek* by ellipsis. Although the anointing is mentioned only briefly, it is apparent that the same form of royal anointing is used which was found earlier in 2 Sam 2:4 and 5:1-3. The verb "anoint" is again used causatively, with the people of Israel as the authoritative, legal body behind the anointing. Nothing is therefore said concerning who actually performed the anointing. The legal function of this anointing was to accomplish the royal status of Absalom.

2.7.3.7 1 Kings 1:39

1 Kgs 1 displays a tripartite structure concerning the description of Solomon's anointing.[65] Firstly, in vv. 32-35 David prescribes how they are

---

[65] So Brettler (1989:128-9), who shows that it is paralleled with a similar threefold repetition of Adonijah's attempts to gain the throne. Brettler (1989:131) has an excellent display of the different elements of all the coronations in the OT.

to go about making Solomon his successor. Secondly, in. vv. 38-40 the
narrator himself describes how it was accomplished. Thirdly, in vv. 43-48
Jonathan gives an eye-witness account to Adonijah. It is important at the
outset to note this structural technique, whereby the event is described
from three different angels. There is the perspective of the king who gives
the orders, the narrator with his sovereign right to focus on precisely the
key issues that are most important to him, and a possible eye-witness
giving a dramatic report of the event and its implications.

There are two things that stand out in a comparative study of the three
versions. In the dramatic report by Jonathan, Adonijah receives the dis-
couraging news that his opponent has not only gained David's support, but
also the strength of the royal 'body-guard', the Cherethites and the
Pelethites.[66] The second point is the detailed description of the anointing in
v. 39. Whereas David prescribes in v. 34 that Zadok the priest and Nathan
the prophet should anoint Solomon, and Jonathan claims the same in his
description in v. 45, the narrator limits his version to Zadok only in v. 39.
His version is not simply an alternate description, however, since what
differs is the detailed description of how Zadok brings out the oil from
hǎ'ōhel, "the tent", obviously a sanctuary, and anoints Solomon.

Excursus: Problem with Numbers in 1 Kings 1:34, 45

In v. 34 the verb "anoint" is in the singular, *ûmāšaḥ*, although the subject,
"the priest Zadok and the prophet Nathan" is plural. In v. 45 the subject is
the same, but the verb is plural, *wayyimšěḥû*. This has caused scholars to
make different alterations to the text. Some would delete "and the prophet
Nathan" from v. 34,[67] but then there remains the problem of what to do
with v. 45. Another alternative is to delete "the priest Zadok and the
prophet Nathan" from v. 45, leaving the verb in the plural.[68] Some scholars
advocate both of these deletions.[69] A fresh look at the text reveals that the
collective singular of the suffix conjugation in v. 34 is part of David's prescription of how Solomon is to be anointed. This could very well be a case
of incongruity in number between predicate and subject, well known in
Hebrew syntax.[70] Verse 45 focuses on a part of the plural subject. In v. 44

---

[66]   Cf. de Vaux (1961:123-4).

[67]   So e.g. Würthwein (1985:16). Jones (1984:99; 1990:54) appears unconvinced by
different attempts to alter the text.

[68]   So Mettinger (1976:203).

[69]   So e.g. Schmidt (1970:176-7).

[70]   See GKC (464-5) and Nyberg (1952:283). This is the view of e.g. Noth (1968:24),
Mettinger (1976:202, n. 40) and DeVries (1985:17). DeVries brings attention to a
similar case earlier in v. 21.

the subject of "had him ride on the king's mule" is Zadok, Nathan, Benaiah, the Cherethites and the Pelethites. In v. 45a the focus narrows down to a more limited subject of "anoint", namely Zadok and Nathan. Then in v. 45b the subject of "have gone up" is again the broader one from v. 44. This focusing on part of a plural subject serves to signal importance and a climactic phase in the narrative. In addition, the plural of the waw prefix conjugation in v. 45, *wayyimšĕḥû* occurs in the context of a vivid and excited description on Jonathan's behalf of what has just happened at Gihon. It is possible that the difference in relation to the singular form in v. 34 is due to the scenic differences as to time, subject, intention and situation.

What v. 39 actually describes is the physical act of anointing, whereas vv. 34 and 45 refer to the whole arrangement around and including the physical act. It could hardly have been said that anyone other than a priest collected oil from the sanctuary and put it to use. Nathan would then have had some part to play in the wider context of the anointing. It has been suggested that he delivered an oracle, which is possible since prophetic activity at royal anointings is nothing unusual in the OT.[71] The narrator apparently thought, however, that it was irrelevant to dwell on Nathan's part in the proceedings, apart from mentioning his participation. The goal of the story is the physical act of anointing, and the narrator goes to great pains to describe this as an act of Zadok the priest, using a particular sacral oil for this purpose. This is the only instance where a particular oil from a sanctuary is said to have been used for royal anointing. It would therefore seem best to presume that the narrator is alluding to a rather normal procedure in his attempt to display the validity of the anointing. The oil is emphasized as sacral in order to make the reader think of Solomon as not only the choice of David, but also of God.[72] This would, then, emphasize a sacral legitimation of the anointing. This is spelled out clearly in the speech by Benaiah, v. 37, in the salutation to David by his servants, v. 47 and in David's final prayer, v. 48. Both of the latter speeches are quotations made by Jonathan and addressed to Adonijah.[73]

---

[71] So Jones (1984:99) and Mettinger (1976:203). Mettinger points to 1 Sam 9:27-10:7; 2 Kgs 9:3; Pss 2:7-9; 110:1-3.

[72] See Halpern (1981:6), who would go as far as to say that the anointing in 1 Kgs 1:39 is as sacral as Saul's in 1 Sam 10:1, but he qualifies this: "The only difference is that the source in Solomon's case does not emphasize divine revelation. It reports, rather, the practical politics of succession."

[73] The sacral legitimation becomes even stronger when the Chronicler's description of Solomon's anointing is taken into account, whether it is meant to be a description of the same event as in 1 Kgs 1:39 or not, see Williamson (1982:187). 1 Chr 29:23 says, "Then Solomon sat on the throne of the Lord, succeeding his father David as king".

Why, then, was the anointing of Solomon given this sacral legitimation? A likely answer lies in the fact that divine anointing appears in the OT when a new dynasty or some form of irregular succession is involved. Jehu, the only king in Northern Israel who is said to have been anointed, foundered a new dynasty. Saul was the first king, which could have legitimated the story of his anointing, and David certainly had no dynastic principle to appeal to. This explains why he was anointed analogously with Saul and possibly also described as adopted by him.[74]

An interesting parallel can be found in an inscription from Harran by Nabonidus. He became king in Babylon without being capable of claiming any dynastic principle.[75] This forced him to argue for his place on the throne by other means, namely by a sacral legitimation:

Sin, the lord of all the gods and goddesses residing in heaven, have come down from heaven to (me) Nabonidus, king of Babylon! For me, Nabonidus, the lonely one who has nobody, in whose (text: my) heart was no thought of kingship, the gods and goddesses prayed (to Sin) and Sin called me to kingship.[76]

What is interesting about this text is that when Nabonidus lacked the proper dynastic origin, he turned to the realm of the sacred to legitimate his kingship. He also emphasizes that he personally was passive in the process and that the gods took the initiative.

The sacral legitimation of Solomon's anointing was therefore a way to counter the irregularities in Solomon's succession to the throne.

After the anointing, Solomon is brought back to sit on the throne. This might be called a coronation, although no stress is laid on it by the narrator. It is only referred to in vv. 35 and 46, and is omitted in the narrator's own report. This indicates that the anointing is more important in 1 Kgs 1 than the placing of Solomon on the throne. The anointing at Gihon is the climax of the outworking of David's orders, both geographically, temporally and literary. That Solomon is said to sit on David's throne after the anointing indicates what the anointing was supposed to accomplish, namely to make Solomon the legitimate king after David.

So far, the focus of this analysis has been upon the sacral character of Solomon's anointing. To balance this presentation, the case of Adonijah

---

Here it is no longer David's throne that Solomon occupies but God's, which makes the divine approval of his kingship explicit.

[74] So Ishida (1977:61-2).

[75] So Hallo & Simpson (1971:147).

[76] *ANET* (562).

will be taken into consideration. He is called king by Nathan in v. 11 and by Bathsheba in v. 18, which is apparently accomplished by other means than an act of anointing. In v. 5 Adonijah displays his intention, and this is worked out in v. 9 through a banquet for all his friends and loyal supporters. The banquet is further referred to in v. 19 by Bathsheba and in v. 25 by Nathan to support the fact that Adonijah has indeed made himself king. A final, climactic factor is also mentioned by Nathan in v. 24, namely the acclamation by Adonijah's supporters. Apparently, the narrator felt no difficulty in giving Adonijah as well as David the epithet King, and he later also ascribes the title to Solomon. In order to make a fundamental difference between these aspirations, it is specified who shall be king "after David". What decides the issue is David's adherence in v. 30 to the promise he has made to Bathsheba, namely that her son, Solomon, shall indeed be king after him.[77]

It then becomes interesting to ask what it is that actually frightens Adonijah. The first thing that Jonathan mentions in his speech to Adonijah in v. 43 is that "David has made Solomon king!",[78] and not that Solomon has been anointed, which could have been expected. Then Jonathan describes how the different parties have shown loyalty to David and by implication to Solomon; the prophet Nathan by attending the anointing, the priest Zadok by performing the act, the body-guard by following Solomon and the people by their acclamation and joy. The decision of David is therefore described as the decisive factor behind Solomon's accession to the throne, and it is recognized as such by Adonijah.

The anointing of Solomon therefore served a propagandistic purpose by showing that his place on the throne has not been taken unlawfully or against the will of David.[79] However, there was nothing this piece of propaganda could do in relation to the dynastic principle concerning the first-born's right to the throne. It could only emphasize the factors mentioned above, namely that Solomon was rightfully made king because of an oath taken by David, and that the anointing was performed as a sacral act. This

---

[77] Cf. Jones (1990:53), who holds that this promise was a fabrication made by Nathan and Bathsheba in order to manipulate the senile king into keeping a promise he had never made. However, Jones has a rather slender base upon which to draw such a conclusion since it is an argument from silence, and especially since Nathan and Bathsheba then become two rather dubious figures.

[78] My translation.

[79] For the term 'propaganda', see Whitelam (1986:166). He defines it as "the process by which a particular worldview (ideology) is disseminated to a specific audience. It is most effective when that worldview reinforces or confirms beliefs or attitudes already held - although often unconsciously - by the audience."

dual legitimation was necessary because Solomon was after all a son of David, and therefore not a clear-cut usurper. The question of proper dynastic succession, therefore, had to be dealt with and the decision of David was given as the answer. Behind this more civil legitimation was put the sacral, as a form of double security for the legitimation of Solomon's accession to the throne.[80]

What remained, then, was a modified form of the dynastic principle. Both the act of royal anointing and the dynastic principle of primogeniture were modified in order to fit together; the anointing was emphasized as sacral, and the dynastic principle was made dependent on the choice of David. Just because the sacral legitimation is emphasized to such an extent in 1 Kgs 1, however, does not necessarily mean that it did not exist earlier. It could just as well have been the case that it was brought forward in 1 Kgs 1 because it was felt needed in order to legitimate the anointing.

It was found above, regarding the anointings in 2 Sam 2:4; 5:3 and 19:11, that the verb "anoint" is used causatively in the phrase "anoint PN king". In this particular case there is no such use of the verb, and instead the act of anointing is described as similar to the divine anointings in 1 Sam 10:1 and 16:13. On the other hand, when the subject of the anointing in 1 Kgs 1:39 is spelled out as being the priest Zadok, it can hardly be said to be in contrast with the earlier texts where the phrase "anoint PN king" is used. In this respect 1 Kgs 1:39 differs from the divine anointings, since they are described as being performed by a prophet. The stock phrase "anoint PN king" is then deliberately avoided in favour of a description of the actual anointing.

The purpose behind the different terminology in 1 Kgs 1:39 resides in its propagandistic tendency. There are simply no elders and certainly no people who can legitimately authorize the anointing of Solomon. At the same time, the anointing is described as a sacral act, although the description is given a veiled and indirect form. The description of the anointing in 1 Kgs 1:39 thereby functions as a hinge between the civil and the sacral legitimation. By emphasizing the fact that Solomon was anointed according to the proper legal convention, e.g. by a priest, and by the order of David, a civil legitimation is indicated. By describing how a priest performs the act by means of holy oil, accompanied by a prophet and at a local sanctuary, the door is opened to a sacral legitimation as well.[81]

---

[80] See e.g. Kuan (1990:35), who also notes the presence of both civil and sacral legitimations.

[81] See Mettinger (1976:201-2) for a similar view.

Therefore, the legal function of the anointing of Solomon is severely restricted by the fact that it has a propagandistic tendency in describing what is actually a usurpation. The ordinary legal authority, which authorized the anointing and thus legitimated the king-making process, is not present. This made the anointing void of any proper legal function.

2.7.3.8 1 Kings 19:15-16 and 2 Kings 9:3, 6

In 1 Kgs 19:15-16 Elijah the prophet receives a divine command to anoint the Israelite king Jehu, the Aramean king Hazael and his own successor, Elisha. It is interesting to note the interchangeability between the anointing of kings and the anointing of a prophet's successor. It implies that anointing could be understood to signal more than just transference of kingly status.

1 Kgs 19:15 says that *ûmāšaḥtā ʾet-ḥăzāʾēl lĕmelek ʿal-ʾărām*, "you shall anoint Hazael as king over Aram." The expression is a conglomerate of the two different forms seen earlier, since the verb "anoint" is used causatively yet has the agent as the subject, namely the prophet Elijah. As such it is similar to the divine command given to Samuel in 1 Sam 9:16, "and you shall anoint him to be *nāgîd* over my people Israel."[82] As was seen earlier regarding the anointings in 1 Sam 10:1 and 16:13, it is a use of the expression "anoint PN king" which serves to emphasize the divine election.

The command given to Elijah to anoint Jehu is not carried out by himself, but by an unnamed disciple of his in 2 Kgs 9:6. In 2 Kgs 8:13 Elisha only notifies Hazael of the fact that he is to be king, without any mention of an anointing. There is also no mention of an anointing of Elisha.

In the description of the anointing of Jehu in 2 Kgs 9:3, 6, the standard phrase "anoint PN king" is used. However, since God is given as the subject, the anointing is another example of divine anointing.[83] This is countered in the text, however, by the use of factors which would imply a proper royal anointing with a legal function, not unlike what was found earlier regarding the anointing of Solomon in 1 Kgs 1. The major elements in implying a legal status are found in v. 13. Jehu's friends, upon hearing what has happened, place their mantles under Jehu's feet, blow a horn and shout the acclamation, *mālak yēhûʾ*, "Jehu has become king!"[84] This is meant to give the anointing an official status, however unofficial it might have been.

---

[82] My translation.
[83] See e.g. Minokami (1989:155). See also the similar statement in 2 Chr 22:7.
[84] My translation.

If the two pretenders to the throne in 1 Kgs 19:15-16 are compared, an interesting similarity is found that might very well lead to the reason for the use of the anointing in the command. Jehu had no dynastic principle whatsoever to rely on, which makes him a usurper of the throne. Hazael was also without any dynastic support, which is evident from the chronicles of Shalmanezer III, where it says that "Hazael, a commoner (lit.: son of nobody), seized the throne".[85] It can hardly have been a coincidence that both kings which Elijah was told to anoint were usurpers, without any dynastic principle to their advantage. This probably shows the reason for the insistence on anointing in 1 Kgs 19:15-16. The anointing in this text is without the legal function of actually making someone king. Instead it strengthens the divine election, which in these cases is very much needed since they both took the throne by force. This might also explain why Elijah is told to anoint Elisha as his successor. There was no principle of succession in passing on the leadership of a prophetic band, which made it necessary to legitimate the choice of Elisha.

The conclusion is, then, that the anointings prescribed in 1 Kgs 19:15-16 and the one performed in 2 Kgs 9:6 are examples of divine anointing which has been found earlier in 1 Sam 10:1 and 16:13. It has no legal function, but serves to strengthen the divine election. In these texts the anointing was particularly necessary since it concerned the sacral legitimation of usurpers and the leader of a prophetic band.

2.7.3.9 2 Kings 11:12

This text will be approached by means of its structure, which is delicately formed in order to enhance the anointing in v. 12. Throughout vv. 4-19 there are several occurrences of the epithets "the king's son" and "the king", which serves to form a climax in v. 12. In v. 4 the king's son Joash is shown to the soldiers. In their eyes he has yet to achieve royal status and is therefore not called king. However, in vv. 7, 8, (2) and 11 he is nevertheless called king, which is somewhat puzzling. In these cases, however, Joash is not actually seen but only referred to as the one who ought to have royal status, and hence the epithet is applied. In v. 12a he is again called the king's son, since Joash appears in person as the pretender to the throne and not yet as the king. In vv. 14-19 Joash is called king even though he appears in public, which only goes to show that the shift from being the king's son to actual king has taken place in v. 12b-c.

---

[85] *ANET* (280).

In this apparently climactic part of the narrative, v. 12b-c, a number of actions are performed. Joash receives the *nēzer* and the *ʿēdūt*, he is said to be made king and anointed, and he is acclaimed by the bystanders through handclapping and shouting. This is the only occurrence of a coronation where the king is said to receive the *nēzer* and the *ʿēdūt*. This is not the place to go into the difficult question as to what these items actually were and what they symbolized, except to say that they must have symbolized the royal status, which is why they are mentioned here.[86] As regards the other four statements, however, they will have to be analyzed more carefully:

a. *wayyamlikû ʾōtô*	a. ... and they made him king,
b. *wayyimšāḥuhû*	b. and they anointed him,
c. *wayyakkû-kāp*	c. and they clapped their hands,

d. *wayyōʾmĕrû*
   yĕḥî hammelek
	d. and they shouted,
	   "long live the king!"[87]

The actions in 12c and 12d are performed simultaneously. The relationship between 12a and 12b is more subtle, however. The waw at the beginning of 12b can hardly imply either consecutiveness or simultaneousness. It would leave the abstract phrase "and they made him king" in mid-air, beside the more concrete statement about anointing which, as has been shown earlier, has much to do with king-making. It would be more natural to understand the waw at the beginning of *wayyimšāḥuhû*, "and they anointed him" in 12b as epexegetical.[88] The meaning would then be, "and they made him king by anointing him". The text then contains an explanation of the legal function of the royal anointing, which is to make someone king. It is by means of this anointing that Joash becomes king since, as was seen above, in the following context he is referred to as such even when be appears in public. This would also mean that the handing over of the *nēzer* and the *ʿēdūt* as well as the acclamation are complementary components in the ceremony, and do not partake in the actual act of making Joash king. No doubt they were necessary in order to make it a legitimate coronation ceremony, but their function was complementary to the anointing in making Joash king.[89]

---

[86] Cf. e.g. Mettinger (1976:287-9) and Cogan & Tadmor (1988:128).

[87] My translation.

[88] So e.g. Würthwein (1984:349). See Waltke & O'Connor (1990:551).

[89] See Brettler (1989:133-4), who notes the prominence of the anointing and how it sometimes is the only procedure given for the king-making, which would suggest that "it was (one of) the main performative rite(s) of the coronation." Using the terms 'rite' and 'ceremony' of cultural anthropology, the anointing is an example of "rituals of

The reason why the anointing of Joash is emphasized so strongly arises from the fact that it is a matter of conspiracy and usurpation against queen Athaliah. In contrast to David and Jehu, however, Joash has the privilege of dynastic primogeniture. Nevertheless, the stress on the anointing serves propagandistically to strengthen the legitimate role of Joash as king. Other strengthening factors are the role of the people in their acclamation and the function of the priests, and especially the priest Jehoiada. The role of the people is related to the reason why the verb forms in v. 12 are in the plural. It seems strange, at first sight, that although the priest Jehoiada is said in the first part of v. 12 to hand over the *nēzer* and the *ʿēdût* to Joash, he is not specified as the one who anoints. The unspecified plural subject in the four verb forms in v. 12 is to be inferred from the royal bodyguard mentioned in v. 11 and the priests that are presumably present. Afterwards, in v. 13, the focus shifts from the coronation scene to Athaliah, who suddenly hears the cries of the royal bodyguard and the people, which is the first time the people attending the coronation are mentioned. This is meant to strengthen the legitimate status of the anointing of Joash, since he has gained the approval of the people. It is therefore not without reason that the narrator makes Jehoiada recede for a moment in v.12, since the purpose is to show the collective and authoritative legitimation of the anointing of Joash, and not just the work of a zealous priest.[90]

Excursus: An Implicit Plural Subject of 'Anoint' in the LXX

It is interesting to note how the LXX has dealt with this matter of the plural forms in 2 Kgs 11:12. It reads ἐβασίλευσεν αὐτὸν, "he made him king" and ἔχρισεν αὐτόν, "he anointed him". The translator has apparently understood the two plural forms in analogy with the earlier ἐξαπέστειλεν, "he brought out" and ἔδωκεν, "he gave", probably due to the implicitness of the plural subject. The same phenomenon can be found in 2 Sam 5:17. The MT has *māšĕḥû ʾet-dāwid lĕmelek*, "they had anointed David king",[91] which is translated in the LXX as κέχρισται Δαυιδ βασιλεὺς, "David had been

---

status transformation", whereas the accompanying acts are "ceremonies confirming the social institution involved and demonstrating the individual person's solidarity with the institution", Malina (1986:140-3).

[90] Most scholars would argue that it was a priest, and then most likely Jehoiada himself, who nevertheless performed the anointing, e.g. Mettinger (1976:145), who holds it probable, and Würthwein (1984:350), who regards what he calls the priestly coronation in v. 12aβ as a later addition. Kutsch (1979:80), however, does not hold that a priest performed the anointing. However, since the text does not say explicitly whether the priest Jehoiada performed the anointing or not, it would seem best not to have a firm opinion, although it is highly likely that he did so.

[91] My translation.

anointed king". It seems therefore that the LXX consistently avoids the plural forms of "anoint" when the subject is only implied. When such a plural subject is mentioned, as in 2 Sam 2:4; 5:3 and 19:11, the LXX has the verb in the plural as well.

This might very well point the way to a solution to the enigma in 1 Kgs 5:15 (LXX 5:1). The MT says that Hiram sent envoys to Solomon because he had heard that *'ōtô māšĕḥû lĕmelek*, "they had anointed him king", but the LXX[B,L] reads that Hiram sent his envoys χρῖσαι τὸν Σαλωμων, "to anoint Solomon".[92] It would seem likely that this is yet another instance where the LXX tries to avoid the awkward plural *māšĕḥû*, "they anointed" without an explicit subject.[93] A supporting fact is that just before the statement in 5:1, the LXX has gathered together two statements concerning diplomatic relations, which in the MT are to be found in different places. In 4:31 the marriage between Solomon and the daughter of Pharaoh is referred to, to be found in 3:1 in the MT. In 4:32-33 it is described how Pharaoh gives Gezer as a dowry, which is found in 9:16-17 in the MT. Apparently these three statements concerning diplomatic relations were meant to strengthen the importance of Solomon. This, together with the difficult plural forms, then lead to the remoulding of 1 Kgs 5:15 in the LXX.

2.7.3.10 2 Kings 23:30

This short text describes how the *'am-hā'āreṣ*, "the people of the land" make Jehoahaz king after his father Josiah. The comment is brief and does not tell very much about the circumstances, but it is possible to discern some interesting facts. There is no emphasis on a sacral character of this anointing. Instead it is the collective legitimation by the people that is emphasized by the explicit mention of the "people of the land" as the subject of the anointing.

The expression *wayyimšĕḥû 'ōtô*, "and they anointed him" is similar to, though shorter than, what has been found above.[94] Then, immediately afterwards, it says that *wayyamlîkû 'ōtô*, "and they made him king."[95] The following phrase, *taḥat 'ābîw*, "in place of his father" modifies both the preceding phrases.[96] This can hardly have been meant as two separate acts

---

[92] LXX[A,O] follow the MT, which is probably the result of a later harmonization, see Kuan (1990:32).

[93] Some scholars would regard the reading of LXX[B,L] as original in relation to the MT, e.g. Mettinger (1976:225-7), Seybold (1986:50), Hayes & Hooker (1988:43-4) and Kuan (1990:31-4).

[94] My translation.

[95] My translation.

[96] Cf. the construction in 1 Kgs 5:15, *'ōtô māšĕḥû lĕmelek taḥat 'ābîhû*, "they had anointed him king in place of his father".

performed consecutively. The same conclusion was drawn above regarding 2 Kgs 11:12, where the two expressions occur in the opposite order. It is more likely that the relationship between the two expressions here, as in 2 Kgs 11:12, is epexegetical,[97] which means that "they made him king" is an explanation of the earlier "they anointed him". The translation would then be: "And then they anointed him, thus making him king after his father." It would then be an explicit confirmation of the legal function of the royal anointing, namely to accomplish the royal status of Jehoahaz.

Why is this anointing referred to at all? The answer lies within the propagandistic purpose of the text. The narrator went to great pains to underline the fact that it was Jehoahaz, and not his elder brother, Eliakim, who was anointed. The dynastic right of primogeniture favoured the elder brother, which is why it had to be noted that the younger brother was actually anointed in the proper manner, i.e., by the authority of the *ʿam-hāʾereṣ*, the "people of the land".[98]

Who actually performed this anointing is as unimportant to the narrator as it was found to be concerning the anointings of David in 2 Sam 2:4 and 5:3, and of Joash in 2 Kgs 11:12.

Excursus: Anointing in Psalms 45:8; 89:21 and 105:15

Ps 45:8 This is a psalm about the king, v. 2. It praises his qualities and encourages him to uphold justice in his kingdom. In v. 8 there is a reference to an anointing of the king. In order to understand that anointing, however, it must be placed in the larger context of two similar statements in vv. 3 and 7:

v. 3 *ʿal-kēn bērakkāʾ ĕlōhîm* *lĕʿôlām*	Therefore, God has blessed you forever.
v. 7 *ksʾk*[99] *ʾĕlōhîm ʿôlām wāʿed*	God has enthroned you forever and ever.
v. 8 *ʿal-kēn mĕšāḥăkā ʾĕlōhîm* *ʾĕlōhêkā šemen śāśôn* *mēḥăbērêkā*	Therefore God, your God, has anointed you with the oil of gladness, beyond your companions.[100]

---

[97] See Waltke & O'Connor (1990:551).

[98] Cf. Mettinger (1976:129-30): "As attested by 2 R 23,30 and Jer ch. 34 the power of the *a.h.* was a 'constitutional' check on governmental authority in Judah. The participation of the *a.h.* in the royal investitures agrees with what we know of the investitures of Saul and David, and so there is a remarkable continuity in this respect."

[99] I read *ksʾk* as a denominative piel, as proposed by Dahood (1966:273) and accepted by Craigie (1983:336-7). For the denominative function of piel, see Nyberg (1952:222) and Waltke & O'Connor (1990:410-14, esp. 413). For other alternatives, see Kraus (1978:487).

[100] My translation.

If *ksᵓ* in v. 7 is read as a denominative piel of *kissēᵓ*, "throne" there is a triad of divine actions related to the king in vv. 3, 7 and 8.[101] In v. 3 God is said to have blessed the king, which is an allusion backward to v. 2, as a consequence of his beauty, and forward to vv. 4-6, as an explanation for his success in battle. In v. 7 the king is said to have been enthroned by God. The basis for the enthronement is given in the second half of the verse, namely because justice rules in the land. This relationship between the legitimacy of a king and his desire for justice can be found throughout the ancient Near East.[102] In v. 8 God, who is given added emphasis by the double mention, is said to have anointed the king. The reason for it is found in v. 7, namely that the king loves justice and hates evil. It is also stated in v. 8 that God has anointed the king with *šemen śāśôn*, "the oil of gladness", which means "oil that brings happiness", or possibly "oil connected with happiness". The oil referred to is the oil used in the anointing ceremony, and the happiness refers to the joyous acclamation which accompanied the royal anointing, as seen above concerning 1 Sam 10:24; 1 Kgs 1:25, 39 and 2 Kgs 11:12. The fact that the anointing of the king has been made "beyond your companions" indicates the election inherent in the making of a king. The conclusion is that the anointing spoken of in Ps 45:8 is the anointing of the king. That God is said to be the subject of the anointing shows that it is used to express the divine election of the king. Similar examples of divine anointings were found earlier in 1 Sam 10:1; 16:13 and 2 Kgs 9:3, 6.

Ps 89:21 This text contains a similar expression to the one found in Ps 45:8: *māṣāᵓtî dāwid ʿabdî bĕšemen qodšî mĕšaḥtîw*, "I have found my servant David; with my holy oil I have anointed him". The subject of the anointing of David is God, which recalls 1 Sam 10:1 where God is said to anoint Saul and above all 2 Sam 12:7. In the first half of v. 21, God is said to have "found" David, implying a search for and selection of the proper candidate for the throne. Another important point in this text is the mention of the "holy oil" by which God is said to have anointed David. The surprising fact here is the combination of phraseology otherwise known from theological comments concerning divine election of kings and the priestly terminology found in Exod 30:25, where it is called "holy anointing oil". This might indicate a mingling of traditions, as well as the continuance of the practice of keeping this particular anointment oil in the sanctuary. The same oil which used to anoint kings was then probably also used to anoint priests as well as cultic objects.

Ps 105:15 The use of anointing to designate election is extended further in this text when God calls the patriarchs *mĕšîḥāy*, "my anointed ones". The patriarchs are earlier in vv. 6 and 11-12 said to have had a special relationship to God as his elected ones. Since divine anointing refers to divine election of kings, it has here been transferred to designate divine election of the patriarchs as well. There is also a similarity between the inviolability of

---

101   So Dahood (1966:273).

102   Cf. de Vaux (1961:146).

the divinely chosen king and the divine command in v. 15: "Do not touch my anointed ones; do my prophets no harm." The patriarchs are also called prophets in v. 15b, another group which is well-known for having a special relationship with God.[103] As was the case above regarding God's command to Elijah to anoint his successor Elisha in 1 Kgs 19:16, the anointing could be used to emphasize the divine election of prophets.

Excursus: Priestly Anointing

According to Exod 28:41; 29:7 and Lev 8:12, the priests were installed in their office through the act of anointing as well as through the filling of hands.[104] This is clearly a case of cultic law, which is not the subject of this analysis.[105] Nevertheless, there are some interesting points to be made in relation to royal anointing.[106] The texts which describe the priestly anointing stress the particular oil that is used. This sacral oil reminds one of the oil which Zadok brought from the tent-sanctuary in 1 Kgs 1:39. The priestly traditions describe the oil used as the *šemen hammišḥâ*, "the anointing oil",[107] or *šemen mišḥat-qōdeš*, "sacred anointing oil",[108] which even receives a detailed description of its composition and proper use in Exod 30:22-33. There is also an interesting expression in Exod 28:41: *ûmāšaḥtā ʾōtām ûmilleʾtā ʾet-yādām wĕqiddaštā ʾōtām wĕkihănû lî*, "and (you) shall anoint them and ordain them and consecrate them, so that they may serve me as priests." The first two statements regarding the anointing and the handfilling, here translated "ordain", refer to concrete acts, while the third statement explains the aforementioned acts. The fourth statement explains the new status and function of the anointed and thus consecrated priests. The last two statements then function explicatively in relation to the aforementioned acts. This is made more explicit in Exod 29:36, concerning the consecration of the altar, *ûmāšaḥtā ʾōtô lĕqaddĕšô*, "and (you) shall anoint it, to consecrate it" and similarly Lev 8:12, by marking the purpose of the

---

[103] Another, very common expression is *māšîaḥ yhwh*, "the Lord's anointed one". Besides referring to the king, it also expresses the divine election of God's own people, Hab 3:13, see de Moor (1990:133, n. 145), or even foreign kings, Isa 45:1. For the use of this expression, see e.g. Kutsch (1963:60-3), Mettinger (1976:191), Seybold (1986:52-8) and Brettler (1989:35).

[104] No satisfying explanation has as yet been given to this expression. Some form of symbolic act was probably performed, analogously to the anointing, see e.g. Gorman (1990:128). Whether the expression gives any clues to the procedure of the act is uncertain, however.

[105] See e.g. Gorman (1990:118-20).

[106] For an analysis regarding the relationship between the anointings in Exod 29 and Lev 8, see Walkenhorst (1969:44-55).

[107] E.g. Exod 25:6; 29:7; Lev 8:2; Num 4:16.

[108] Exod 30:25, 31. There are some variants of this formulation where *qōdeš*, "sacred" is replaced, in Lev 10:7 with *yhwh* and in Lev 21:12 with *ʾĕlōhāyw*, "his God".

anointing with the preposition *lĕ*.[109] In Exod 29:44 it says that "Aaron also and his sons I will consecrate, to serve me as priests", but later on in Exod 30:30 it says that "You shall anoint Aaron and his sons, and consecrate them, in order that they may serve me as priests." The subject of the verb "consecrate" is then said to be both God and Moses. Moses is the agent of the consecration as the performer of the anointing and handfilling which achieves the consecration. However, the actual consecration is done by God, which is why he is also the subject. A similar case was found above regarding royal anointing, when it was given subjects both in the plural and in the singular, and both God and a human appeared as subjects. The differences to be noted here are that in the priestly tradition God is never said to have anointed a priest, and the verb "anoint" is always used with a human subject and never causatively, as in the royal anointings.[110] The conclusion is that, although the descriptions of the royal and priestly anointings vary somewhat, they are very much the same. This is relevant for the historical explanation below.

2.7.4 Historical Explanation

The historical explanation of the legal symbolic act of royal anointing remains very much in the dark. One possible way of explaining the relation between the performance of the act and its legal function, however, is to focus on the practice of anointing the head.[111] The Sumerians already in their time had the custom of shaving their heads in order to keep free of lice and wear wigs instead. This hygienic use was then transferred to the sphere of priestly rituals, where it served to symbolize cultic purity. The priest therefore came to be called in Akkadian *pašīšu*, "the anointed", from the verb *pašāšu*, "anoint". The act of anointment was then used to consecrate the priests into their office, and similarly as a means of installing the king into his office. The act of making someone king would then have been expressed visually by means of the anointing.

---

[109] See Gorman (1990:119).
[110] See Seybold (1986:52).
[111] The following explanation is based on Jacobsen (1987:3). See also Pardee (1977:17) for a similar line of reasoning.

2.7.5 Summary and Conclusions

1. The anointing was performed by pouring a container of oil over the head. In the only text which describes the procedure for a royal anointing with an intended legal function, namely 1 Kgs 1:39, a priest performs the act. This was probably the case in all royal anointings with a legal function.

2. Anointing with a legal function is known from extra-biblical material, although not with the same frequency as in the OT. From Ugarit traces have been found of what might be a reference to a royal anointing of Baal. According to the Amarna-letters, the Egyptian Pharaoh had his vassals anointed as a way of installation. The description of the anointing does not, however, mention who actually performed the act, but only that the Pharaoh legitimated it. Among the Hittites, royal anointing was apparently practised. The descriptions, although fragmentary, have the same implicit plural subject of the act of anointing as in the OT. This shows that the texts were more interested in the legitimating factor behind the anointing than who actually performed the act.

3. Royal anointing is portrayed as the climax of king-making in the OT. The best argument for this is the explicative relationship between the two expressions "they anointed him" and "they made him king" in 2 Kgs 11:12 and 23:30, and interestingly enough also in one of the Amarna letters, *EA* 51:6-7. By this connection, a common reference is given for these two expressions, which indicates that by means of anointing the person in question was indeed made king. The legal function of royal anointing was therefore to accomplish the royal status of someone.

4. The proper royal anointing needed a civil legitimation in order to fulfil its legal function, as in 2 Sam 2:4; 5:3; 19:11; 2 Kgs 11:12 and 23:30. When a sacral legitimation was given, as in 1 Sam 10:1; 16:13 and 1 Kgs 19:15-16, no legal function was involved. The divine anointing was modelled in these latter texts after the proper royal anointing and served to emphasize the divine election. In 1 Kgs 1:39 an attempt was made to provide the anointing of Solomon with both a civil and a sacral legitimation. As a royal anointing, however, it failed to fulfil the requirements for accomplishing the legal function of making Solomon king.

5. Royal anointing is only mentioned when there is a case of irregular succession to the throne. The allusion to an anointing is meant to strengthen the legitimate royal status of the king in question. This is found in 2 Sam 2:4 and 5:3 since David was not in any way related to Saul, in 1 Kgs 1:39 since Solomon was the younger brother, in 2 Sam 19:11 since Absalom was a usurper, in 2 Kgs 11:12 since Queen Athaliah was still on the throne and in 2 Kgs 23:30 since Jehoahaz was the younger brother. It is also found in the texts which describe divine anointing, namely 1 Sam 10:1, since Saul was the first king, in 1 Sam 16:13 for the same reasons regarding David as given above and in 1 Kgs 19:15-16, since Jehu and Hazael were usurpers and Elisha the successor of a prophet.

6. The priestly anointing served to consecrate priests to their cultic service. The legal function of the act was therefore part of cultic law. The formulation of the description of priestly anointing shows several parallels to the way the royal anointing is described.

7. The historical explanation of the royal anointing could very well be based on the old custom of anointing the head to keep it free from lice. It was then used as a symbolic form of achieving cultic purity, which served to install the priest into his office. This use of anointing, namely to visualize and accomplish the installation of a person into an office, would then have been used for the installation of kings as well.

2.8 Grasping the Horns of the Altar

2.8.1 Introduction

The legal symbolic act of grasping the horns of the altar is naturally connected with the possibility of achieving asylum at the sanctuary.[1] The following analysis of the act will also bring attention to other intricate questions.

There may be an allusion to this act in Exod 21:12-14, which is the law that prescribes the conditions under which the right to asylum could or could not be claimed. However, it is only in 1 Kgs 1:50 and 2:28 that we find actual occurrences of the act. The problem is, however, that the legislation in Exod 21:12-14 does not seem to concur with the circumstances surrounding the two examples of the act in 1 Kgs 1:50 and 2:28. Furthermore, the fact that horned altars are thus far a Palestinian phenomenon explains why no relevant extra-biblical examples of the act are available.[2]

2.8.2 Procedure

In Exod 21:12-14 there is most likely an allusion to this symbolic act. The person seeking asylum is said in v. 14 to be taken *mēʿim mizbĕḥî*, "from my altar". This probably implies that the person in question has earlier taken hold of the horns of the altar.[3]

The expression used for describing the symbolic act in 1 Kgs 1:50 and 2:28 is straightforward enough. The person seeking asylum entered the shrine, went up to the altar and took hold of its horns. However, it is uncertain whether the person seeking asylum used one or both hands and, if he used both hands, whether he took hold of one horn or two. The expression used in I Kgs 1:50 and 2:28, *wayyaḥăzēq bĕqarnôt hammizbēaḥ*, "and he grasped the horns of the altar"[4] argues for that two horns were grasped. It

---

[1] For the function and use of asylum in the OT, see Löhr (1930), Nicolsky (1930), Greenberg (1959) and Houtman (1990).

[2] See Aharoni (1974), DeVries (1987:31) and Mazar (1990:500) for various horned altars found in Palestine. For horned incense altars found at the ancient Philistine city of Ekron, now Tel Miqne, see Gitin (1989:32-5, 46, 50). For an inventory of horned incense altars, see Zwickel (1990:110-28). There could be earlier examples of horned altars from Mesopotamia, but the material is not clear, see Goff (1963:34-5). For horned buildings in the ancient Near East, see Potts (1990).

[3] So e.g. Houtman (1990:19).

[4] My translation.

could also be referring to one of the horns indeterminately.[5] However, the text may also be indeterminate as to whether one or two horns are grasped.

2.8.3 Legal Function

2.8.3.1 Exodus 21:12-14

In Exod 21:12-14, three assertions are made. Firstly, he who intentionally kills another person will himself die, v. 12. Secondly, he who kills unintentionally will be shown an escape route, v. 13, thus making an exception to the earlier law in v. 12. Thirdly, returning to the statement in v. 12, it is explained in v. 14 that the way of escape in v. 13 does not apply to the one who has killed intentionally.[6] This third assertion is then the negative counterpart of the one in v. 13.[7]

Verse 13, "I will appoint for you a place to which the killer may flee", might allude to the cities of asylum described in Num 35:9-29, Deut 4:41-43 and 19:1-13.[8] However this may be, the word for "place", māqôm, is further specified by the mentioning of the altar in v. 14.[9] The right of asylum is then connected to the altar.

The following phrase in v. 14, mēᶜim mizbĕḥî tiqqāḥennû lāmût, "you shall take him from my altar, that he may die"[10] is somewhat unusual, since it does not say who would perform the execution. This is probably due to the fact that the accused was turned over to the family of his victim to suffer blood vengeance, according to Deut 19:11-12.[11] The phrase probably means that in order for the instructed execution in v. 12 to be carried out

---

[5] See GKC (400).

[6] Cf. Löhr (1930:35) who considers it an attempt to come to grips with an abuse of the law of asylum at the altar.

[7] Verses 13-14 are usually regarded as secondary, so e.g. Schwienhorst-Schönberger (1990:40-2) with further discussion and literature. Osumi (1991:122) holds that vv. 13-14 were added in a literary stage in the history of the formation of the law. Otto (1988:32) holds that the law in v. 12 originally belonged to family law. Verses 13-14 were then added through a traditio-historical process. Since vv. 13-14 put a limit to the blood-revenge presupposed in v. 12, vv. 12-14 thus came to be related to the local jurisdiction.

[8] See e.g. Greenberg (1959) for a treatment of these cities.

[9] Schwienhorst-Schönberger (1990:40-1) explains the use of these terms as due to the fact that God does not erect an altar, but he may appoint a place, whereas man erects an altar to God. Salmon (1969:161-3) interprets the māqôm, "place" as a permanent place of rescue, whereas the altar is only a temporary measure. This is, however, an unlikely reading of the text.

[10] My translation.

[11] So e.g. Schwienhorst-Schönberger (1990:123).

the killer had to be removed from the altar, since it would otherwise be considered a sacrilege.[12]

2.8.3.2 1 Kings 1:50

1 Kgs 1 describes how Adonijah makes a claim to ascend the throne after his father David and how he invites his allies in this attempt to a banquet, v. 41. When they are told that Solomon has become king, vv. 43-48, the gathering is dispersed, v. 49. Adonijah considers his life threatened with Solomon now on the throne, and goes to the temple to take hold of the horns of the altar, v. 50. The act thereby implies asylum from capital punishment.

Adonijah subsequently makes it clear that Solomon must swear an oath to him that he will not be executed. This rash claim of Adonijah to an oath is, however, deliberately counterbalanced by several factors introduced by the narrator. Firstly, Adonijah calls Solomon king, v. 51, thereby accepting his claim to the throne. Secondly, Adonijah calls himself a servant of the king in v. 51, thereby subjugating himself to Solomon. Thirdly, when the two meet in v. 53, Adonijah shows his total surrender by prostrating himself in front of Solomon. The oath demanded by Adonijah from Solomon is therefore in reality transformed into a plea for pardon.

Solomon's answer in v. 52 is somewhat ambiguous. It could be seen as the oath which Adonijah demanded, but at the same time it could merely be stating the law which governed the possibility of asylum, as it is found in Exod 21:12-14.[13] Adonijah apparently accepts this, since he leaves the altar to receive his pardon from the king. The striking fact is that it is the fear of the wrath of Solomon that makes Adonijah run for the altar, and not that he has killed unintentionally. What he is claiming is not, therefore, so much the asylum which is open to the one who has killed unintentionally, but instead a more general form of asylum at the altar. What was laid down in the law of Exod 21:12-14, as applied to unintentional killing, was probably only a special case of a wider use of this symbolic act, namely to make use of asylum at the altar in a more general sense. This wider use is best described as part of customary law, which will be discussed further

---

[12] Sacrilege is considered here as any dishonour done to the sanctuary, such as killing, e.g. 2 Kgs 11:15.

[13] Fokkelmann (1981:379) holds that Solomon "is not prepared to make this oath and answers the request for an unconditional statement with two conditional sentences, 52bc and de." Conroy (1985:62), on the other hand, argues that "the solemn public statement of a king may have been regarded as equivalent to an oath."

concerning 1 Kgs 2:28 below.[14] The restriction in Exod 21:12-14 is then an example where customary law has been limited. Whether this limitation was ever put into practice is impossible to determine.[15]

The legal function of the act is thus for Adonijah to accomplish his right to asylum at the altar, to the effect that he will indeed be treated fairly by Solomon. It has no apparent relation to the legislation in Exod 21:12-14.

2.8.3.3 1 Kings 2:28

1 Kgs 2:28-34 describes how Joab fears Solomon because of his support of Adonijah, and how he therefore takes hold of the horns of the altar, v. 28. Solomon then orders Benaiah to execute him. From Benaiah's argument with Joab in v. 30, it is apparent that the execution was not meant to take place at the altar, but that Joab had to leave the altar before his execution. This he refuses to do, v. 31, and expresses his wish to die at the altar. The premeditated murders which Joab is accused of are then described in a speech by Solomon, vv. 31-33, who subsequently has Joab killed at the altar, v. 34.

It is interesting to note, in relation to 1 Kgs 1:50, that when Solomon needs a reason to remove Joab from the altar he appears to follow the law in Exod 21:12-14, namely that he who has committed premeditated murder cannot be guarded by asylum of the altar.[16] However, there are some problems that occur at this point. Why could Joab not be removed from the altar when he was accused of premeditated murder, since this was allowed by the law in Exod 21:12-14? Also, if Joab was aware of this accusation and that the law in Exod 21:12-14 was applicable, why did he take refuge at the altar, knowing that it would be of no avail? The answers to these questions lie in the fact that there is a discrepancy between the reason why Joab sought refuge at the altar and the reason Solomon provides for killing Joab. Joab is asking for asylum in general, based on the sanctity of the altar,[17] whereas Solomon refers to the law in Exod 21:12-14, which makes

---

[14] Similarly Houtman (1990:42), who holds that Solomon's actions in 1 Kgs 1-2 are based on customary law and not on the law in Exod 21:12-14. Nicolsky (1930:149) recognized this distinction between a customary law that allowed asylum indiscriminately, and the innovation of Exod 21:12-14, which limited the right to asylum.

[15] Houtman (1990:38) holds that Exod 21:12-14 describes the desired legal practice, which was not necessarily applied.

[16] That the act in 1 Kgs 2:28 does mirror the law in Exod 21:12-14 is held by e.g. Phillips (1970:100), Childs (1974:470) and Whitelam (1979:153).

[17] This is usually overlooked by scholars. Whitelam (1979:153) holds that it appears evident that the right to asylum was not automatic. However, if it was the law in Exod 21:12-14 that provided the legal justification of Joab's execution, why could Joab not

an exception from the general right to asylum at the altar. However, Solomon's use of this law fails to be applied appropriately since Joab is not removed from the altar.[18] This makes it likely that Solomon's use of the law in Exod 21:12-14 in order to execute Joab at the altar is actually an attempt to justify both murder and sacrilege. It is left undecided here whether this attempt to whitewash Solomon was of his own doing,[19] the work of a contemporary author, or a later deuteronomistic author or redactor. Whoever made this attempt at a justification, however, did not conceal the fact that Joab appeals to a general form of asylum, which could only be broken by committing sacrilege and murder.

The legal function of the act of grasping the horns of the altar by Joab is then the same as was found in 1 Kgs 1:50, namely to accomplish the right to asylum at the altar. The legal function of the act apparently had no connection to the law in Exod 21:12-14, since Joab does not seem to be aware of its relevance. It is more likely that the application of the law is an attempt to justify Solomon's behaviour.

2.8.4 Historical Explanation

The most profound symbolism of the altar is the divine presence. In order for the altar to be suitable for the divine presence, however, it must be consecrated with blood, Lev 4:7, 18, 25, 30, 34; 8:15; 9:9 and 16:18. In all these instances the blood is put on the horns of the altar, which means that the horns represent the whole altar. There are also some texts which might show the way to a further symbolic meaning of the horns of the altar.

According to Amos 3:14, the judgement would cause the horns of the altars of Bethel to be cut off. This could mean that the possibility of asylum would cease to be available.[20] The horns then symbolize the possibility of rescue, inherent in the institution of asylum at the altar. Alternatively, it could be held that by cutting off the horns any proper use of the altar was

---

have been removed from the altar, as the law stated? And why is he said to have gone there in the first place?

[18] It is the discrepancy between the execution at the altar in 1 Kgs 2:34 and the law in Exod 21:12-14, together with the fact that King Solomon himself interacts with the proceedings, that make Houtman (1990:42) draw the conclusion that Solomon's action is not based on the law in Exod 21:12-14.

[19] See e.g. Whitelam (1979:152-4), who notes the pretence of monarchical judicial authority to function within the law when it strove to remove dangerous rivals: "The fact that this execution laid strong claim to legal justification does not detract from the view that the ulterior motives behind the act were all important."

[20] So e.g. Soggin (1987:65) and Andersen & Freedman (1989:411).

made impossible.[21] The horns would then refer to the altar itself and, in extension, to the cultic practices attached to it. This interpretation is supported by the fact that the cutting off of the horns stands in parallelism with the preceding phrase in v. 14, "I will punish the altars of Bethel". This phrase is, incidentally, also in parallelism with yet another preceding phrase in v. 14, "On the day I punish Israel for its transgressions". The three statements then go from the general "Israel" to the more specific "altars" to the particular, "the altar". This latter view is therefore to be preferred.

In Jer 17:1 the prophet comments ironically on the sins of the people, "with a diamond point it is engraved ... on the horns of their altars". The relationship between people and God cannot be re-established as long as their sins defile the very center of the divine presence. However, there is no reason to see an allusion to asylum in this text.[22]

In Ps 18:3 (= 2 Sam 22:3) God is described as *qeren-yiš'î*, "the horn of my salvation", which means "the horn that saves me". Since the act of grasping the horns of the altar could achieve asylum, the horns came to symbolize that which rescues. When this was applied to God's salvation in Ps 18:3, God is metaphorically described as the horn which saves.

The horns of the altar thus symbolize the divine presence. The act of grasping the horns was a way of taking hold of not only the horns physically, but also the divine presence. The act would then be based on the belief that God protects those who seek refuge with him, and that his sanctuary is therefore a place of asylum. It is probable that the horns in this way also came to symbolize the possibility of rescue. The act of grasping the horns would then be a way of taking hold of the possibility of rescue. This historical explanation of the act would then make it understandable why the procedure of grasping the horns of the altar was connected to the legal function of accomplishing asylum at the altar.

---

[21] So e.g. Stuart (1987:332). Wolff (1969:239) suggests both possibilities.

[22] See Carroll (1986:349), who considers the horns as signs of cultic protection in asylum to be used here as signs of Judah's sin.

2.8.5 Summary and Conclusions

1. The act was performed by grasping one or more of the horns of the altar in the sanctuary.

2. The legal function of the act of grasping the horns of the altar is to accomplish the performer's right to asylum at the altar.

3. Both Adonijah, in 1 Kgs 1:50, and Joab, in 2:28, are trying to avoid Solomon's revenge by seeking rescue at the altar. These examples of the act do not show any relation to the law in Exod 21:12-14, but appear to be based on a more general right to asylum at the altar.

4. The attempt to justify Solomon's behaviour in executing Joab by making use of the law in Exod 21:12-14 is not a correct description, but an attempt to free Solomon from accusations of murder and sacrilege.

5. The historical explanation of the act is based on the fact that the horns of the altar symbolized God's presence. Since God was believed to help those who seek refuge with him, the horns came to symbolize divine rescue as well. By grasping the horns of the altar, a person was then invoking what they symbolized, namely the possibility of rescue.

2.9 Transferring the Mantle

2.9.1 Introduction

Some of the acts that are studied in this analysis are clearer than others, as far as their legal characters are concerned, because their contexts are unambiguously legal. Others, like in the present case, produce difficulties since their contexts are not primarily legal. This is the case as well with the other act connected with a mantle in this analysis, namely to cover the woman with a mantle. Even further removed from a legal function are acts such as to grasp or to cut the hem of the mantle.

> The reason for not including the acts of grasping or cutting the hem of the mantle in this analysis is that the occurrences of these acts in the OT do not describe the acts as having a legal function. Furthermore, the acts as they are described do not even exemplify a reusing of a legal symbolic act.[1] The act by Saul in 1 Sam 15:27, as well as the act mentioned in Zech 8:23, are examples of a symbolic act which symbolizes subordination and supplication.[2] The symbolic act by David in 1 Sam 24:5 displays authority over Saul.[3] In neither of these cases is there any reason to see a reusing of a legal symbolic act in a non-legal context.

The text that will be studied here is 1 Sam 18:4, where Jonathan transfers his mantle to David. The major difficulty with this act is whether or not a legal function has been associated with the performance of the act.

Because there is only one text to study regarding this legal symbolic act, and even that text is without a proper legal context, extra-biblical material will be used that refer to a similar act with a legal function.

2.9.2 Performance

The performance of the act in 1 Sam 18:4 is clear enough. Jonathan takes off his *měʿîl*, the outer mantle, his *maddâ*, the mantle worn below, his bow, sword and belt, and hands them over to David. The text stresses the fact

---

[1] For a non-legal use of the act of grasping the hem of the mantle, see *KTU* 1.6.II:9-11, cf. Greenstein (1982), and Ahiqar 171. For a legal use, see *KAI* 215:11 and the various texts in Malul (1988:420-31). For legal uses of cutting the hem of the garment, see Malul (1988:139-59, 197-208). For the use of these different acts in ancient Near Eastern diplomacy, see Munn-Rankin (1956:85, 91-2).

[2] So e.g. Brauner (1974:36) and Kruger (1986:112). See also Conrad (1969) for a somewhat different view.

[3] Cf. Gordon (1980:56).

that it was Jonathan himself who took them off by using the hithpael stem of the verb, *wayyitpaššēṭ*, which is the only occurrence of the verb *pāšaṭ* in this stem. Since the verb is used in the qal stem in 19:24, when Saul is said to take off his clothes, it would seem probable that the author wanted to stress the independent decision and performance of Jonathan, and that it was Jonathan's own belongings that were handed over.[4]

Another interesting fact is that Jonathan is said to take off the mantle *ʾăšer ʿālāyw*, "that he was wearing", which would seem to be a rather superfluous comment, especially since the hithpael stem was used immediately before to strengthen the reflexive character of the act. The author is therefore not only stressing the fact that Jonathan was handing over his mantle to David, but the performance as such, namely that Jonathan was accomplishing a particular kind of act. Therefore it is important for the author to note as well that the mantle which was handed over had to be taken off by Jonathan himself. The description of the procedure of the act therefore argues for the performance of a symbolic act.

2.9.3 Legal Function

It has been noted that Jonathan's relation to David is described in 1 Sam 18:1 and 3 by means of strong emotional terminology, such as "the soul of Jonathan was bound to the soul of David",[5] and that "he (Jonathan) loved him as his own soul." The use of the verb *ʾāhab*, "love" in this text has been considered by some to denote not so much an affectionate relationship but a covenant made between them.[6] As has been noted by Gordon,[7] however, it is a remarkable fact that almost everyone seems to "love" David in 1 Sam 18. In v. 16 the whole of Israel and Judah are said to love him, in v. 20 Michal does so as well, and in v. 22 Saul secretly has it told to David that all the servants of the king love him. It could very well be that Saul is the only one not described as lovingly attached to David. However, it is interesting to note what is said in v. 2, namely that "Saul took him that day and would not let him return to his father's house." This should most likely be described as an act of affection on behalf of Saul. It was also stated earlier in 16:21 that Saul "loved" David.[8]

---

[4] See Waltke & O'Connor (1990:430), where this example is categorized as indirect reflexive.

[5] This expression is only used once more in the OT, namely in Gen 44:30 where it describes Jacob's deep paternal affection for Benjamin, see McCarter (1980:305).

[6] So e.g. Thompson (1974) and Ackroyd (1975).

[7] Gordon (1986:159).

[8] It would seem that Saul's appointment of David in v. 5 is not the same as the one in

Too much stress therefore must not be put on the use of "love" in this text, since the author seems to have had an overall purpose to display David as everyone's favorite, and in particular Jonathan's.[9] It seems that the affection shown towards David by apparently all participants in 1 Sam 18 is a sign of loyalty and admiration. In this sense, the use of "love" might, at most, strengthen the more official ties between David and those who love him, and above all, Jonathan.[10]

In 18:3 Jonathan and David are said to make a covenant, *wayyikrōt yĕhônātān wĕdāwid bĕrît*, which does refer to some form of legal bond on a personal basis. The question is, however, whether it is Jonathan who makes a covenant with David,[11] or whether they make the covenant together, on an equal basis.[12]

The former alternative is favoured by the following causal clause, "because he loved him as his own soul." This could imply that Jonathan was the subject already in the previous clause. On the other hand, this alternative would have to consider the waw in *wĕdāwid* as a case of waw concomitantiae,[13] a use which is not elsewhere attested in the phrase "make a covenant with someone". Elsewhere the phrase is always constructed by means of prepositions, mostly *lĕ*,[14] *ʿim* [15] or *ʾet*.[16] The translation would then be, "with David".

The latter alternative interprets the waw in an easier way, but runs into trouble with the subsequent causal phrase. On the whole, however, it would seem less problematic to choose the latter alternative. The causal construction may be due to the fact that it was Jonathan who took the initiative to the covenant with David, and nothing more. The covenant is

---

v. 13. The former is a sign of affection and approval, the latter an attempt to have him killed.

[9] McCarter (1980:342) calls it "the irresistible charm of the man who has Yahweh's favor."

[10] Thompson (1974:338) considers the use of "love" in this context as ambiguous, and "pregnant with political significance." That may be as far as the comparison with the more technical use of the verb will take us.

[11] So e.g. Stoebe (1973:343) and Klein (1983:231-2). Klein considers it implicit, although he translates it as "Jonathan and David made a covenant" (1983:171).

[12] So e.g. McCarter (1980:300, 304).

[13] Cf. GKC (484).

[14] E.g. Exod 23:32; 34:12, 15; Deut 7:2; Josh 9:7, 15; 24:25; 1 Sam 11:1; 2 Sam 5:3; 1 Kgs 20:34; 2 Kgs 11:4; Ezra 10:3; 1 Chr 11:3; 2 Chr 21:7.

[15] E.g. Exod 24:8; Deut 4:23; 5:2; 9:9; 29:11, 24; 1 Kgs 8:21; Job 40:28; 2 Chr 6:11; 23:3.

[16] E.g. Gen 15:18; Deut 5:3; 28:69; 29:13; 2 Sam 3:13; 2 Kgs 17:15, 35; Jer 31:33; 34:8; Ezek 17:13.

therefore meant to be on an equal basis between Jonathan and David, with a certain stress on the initiative of Jonathan.[17]

Excursus: The Covenant Between Jonathan and David

The covenant between Jonathan and David is a thread that runs through a large part of 1 and 2 Samuel, beginning here in 1 Sam 18:1-3. A covenant is said to be made three times, in 1 Sam 18:3, 20:16, where it refers to the immediately preceding oath in v. 12-13, and 23:18. The two latter cases are best seen as a renewal of the original covenant made in 18:3. It is also described as an oath that is sworn in 1 Sam 20:17,[18] 42 and 2 Sam 21:7. The covenant is said to be performed "before the Lord" in 1 Sam 23:18 and it is called lit. "a covenant of the Lord" in 1 Sam 20:8. As an oath it is said to have been "sworn in the name of the Lord" in 1 Sam 20:42, and in 2 Sam 21:7 it is described as an "oath of the Lord". God is said to be a witness to the covenant in 1 Sam 20:23 and 42. David appeals to the covenant made by asking Jonathan to perform *ḥesed*, fidelity to the covenant made, in 1 Sam 20:8, and in 2 Sam 9:3 he refers to his own act of *ḥesed* as *ḥesed* of God.[19] The same is done almost immediately afterwards by Jonathan in 1 Sam 20:14-15. David, finally, describes himself as an *ʿebed*, "servant", of Jonathan in 1 Sam 20:7-8[20] and calls Jonathan his "brother" in 2 Sam 1:26. These are references or allusions, some implicit and some explicit, to a covenant between David and Jonathan that must have been meant to be more than just a sign of affection between friends. It appears to have created a bond between the two that could be called upon in times of trouble. Adherence to the covenant meant not only help for the other party of the covenant personally, but it also included his descendants, as can be seen from David's treatment of Mephibosheth in 2 Sam 9.

---

[17] Later references to this covenant may support both of the alternatives discussed above. In 1 Sam 20:16 Jonathan is said to take the initiative in making a covenant with David, whereas in 23:18 it is expressly stated that Jonathan and David entered the covenant together.

[18] The LXX reading, Ιωναθαν ὀμόσαι τῷ Δαυιδ, "Jonathan swore to David" is to be preferred to the MT reading, *yĕhônātān lĕhašbîaʿ ʾet-dāwid*, "Jonathan made David swear", since what is said to be the reason afterwards in v. 17 is not David's love but Jonathan's. So e.g. McCarter (1980:337) and Klein (1983:203).

[19] Gordon (1986:248) notes that by this phrase a reference is made to the *ḥesed* of God in 1 Sam 20:14, which seems to function for Jonathan as the measure for David's future handling with his descendants. Sakenfeld (1978:91) says regarding the relationship between the covenant made and the fidelity to it, that "the *bĕrît* relationship is the basis for the obligation to do *ḥesed*."

[20] Riesener (1979:159, n. 12) prefers to see the use of *ʿebed* in these verses as due to the fact that David is addressing a member of the royal family. But although that may be possible, it does not take into account the more overall perspective of the covenant between the two and the fact that it is David and not Jonathan that will succeed Saul. A certain ambiguity may very well remain, however.

Turning now to the close context of the act in v. 4, it is interesting that vv. 1-5 can be divided into David's relations with Jonathan and then Saul, namely with Jonathan in vv. 1 and 3-4 and with Saul in vv. 2 and 5. The relationships between these different persons seem to be that in v. 1 Jonathan displays his affection for David, and somewhat similarly, but more withdrawn is Saul's display of affection in his refusal to let David return to his home in v. 2. In v. 3 Jonathan takes action on the basis of his affection for David and the two enter into a covenant. Saul in a similar vein takes action in v. 5 and puts David in charge of the army. This leaves v. 4 in between the actions taken by Jonathan and Saul. The most natural relation for v. 4 would then be to the preceding v. 3, since they both describe actions taken by Jonathan. The question is, then, what relation is there between vv. 3 and 4?

No explanation of the act in v. 4 is given, but that is not unusual regarding symbolic acts, especially if they are considered conventional and therefore well-known in the cultural context. Again, any possible explanation must therefore come from how the act functions in the context. The relation of the act in v. 4 to the covenant in v. 3 is then of vital importance. On formal grounds it seems best to consider the waw plus prefix conjugations which introduce vv. 3 and 4 as dependent upon the temporal clause in v. 1.[21] Verse 4 should therefore be considered as successive to v. 3, most likely temporally.[22] This would mean that Jonathan and David began by making a covenant and then Jonathan performed his act of transference. The covenant should then be regarded as some form of prerequisite for Jonathan's act. The love Jonathan has for David should therefore be seen as taking material form in the act in v. 4. The function of the act, however, is still to be sought for.

The wider context can be helpful. In 1 Sam 20:14-15 Jonathan assures himself of the fact that David will remember their covenant in the future, whether he himself is alive or not, which implies that David and not Jonathan will be reigning after Saul. In 1 Sam 23:17, Jonathan tries to comfort David, who is being pursued by Saul, by telling him that "you shall be king over Israel, and I shall be second to you". Both these texts confirm the interpretation of the act in 18:4 as a deliberate and free transference of the right to the throne by Jonathan to David.[23]

---

[21] See Waltke & O'Connor (1990:553-4).

[22] There is an incongruity of numbers in v. 3 since the predicate has singular and the subject plural, a well-known phenomenon in Hebrew syntax, see GKC (464-5), and Nyberg (1952:283-4).

[23] So e.g. Klein (1983:231) and Gordon (1986:177). See also Mettinger (1976:39), who considers the act to contain the legal symbolism of transferring the position as heir

The question that must be put at this point, however, is why this particular symbolic act is used to convey this message? There are two possible answers. The first is that Jonathan's act is similar to the symbolic acts of the prophets, which makes the interpretation rather straight-forward. The mantle, as a symbol for Jonathan's right to the throne as heir, is transferred to David.[24] Then, however, the act does not belong in the category of legal symbolic acts. The second alternative is to consider the act as being based on a legal symbolic act. This legal symbolic act would then have been reused in a non-legal context. It is not possible to understand the act as having a proper legal function, since the context is void of any indications of a proper legal proceeding. On what grounds, then, could the second alternative be made plausible? Since the context will not contribute sufficient information, extra-biblical material will be used.

The act performed by Jonathan may very well be based on a legal symbolic act which is also known from Ugarit, Emar and El-Qiṭār. There are three texts from Ugarit that are relevant, PRU IV, 17.159; RS 8.145[25] and Ugaritica V, 83 (RS 20.146). Of these RS 8.145 and Ugaritica V, 83 are wills, describing how a son who refuses to obey his father is forced to leave the house and deposit his mantle on the stool or the door-bolt. The legal function was to expel a member from the family, thus depriving him of his legal status as member of the family.[26]

In PRU IV, 17.159, the prince and heir to the throne of Ugarit called Utrišarruma, is given an ultimatum, ll. 22-31.[27] Either he stays with his father Amistamru, King of Ugarit, or he follows his mother Bentešina, who has been divorced from the king, ll. 8-10. If the prince chooses to follow his mother, he is told to put his mantle on the throne and leave, l. 26. Ammistamru will then make another son the heir to the throne, ll. 27-31.

The texts from Emar are mainly wills, containing clauses that regulate the inheritance in the case of certain changed circumstances. One of these wills states that a daughter who does not accept the mother after the death of the father, must put the mantle on a chair and leave the house.[28] The

---

apparent.

[24] For the mantle as symbol of personality in this text, see e.g. Kruger (1984:79, n. 4). See also Koschaker (1940; 1942), Finet (1969) and Malul (1988:114-6). For clothing as an expression of personality in the general area of folkloristics, see Horn (1977).

[25] Thurau-Dangin (1937:249).

[26] See Malul (1988:93-116), which is the most thorough study of these texts. His conclusions have been followed here.

[27] The parallel between 1 Sam 18:3-4 and PRU IV, 17.159 was first brought to attention by Knutson (1975:120-2). See also Rummel (1976).

[28] Arnaud (1986), 31:15.

same is applied to a child who does not accept the father,[29] the husband in the will of the wife,[30] and the wife in the will of the husband.[31]

The text from El-Qiṭār, although difficult to understand because of its broken state, also deals with inheritance.[32] Anyone among the inheritors who does not agree with the decision of the father must put his mantle on the chair and leave the house, presumably without any legal status as member of the family.

In the light of this extra-biblical material, it seems possible that such a legal symbolic act was known in ancient Israel. It explains how the transfer of Jonathan's mantle to David in 1 Sam 18:4 could be seen as symbolizing the transference of the legal status as heir to the throne.[33] At the same time, however, there is one important aspect that does not fit in, namely that the extra-biblical texts do not say that the mantle is transferred. It is possible, however, that even the transference of the mantle in 1 Sam 18:4 was considered to be part of the legal symbolic act. It should be kept in mind that the extra-biblical examples are few in number, and may very well describe an alternative procedure. That the mantle would have been transferred to the person who was already known to be the successor, as in 1 Sam 18:4, would seem reasonable. That the mantle was to be put on the chair or throne[34] in the extra-biblical examples would also be understandable, if it was not yet evident who the successor would be. If transference was indeed part of the procedure for the legal symbolic act which is reused in 1 Sam 18:4, it would explain the procedure of Jonathan's act.

The conclusion is, then, that the act in 1 Sam 18:4 does not appear to be meant as a proper legal symbolic act. However, it can be understood as a reuse of a certain legal symbolic act in a non-legal context. This would have been done in order to strengthen the decision of Jonathan.[35]

In the end, however, this must be considered as rather hypothetical reasoning, since it is based on some extra-biblical material. It still remains

---

[29] Arnaud (1986), 5:21.

[30] Arnaud (1986), 30:9.

[31] Huehnergard (1983), 2:21-22; 3:16. See also Huehnergard (1983:30-1; 1985:431-4).

[32] Snell (1983-84), ll. 16-17. Snell (1983-84:164) draws the analogy between his text and similar formulations in texts from Emar and Ugarit.

[33] So Rummel (1976:7).

[34] From an historical point of view, it would seem that when the mantle was to be put on the throne in PRU IV, 17.159:26, it was meant to refer, by metonymy, to the one who would be the next heir to the throne. This would then argue for that the transference was part of the procedure of the legal symbolic act which is reused in 1 Sam 18:4.

[35] Knutson (1975:121-2) argues similarly that the author "draws upon an old court custom to buttress his legitimization of the Davidic dynasty."

possible that what is described is a symbolic act not unlike the symbolic acts performed by the prophets. What has been described above is regarded as most probable, but is without support comparable to that which could have been provided by the context, or at least comparable material from the OT.

2.9.4 Historical Explanation

The historical explanation of this act is quite simple. The mantle is a well-known symbol for the identity and status of the person who is wearing it. When someone's mantle is transferred to another person, or simply removed, his status is transferred, or removed. This suits well the legal function of having to abstain from a legal position to the benefit of someone else.

2.9.5 Summary and Conclusions

1. The detailed description of the performance of the act in 1 Sam 18:4 argues for the fact that it was meant as a specific symbolic act.

2. There is nothing in the context to indicate that Jonathan's act of transferring the mantle to David has a legal function. It is likely that Jonathan's act was based on a legal symbolic act for a purpose other than legal. However, the argument is based on extra-biblical material for the legal function, and therefore it remains inconclusive. Nevertheless, this forms the basis for the following conclusions.

3. The symbolic act performed by Jonathan was meant to make an association to a legal symbolic act, whereby a member of a family was expelled along with the incurring of the loss of rights that belonged to such a status.

4. The legal symbolic act was then reused in order to emphasize Jonathan's decision to hand over his right to the throne to David. The association to the legal symbolic act also served to highlight the status of the covenant between Jonathan and David. This is part of the over-arching theme of displaying David as the proper and righteous successor to the throne.

5. The historical explanation is that the status of a person, symbolized by his mantle, was removed or transferred to the benefit of someone else.

2.10 Covering a Woman with the Mantle

2.10.1 Introduction

There are two texts that are of interest here, namely Ezek 16:8 and Ruth 3:9. It should be clear from the outset that neither of these texts occurs in a legal context. What may be relevant is therefore a secondary use of a legal symbolic act. Since these texts have recently been studied by Kruger in the light of extra-biblical material, especially of the opposite type where the hem of the mantle of the wife is cut by the husband as a way of dissolving the marriage, it will not be done in this analysis.[1] Besides, the legal symbolic act of cutting the hem of the mantle is not known from the OT. To then argue as if it had been known would be too hypothetical, since, as has been described above, these texts themselves do not occur in a clearly legal context.

2.10.2 Performance

In both Ruth 3:9 and Ezek 16:8 the same expression is used, namely *pāraś kānāp ʿal*, lit. "spread the *kānāp* over". Although the performance of the act seems rather straightforward, in that the *kānāp* is spread out by the man over the woman, who is presumably lying down, it is this formulation that presents a problem. Does *kānāp* in these texts refer to the "hem" of the mantle or to the mantle itself, by way of synechdoche?[2]

It is significant that in these two texts *kānāp* is used without a specifying genitive, which is found, e.g. in 1 Sam 15:27, *biknap-měʿilô*, "the hem of his mantle".[3] In this case it is specified that a part of the mantle is being torn off, whereas in Ruth 3:9 and Ezek 16:8 it is spread out. The fact that no genitive is given in these two texts indicates that no clear-cut distinction was considered by the authors between the part of the mantle that was to cover the woman and that which was not. On the other hand, in Ruth 3:4 and 7 it is emphasized that Ruth lies down at the feet of Boaz. This suggests that it was the lower part of the mantle that was used by Ruth to cover herself. If her act was meant to imitate the one which she asked Boaz to perform in v. 9, then *kānāp* might refer to this lower part of the mantle. However, it remains uncertain whether the act of Ruth carries this analogy. In Ezek 16:8 it is said that the *kānāp* serves to cover the nakedness of the

---

[1] Kruger (1984).

[2] For the latter view, see Wellhausen (1904:40).

[3] My translation.

woman, which could hardly have been the case if only the corner of the mantle was used. It seems probable, therefore, that the whole mantle is referred to in Ruth 3:9 and Ezek 16:8.

> Malul has made an interesting comparison with the use of the *sissiktu*, "hem" in Mesopotamian sources. He concludes that the *sissiktu* was originally used for the whole of the under-mantle, but it came to be used for the important part, namely the corner of the mantle: "Thus, the functioning of the lap-garment in certain very common legal symbolic acts may well have caused, by way of metonymy, its name to be restricted to only that part of it which was frequently involved in the various symbolic acts."[4] The use of *kānāp* would then display the opposite development. He notes that sometimes "the word *kānāph*, which elsewhere is used to mean the corner of the garment, means some type of garment related to one's lap. ... Here it is clear that *kānāph* does not mean just the corner of the garment, and may be interpreted as referring to the undergarment of the lap."[5]

The reason why *kānāp* is used and not a term which is commonly used for the mantle, such as *mĕʿîl*, has to do with the fact that there are two uses of the expression "spread the *kānāp*". The one occurs here in Ruth 3:9 and Ezek 16:8, and the other describes how a bird spreads out its wings.[6] The relationship between these two variant uses of the expression will be discussed further below, under Historical Explanation.

> In a recently published text from Mari, ARM 26.251:16-18, the queen is quoted as saying concerning her husband, King Zimri-Lim: "Depuis que mon Seigneur Zimri-Lim a posé le pan de son habit sur moi". The description of the procedure of the act is remarkably similar to the one found in Ezek 16:8 and Ruth 3:9. However, the highly fragmentary state of the text makes it hard to decide with any certainty whether the phrase is idiomatic or whether it does refer to an act. There are no clues to the function of a possible act, except that it is said to be performed by a man in relation to his wife. Still, it does give an example of a similar expression as in the biblical texts, and probably also of a similar act.

---

[4] Malul (1986:34-5).

[5] Malul (1986:35, n. 89).

[6] See e.g. Joüon (1935:202).

2.10.3 Legal Function

It has long since been recognized that the act of covering a woman with a mantle has to do with marriage.[7] To be correct, a differentiation should be made between betrothal and marriage. However, since so little is known about these customs in ancient Israel, and since no particular reference to betrothal is indicated in Ruth 3:9 and Ezek 16:8, marriage will be used as an overall concept. It should be kept in mind, nevertheless, that betrothal held a very high legal status, and could very well be referred to in these texts.[8]

2.10.3.1 Ezekiel 16:8

Ezek 16:8 is a tightly structured unit which needs to be unwrapped in order for the function of the symbolic act to be understood, and then especially in relation to other parts of v. 8.[9] The text is as follows:

a. *wāʾeʿĕbōr ʿălayik*	a. I passed you by again
b. *wāʾerʾēk*	b. and looked at you;
c. *wĕhinnēh ʿittēk ʿēt dōdîm*	c. you were at the age of love!
d. *wāʾeprōś kĕnāpî ʿălayik*	d. I spread my mantle over you,
e. *wāʾăkasseh ʿerwātēk*	e. to cover your nakedness.
f. *wāʾeššābaʿ lāk*	f. I swore to you,
g. *wāʾābôʾ bibrît ʾōtāk*	g. thereby entering into a covenant
nĕʾum ʾădōnāy yhwh	with you, says the Lord God,
h. *wattihyî lî*	h. and so you became mine.[10]

In 8d the mantle is said to be spread out over the woman. This receives an explanation in 8e, focusing on the purpose of the act. In 8f an oath is taken, which receives a following explanation in 8g, focusing on its purpose. The final phrase in 8h seems to function as a climax to the whole description in 8d-g, describing the logical consequence of both the symbolic act in 8d-e as well as the oath in 8f-g.

That God's covenant relationship with Israel is described as a marriage in this text is obvious, not the least from the final statement in 8h, "and so you became mine." What comes before this statement should then be

---

[7] See e.g. Finet (1969:127), Lindström (1983:50), Dommerhausen (1984:246) and Malul (1985b:197-8).

[8] Cf. Neufeld (1944:142-4) and de Vaux (1961:32-3).

[9] For a thorough analysis of the immediately preceding part of this story, see Malul (1990a).

[10] My translation.

related to the consummation of the marital relationship. There are two major items described before 8h, an act of spreading the mantle over the woman and an oath-taking, both of which receive a subsequent explanation. The second item, where an oath is taken towards the woman, is explained as entering into a *bĕrît*, "covenant" with her. This presents a problem, however, since marriage is nowhere else in the OT described with the word *bĕrît*. This is not to say that the marital relationship is not meant to be of a legal status, which it surely is. The reason why *bĕrît* is used here is that what the marriage metaphor is meant to describe, namely the covenant relationship between God and Israel, shines through in the metaphor.[11] The first item, the spreading of the mantle over the woman, is subsequently explained as a way of hiding the nakedness of the woman. The act is therefore described as functioning in a non-symbolic way. However, this is probably also due to the metaphorical use of the marriage motif. The relationship between God and Israel is described metaphorically as when a man meets a helpless and naked woman on the ground and falls in love with her. This dramatic description has probably caused the act to be used in a literal sense, in order to heighten the literary effect of the description. However, in the light of what follows upon this act in v. 8, namely the oath-taking and especially the statement in 8h, "and so you became mine", it would seem strange if the act did not have a further, symbolic meaning. It would seem reasonable that this act, together with the oath-taking, is included in the final statement, which would give the act the symbolic meaning of entering marriage.

The conclusion is, then, that the act which is described in Ezek 16:8 reflects a legal symbolic act. When a man performed this act by covering a woman with his mantle, the legal function of the act was to accomplish the marital relationship between the two.[12]

Excursus: Removing the Mantle and Uncovering the Nakedness

There is an interesting expression in Deut 23:1 and 27:20, which might be relevant to the act under discussion here. Deut 23:1 says, *lō'-yiqqaḥ 'îš*

---

[11] So Greenberg (1983:278): "Through the terminology of oath and covenant, which does not belong to the realm of marriage, glimmers the reality underlying the metaphor." The texts that seem to say that marriage was conceived as a *bĕrît*, "covenant" are, apart from the text studied here, Mal 2:14 and Prov 2:17. Greenberg is probably right in that these texts do not necessitate such an explanation. So also Milgrom (1976:134), who considers the use of *bĕrît* in these texts to be a metaphor without any legal value.

[12] Kruger (1984:85-6) reaches a similar conclusion when he says that the act signified the establishment of a new relationship. See also Korpel (1990:228-9).

ʾet-ʾēšet ʾābîw wĕlōʾ yĕgalleh kĕnap ʾābîw, "A man may not take his father's wife, that is, he should not remove his father's mantle."[13] Here it is best to take the waw in wĕlōʾ as explicative, which means that the second phrase has to do with marriage. To remove the father's mantle might then refer, by opposition, to a legal symbolic act where the man covered the woman by his mantle and thereby entered into marriage with her.[14] However, the use of the expression in this particular text is idiomatic, being roughly synonymous with the first statement. In Deut 27:20 there is an almost duplicate of 23:1.

In Lev 18:8 and 20:11 there is an expression that has caused some difficulties, and especially in relation to the expression in Deut 23:1 and 27:20. Lev 18:8, which deals with illegitimate relations between son and stepmother, says as follows; ʿerwat ʾēšet-ʾābîkā lōʾ tĕgallēh ʿerwat ʾābîkā hîʾ, "You should not uncover the nakedness of your father's wife, since it is your father's nakedness."[15] In v. 7 there is a similar expression regarding illegitimate relations between son and mother: ʿerwat ʾābîkā wĕʿerwat ʾimmĕkā lōʾ tĕgallēh ʾimmĕkā hîʾ lōʾ tĕgalleh ʿerwātāh, "You should not uncover the nakedness of your father, which is the nakedness of your mother. Since she is your mother, you should not uncover her nakedness."[16] This is then repeated concerning several different relations within the larger family, which makes it impossible to hold that it only refers to blood relationships. Instead, it refers to the illegitimate relationships that could occur within the larger family, ruled by the paterfamilias. Marriage therefore seems to have been regarded as solemn as blood relationships.

This latter expression is often mentioned in connection with the former expression from Deuteronomy.[17] However, it has not been sufficiently recognized that the two expressions use the verb gālâ with different meanings, namely "remove" and "uncover".[18] There is, therefore, no inherent reason why the two expressions should depend on each other. The expression "to remove the father's mantle" is probably derived from the legal symbolic act of covering a woman with the mantle, with the legal function of entering marriage with her. The expression "to uncover the father's/mother's nakedness" is probably a figurative way of explaining the seriousness of the marriage relationship. It might also be related to Hos 2:3, where Hosea takes the clothes off his wife as a punishment for adultery.

Therefore, these two expressions should not necessarily be related to each other on any other ground than that they both treat illegitimate sexual

---

[13] My translation.

[14] So e.g. Craigie (1976:333) and Mayes (1979:313).

[15] My translation.

[16] My translation. The waw in wĕʿerwat is taken as explicative before an apposition, see Waltke & O'Connor (1990:648-9), although it could also be emphatic, as in v. 47.

[17] See Zobel (1973:1021) and Westermann & Albertz (1971:422).

[18] In e.g. Isa 47:2-3, both meanings are used, "remove (gallî) your veil, ... uncover (gallî) your legs, ... your nakedness shall be uncovered (tiggāl)".

relations.[19] Only the expression "remove the father's mantle" is related to the legal symbolic act of spreading the mantle over the woman.

2.10.3.2 Ruth 3:9

The act in Ruth 3:9 is related to the intricate question of the institution of *gᵊʾullâ*, "redemption" in Israel, and in particular the role of the so-called *gōʾēl*, "kinsman-redeemer". When Naomi, Ruth's mother-in-law, realizes that Ruth has awakened the attention of Boaz, she rejoices, 2:20, because she knows that Boaz holds the position of kinsman-redeemer in relation to her family. A marriage between Ruth and Boaz would therefore mean much more for Naomi than seeing her daughter-in-law being cared for. It would mean that the name of Elimelech, Naomi's late husband, would continue to be upheld by the offspring of Ruth. It would also have as its consequence that the field, which belonged to Naomi and Elimelech before their move to Moab, would be redeemed to the benefit of Naomi. There is no need here to delve any deeper into the question of the *gᵊʾullâ* institution as well as Boaz' role as kinsman-redeemer, except to note the fact that it provides the legal force behind Ruth's request for a marriage with Boaz in 3:9. A close analysis of this verse shows that it contains a delicately structured statement by Ruth:

a. *wayyōʾmer mî-ʾătt*	a. He said "Who are you?"
wattōʾmer	And she answered,
b. *ʾānōkî rût ʾămāteka*	b. "I am Ruth, your servant;
c. *ûpārastā kĕnāpĕka*[20]	c. spread your mantle
ʿal-ʾămātĕkā	over your servant,
d. *kî gōʾēl ʾāttâ*	d. for you are kinsman-redeemer."[21]

Boaz' question in a is answered primarily in 9b. This answer is then given a consequence in 9c, which in its turn is given a cause in 9d.[22] The answer thus displays a chiastic structure, cause-effect-cause, where the climax

---

[19] Malul (1988:152), failing to grasp the diversity of the denotations of the verb *gālâ*, claims that the law in Lev 18:8 and 20:11 "substitutes the word *ʿrwh* 'nakedness' for the word *knph*."

[20] The singular of the Qere is followed, see the excursus below.

[21] My translation.

[22] The waw relative suffix conjugation often expresses a consequent situation when it follows upon a nominal clause, which is the case here with *ûpārastā*, "spread", see Waltke & O'Connor (1990:534). According to Joüon (1923:334) the waw relative suffix conjugation may, in this case, have a modal nuance, in the sense that Ruth declares Boaz' obligation to act as *gōʾēl*, "kinsman-redeemer".

resides with the middle statement, the consequence of the fact that Boaz is indeed the kinsman-redeemer of Ruth. This can also be seen from the fact that 9b and 9d are nominal clauses, whereas c is a verbal clause.

Ruth is here entreating Boaz to perform his legal duty as kinsman-redeemer. This is shown by the emphasis on Boaz' part when Ruth says that she is *his* servant, that *he* should spread *his* mantle over her because *he* is kinsman-redeemer. It is also shown by the fact that Ruth does not say that Boaz is "my kinsman-redeemer" which could be expected in 9d because of the analogy with "your servant" in 9b. Instead, Ruth's part is played down in order to emphasize the active role of Boaz.

The expression used in vv. 4 and 7 in the description of Ruth's act at the threshing-floor, is *gālâ margĕlōtāyw*, "uncover the place of his feet".[23] It is interesting to note that the verb used is *gālâ*, "uncover/remove". It may very well be that this use of the verb *gālâ* is meant to bring with it certain sexual connotations.[24] These sexual connotations, together with the act of Ruth, would then serve to strengthen her plea in v. 9 for Boaz to marry her.

By her act in v. 7 Ruth tries to imitate the act which she hopes Boaz will perform, and which she also asks him to do in v. 9c, *ûpārastā kĕnāpĕkā ʿal-ʾămātĕkā*, "spread your mantle over your servant". From the reaction of Boaz in vv. 10-13, and his dealings in Ruth 4, especially v. 10, it becomes obvious that what Ruth is asking for in 3:9c is for Boaz to marry her.[25] Boaz' act of spreading the mantle over Ruth, if indeed it was performed, would therefore have been tantamount to marry her.

The act would then be a legal symbolic act, with the legal function of accomplishing a marital relationship.

2.10.4 Historical Explanation

The expression which is used in both Ezek 16:8 and Ruth 3:9 is *pāraś kānāp ʿal*, "spread a mantle over". A shorter form of this expression is used to

---

[23] My translation. The noun *margĕlōtāyw*, "the place of his feet" is an adverbial accusative, see Waltke & O'Connor (1990:170). The locative function is usual with the ma-nominal construction, see Nyberg (1952:207) and Waltke & O'Connor (1990:90). Besides Ruth 3, this word is only found in Dan 10:6 where it seems to be synonymous with *regel*, "foot".

[24] So e.g. Leggett (1974:192, n. 37) and Hubbard (1988:203-4). Hubbard notes that "foot", often used euphemistically for the male genitals, and the expression "to lie down" at Boaz' feet may also give sexual connotations. Carmichael (1980:257-8), however, goes too far when he says that Ruth was actually removing Boaz' sandals, thus telling him that she should be used in a similar sexual sense.

[25] So e.g. Gow (1983:153) and Kruger (1984:84). See also Tosato (1982:107). This appears to be the scholarly consensus.

describe birds spreading their wings in Deut 32:11; Jer 48:40; 49:22 and Job 39:26, and similarly for cherubs in Exod 25:20; 37:9; 1 Kgs 6:27; 8:7; 2 Chr 3:13 and 5:8. However, when birds or cherubs are referred to, the plural of *kānāp* is used, as in Deut 32:11 where an eagle *yiprōś kĕnāpāyw*, "spreads its wings". When a mantle is referred to, as in Ezek 16:8 and Ruth 3:9, *kānāp* is used in the singular. Ruth 3:9 presents a text-critical problem, however, the solution of which might argue against this.[26]

> There are some manuscripts which support the plural form. *kĕnāpêkâ*, instead of the singular form, *kĕnāpĕkâ*, which has the support of the LXX and the Peshitta.[27] From the context it would be hard to understand the use of the plural form, since otherwise the plural is used in reference to wings and the singular in reference to a mantle. Why, then, do some manuscripts have a plural? Earlier, in 2:12, Boaz prays that Ruth will be rewarded for her deeds by God, *bāʾt laḥăsôt taḥat-kĕnāpāyw*, "under whose wings you have come for refuge!" This is the well-known motif of the protecting God, metaphorically described as a bird who provides protection by spreading out the wings, as, e.g. in Deut 32:11, discussed above.[28] The analogy between 2:12 and 3:9 has thereby been made more obvious than it should have been by reading a plural in 3:9 as well.[29] The singular is therefore to be preferred in 3:9.[30]

The act can then be explained historically as an attempt to imitate the protective behaviour of a bird when it spreads out its wings. This is also used of God to express his protective care. When a man then spreads his mantle over the woman, he would be expressing his willingness to provide the woman with protection and shelter. This would have been a logical connection with entering marriage, since in Israelite marriage the husband was obliged to provide security and protection for his wife.[31]

---

[26] See Witzenrath (1975:217, n. 99). She shows that most scholars prefer the singular form. See also Leggett (1974:192-201).

[27] See *BHS*.

[28] See e.g. Woude (1971:835) and Dommerhausen (1984:246).

[29] The word-play produces a rather humorous effect, since the very thing that Boaz is asking from God in 2:12 in general terms is what Ruth asks him to perform, but now in more perceptible terms, so Hubbard (1988:212). Sasson (1989:81) considers Ruth's statement to be a case of irony, but it is difficult to see how irony fits into this context.

[30] So e.g. Witzenrath (1975:217), Hubbard (1988:207, n. 9) and Sasson (1989:81).

[31] So e.g. Kruger (1984:81-2). In Hos 2:8-9 it is this provision that is alluded to when the relationship the Lord-Israel is described as a marriage relationship. The Lord ceases to provide the wife with the basic necessities, and the marriage seems to be terminated. See also Exod 21:7-11 for the husband's obligation towards his wife. Cf. Kruger (1988) for metaphors and similes in Hosea, and concerning marriage in particular. Freedman &

2.10.5 Summary and Conclusions

1. In Ezek 16:8 and Ruth 3:9 the word *kānāp* is used for the mantle in general and not specifically for the hem of the mantle. It is possible that the lower part of the mantle is indicated in Ruth 3:9, but it remains uncertain.

2. The texts Ezek 16:8 and Ruth 3:9 both relate to the legal symbolic act of covering a woman with the mantle. The legal function of this act would be for a man to accomplish his marriage with the woman. However, in neither of these cases is the act described as actually performed. In Ezek 16:8 the act is part of a metaphorical description of the relationship between God and Israel, and in Ruth 3:9 it is an act which Boaz is requested by Ruth to perform. Although this makes the conclusion that Ezek 16:8 and Ruth 3:9 refer to a legal symbolic act less certain, the conclusion regarding the legal function is still the most probable.

3. The historical explanation of the act is based on the image of birds who spread their wings in a protective manner. In a similar way the man symbolizes his protection for the woman by spreading his mantle over her. This would be the historical connection with the legal function of accomplishing a marriage, since the man had the responsibility to care for his wife and supply for her needs.

Andersen (1980:218-90) argue that it is not a matter of divorce in Hos 2, but recently Westbrook (1990:577-80) has shown it to be still the best interpretation.

2.11 Removing the Sandal

2.11.1 Introduction

The act of removing the sandal occurs in two clearly legal contexts; Ruth 4 is explicitly describing a legal procedure at the city gate, and Deut 25:5-10 is part of the deuteronomic laws. The vast literature surrounding these texts is an indication that there are some unsolved problems, and in particular some legal problems in the book of Ruth. This is mainly due to the question of the levirate, which is undoubtedly found in Deut 25:5-10, but what about the book of Ruth? Scholars seem to be as divided as ever on this issue. However, since it is not a primary focus in this analysis, it will, for the most part, be avoided.

2.11.2 Procedure

2.11.2.1 Ruth 4:8

There are several problems pertaining to the procedure of the symbolic act in Ruth 4:8 that must be dealt with. Who removed whose sandal, and to whom did he give it, if indeed it was handed over to someone? Could it have been a reciprocal act? Was a single sandal used, or a pair, referred to collectively? The many alternatives are mainly due to the lack of clarity in the description of the procedure of the act.

To begin with the agent of the act, the text is not clear as to who removed the sandal, and indeed whose sandal it was. The natural alternative, and the consensus view, is the kinsman, since he is the explicit subject earlier in v. 8a. A shift of subject from the first half of v. 8 to the second, from the kinsman to Boaz, would seem rather strained. At the beginning of v. 9, the subject changes and so it is stated explicitly, "Then Boaz said".

The LXX tries to make v. 8 more in accordance with v. 7 by adding καὶ ἔδωκεν αὐτῷ, "and he gave to him", since the MT in v. 8 does not explicitly say that the sandal was given to someone. It is possible that this could be presupposed from v. 7 and therefore it need not have been part of the original text. However, the interesting fact is that if the procedure of the act was to hand over the sandal to the opposite party, it is strange that it does not say so in v. 8. This makes it less likely that the sandal was handed over by the kinsman to Boaz, and instead he probably only removed his sandal. The fact that this is not in line with the description in v. 7 could very well be because v. 7 provides a more general description, suitable for several different legal contexts. This also applies to the question whether the act was reciprocal. A reciprocal act is probably what is described in

v. 7, which could be brought out by the translation "Men took off their sandals and gave them to each other."[1] However, there is no hint of a reciprocal act in v. 8. This makes it even more likely that what we have in v. 7 is a general statement, whereas what is found in v. 8 is a more specialized version, suitable for a particular legal function. This will be argued further below, under Legal Function.

Speiser and Lacheman have brought forward some comparative material from Nuzi which they consider relevant to this discussion.[2]

Speiser finds two texts that tell about different ways to avoid breaking the law in a legal procedure. A father gives his daughter away in marriage and provides her with part of the inheritance as a dowry.[3] This would not do according to Nuzi Law, and thus to avoid breaking the law, the daughter gave her father one pair of shoes and one garment, among other things. In another text the father gives his daughter away and receives in return a garment and a pair of shoes.[4] Speiser views the garment and the shoes as token payments to validate special transactions by lending them the appearance of normal business practice. That would mean that Boaz gives his sandal to the kinsman as a form of payment for the right to acquire Ruth and marry her.[5] Speiser's comparison has the advantage of including sandals. However, the use of the sandals in these texts, and the possible symbolism that lies behind the symbolic acts, do not seem to be the same as in Ruth 4:8 and Deut 25:9.[6] Speiser must claim that it is Boaz who pulls off his sandal and gives it to the kinsman, since otherwise it would not be a payment. It is difficult to understand such an abrupt shift of subject in v. 8, however, although it is not impossible.

Lacheman uses other Nuzi-texts to give another solution. There seems to have been a custom in Nuzi for a seller of land to lift his own foot from the ground and place the foot of the purchaser in its place, thus symbolizing the new owner's right to the property.[7] Lacheman claims that this practice was taken up in Israel and developed further, so that now the sandal was removed from the foot, not the foot from the land, in order to make the symbolism more concrete. Lacheman suggests a parallel symbolic act in the Old Babylonian tradition of "handing over the bukannum" at the sale of a piece of land.[8] However, Lacheman's thesis is unconvincing. It is obviously a different symbolic act altogether from those in Ruth 4:8 and Deut 25:9.

---

[1] My translation.

[2] Speiser (1928-29; 1940) and Lacheman (1937).

[3] Speiser (1928-29:65-6).

[4] Speiser (1928-29:63-4).

[5] Speiser (1940:18).

[6] So e.g. Deroy (1961:375, n. 7).

[7] Cf. also Cassin (1987:294-8).

[8] Cf. Malul (1985a) for a recent analysis of this legal symbolic act.

The conclusion is that the kinsman removed his own sandal, according to v. 8. It is not likely that he handed it over to Boaz, although this could be implied from v. 7. The problem would be, however, why it is not stated to be the case in v. 8. Verse 7 most likely describes a reciprocal act.

2.11.2.2 Deuteronomy 25:9

The procedure of the legal symbolic act in Deut 25:9 is in some respects similar to the act in Ruth 4:8, although the differences are more important than the similarities. It is a sandal that is removed, but this time it is done by the other party, the widow, and not the owner of the sandal, the brother-in-law. Since it is stated that the widow removed "his sandal" from "his foot", it would seem unlikely that both the sandals were removed. A reciprocal act is similarly not to be considered in this case.

The verb used in Ruth 4:8 for the removal of the sandal was *šalap*, its only occurrence with this meaning, whereas the verb used in Deut 25:9 is *ḥalaṣ*, also found with this meaning in Isa 20:2. It is hard to detect any relevant difference between these two verbs, since they appear to be roughly synonymous. The difference in terminology could be seen as an indication that there is no obvious relation between the two texts. It should also be noted that in Deut 25:9 the act of removing the sandal is not followed by a transference of it, which seems natural since it is not the owner of the sandal who removes it. The act here is also followed both by the widow spitting at the brother-in-law and a statement made by the widow.

> As far as I know there is only one example of a similar symbolic act found in extra-Biblical texts. It comes from a Hittite text, the so-called Mešedi-Protocol:[9]

>> If a guard deserts (his post) and carries off a lance from the postern, and the gateman catches him in the sin, he (the gateman) shall remove his (the guard's) shoe.[10]

> The removal of the shoe in this text functions as a punishment of the guard.[11] This would fit in well with the spitting done by the widow in Deut

---

[9] See Jakob-Rost (1965:178). The text is IBoT 1.36.1:53-54.

[10] The translation is from Hoffner (1969:42-4), who also sees a connection with Deut 25:5-10. Some scholars would regard Hittite texts as a priori irrelevant for the OT, e.g. Boecker (1984:13). For a different view from a Hittitologist, see Hoffner (1969; 1973:221).

[11] According to Jakob-Rost (1965:209) the punishment consists in the way the missing sandal calls attention to the mistake made by the guard.

25:9, which functioned as a sign of the contempt that thereafter would meet
the brother-in-law. This is also expressed by the widow's statement in Deut
25:9.

2.11.3 Legal Function

2.11.3.1 Ruth 4:8

The book of Ruth is full of information concerning the ordinary way of
dealing with legal matters in a small town in ancient Israel. Unfortunately,
this information is packed into a small amount of space and too much is
presupposed for the original readers, making it difficult for us to understand it all. It therefore comes as no surprise that scholars disagree concerning those legal matters which are described in the book of Ruth. This
poses a problem, since the understanding of the whole of Ruth 4, and for
that matter, the whole book, influences the understanding of the legal
function of the symbolic act in 4:8. Positively it should be noted that in this
case there is no doubt concerning the legal and symbolic nature of the act.
All scholars seem to agree that there is some legal force behind the act.
What then does it symbolize?

The dubious theory of Carmichael, namely that the sandal symbolizes
Ruth, who is handed over to Boaz, has already been criticized by Phillips
and need not be repeated here.[12] The view of Speiser that the sandal was
the price paid by Boaz fails because, as was shown above, it was the
kinsman who removed his sandal and not Boaz.[13]

The more serious question, however, deals with the role of the *gōʾēl*, the
"kinsman-redeemer."[14] Some hold that the act functions as the kinsman's
renunciation of his right to serve as *gōʾēl*.[15] On the other hand, some would

---

[12] Phillips (1986:11-3).

[13] Speiser (1940:18).

[14] Joüon (1953:82) is right in that the land is not alienated, so it cannot properly be
said to be redeemed. Hubbard (1988:237, n. 5) translates the verb *gāʾal* as "serve as
kinsman-redeemer", which gives the verb an intransitive meaning. This is probably
correct, since in 4:4 and 6 *gāʾal* is used without an object, whereas *qānâ* has one in
vv. 5, 9 and 10. Therefore Hubbard's translation is followed here. In 3:13 *gāʾal* occurs
with an object, when Boaz tells Ruth that the kinsman may want to *yigʿālēk*, lit. "re-
deem you". This does not mean that Ruth was alienated, so it should more properly be
translated according to Hubbard (1988:208, n. 17, 219) as "execute the kinsman's
duty".

[15] So e.g. Neufeld (1944:42-3), Rowley (1947:86-7), de Vaux (1961:22), Gray
(1967:421-2), Westbrook (1971:375) and Sasson (1989:146).

see it as a transference of these rights from the kinsman to Boaz.[16] The latter view implies that the sandal was given by the kinsman to Boaz.

To begin with, the structure of Ruth 4:4-10 will be scrutinized for contextual clues to the legal function of the act in v. 8. This will be done by means of the following outline. It should be noted that this outline is selective, in that only the relevant phrases are included.

	qānâ, acquire	*gāʾal*, serve as kinsman-redeemer
v. 4 (Boaz)	*Acquire!*	
		Whether You *serve as kinsman-redeemer* or not, tell me so, because I am next in line.
(kinsman)		I will *serve as kinsman-redeemer.*
v. 5 (Boaz)	When You *acquire* the field from Naomi You also[17] *acquire*[18] Ruth...	
v. 6 (kinsman)		I cannot *serve as kinsman-redeemer!* You perform my right of redemption! I cannot *serve as kinsman-redeemer!* (the act)
v. 8	You *acquire!*	
v. 9 (Boaz)	I hereby *acquire* the belongings of Elimelech ...	
v. 10	I also hereby *acquire* Ruth as wife...[19]	

---

[16] So Joüon (1953:87-8), Rudolph (1962:68), Boecker (1964:161), Gordis (1974:258), Carmichael (1977:324) and Hubbard (1988:250).

[17] The common emendation of *ûmēʾēt*, "and from" to something like *gam wēʾēt*, "also" is followed here in line with most scholars, see e.g. Hubbard (1988:237, n. 8). The MT is retained by some, e.g. Sasson (1989:120-2) and Gow (1990:310-1).

[18] The Qere is followed, see *BHS*. So also e.g. Davies (1983:232), Gow (1983:165) and Hubbard (1988:237, n. 9). For thorough discussions, see Beattie (1971) and Sasson (1989:119-36), who both prefer the Kethib.

[19] My translation.

Verse 7 is an interruption, which functions as an explanation of the symbolic act in v. 8. Therefore it is not part of this structure, especially since v. 7 has its own coherent structure, as will be shown below. It is clear that the text is structured by means of the two verbs *qānâ*, "acquire"[20] and *gā'al*, "serve as kinsman-redeemer".The verb *qānâ* is used in relation to its antonym in v. 3, *mākar*, "sell". These two verbs are here used in a particular legal form, which will become clearer in the following.

In vv. 4-10 there seems to be a mingling of two forms of speech, analogous to the use of the verbs *qānâ* and *gā'al*. One form is more formal, and seems to function as the more technical speech as far as the legal transactions are concerned. This form uses the verb *qānâ*. The other form seems somewhat less formal, and uses *gā'al*.[21] In v. 4, Boaz begins formally by asking the kinsman to acquire the field from Naomi.[22] He then turns to less formal language and informs himself as to whether the kinsman will exercise his right, which the kinsman affirms. In v. 5 Boaz returns to the formal legal language and specifies the task lying before the kinsman by adding marriage to Ruth to the purchase of the field.[23] The kinsman then responds less formally in the negative, asking Boaz to act in his place. This is then said formally in v. 8, when the kinsman asks Boaz to acquire, which he does in vv. 9-10.

The important point to note, regarding this distinction between formal and less formal language in vv. 4-10, is that the kinsman does not say he will acquire, using *qānâ*, but only that he will serve as kinsman-redeemer, using *gā'al*. He has thereby not said anything that would be considered legally binding, in contrast to what he says in v. 8, using the formal

---

[20] This sense of the verb should not be limited to the meaning "buy", which should be regarded as a specialized form of "acquire". So e.g. Joüon (1953:88), Lipiński (1988:65), Witzenrath (1975:266, n. 118) and Hubbard (1988:244).

[21] See Levine (1983:100), "In Ruth, the verb *gā'al* describes the overall process, whereas *qānâ* specifically refers to the element of purchase."

[22] Here the verb *qānâ* could be translated "buy", since it seems to be a matter of purchasing the field for money. Later, when Ruth is the object in vv. 5 and 10, this would not do, however. The same term "acquire" is used here for both cases, although the different senses should be noted. For a different view, see Campbell (1975:145-7). Sasson (1989:124-5) prefers to view the use of Ruth as object of *qānâ* as Boaz' purchase of Ruth from Naomi. Weiss (1964:246), argues, on the basis of Mishnaic texts, that *qānâ* is used for marrriage "only in contexts embracing other transactions in which *qnh* in its proper sense of 'purchase' (acquire property) is applicable." The problem with Weiss' approach is that the texts he uses may very well have been influenced by the language in Ruth.

[23] Porten (1978:43), Gow (1983:66-7; 1984:316-7) and Sasson (1989:119) are correct in seeing v. 5 as the pivotal point of the story.

speech.[24] It is here in v. 8, then, in his only use of the formal language, that the kinsman officially waives his right to serve as kinsman-redeemer. It is also here that the legal symbolic act occurs.

This can also be seen from the use of the verbal conjugations. In vv. 4, 6 and 8 imperatives are used to exhort the other party to fulfil a certain legal function.[25] The prefix conjugation is used in v. 4, when the kinsman states less formally that he will serve as kinsman-redeemer, although without it being legally binding, since he can apparently abstain from this later on in v. 6. The suffix conjugation is used only in vv. 5 and 9-10.[26] These utterances in vv. 9-10 should be considered as performative, whereby the legal function is accomplished by means of the utterance.[27] This should be seen in relation to the suffix conjugation in v. 3, *mākĕrâ*, "is about to sell".[28] It is no coincidence that these two antonyms occur closely with suffix conjugations, and the reason is that they belong to the technical terminology for transactions such as this.[29]

Excursus: Technical Terminology in Jeremiah 32:8

A somewhat similar structure can be detected in Jer 32:8. Jeremiah is offered the opportunity to buy a piece of land from his uncle Hanamel according to the law of *gĕ᾽ullâ*. The following structure, again selective, appears:

---

[24] Similarly Hubbard (1988:242), who suggests (1988:246) that the kinsman declines from his intention whereas the formal transfer occurred in v. 8. The other possibility given by Hubbard, that it would be a mere rephrasing, is unconvincing in the light of the distinct uses of both *qānâ* and *gā᾽al* in the context.

[25] Boecker (1964:168) calls this "Kaufaufforderung". Cf. Jer 32:7-8 and 25.

[26] Of course v. 5 only describes the alternatives open to the kinsman, but the reference is to the possibility that the kinsman will make the formal declaration, "I hereby acquire".

[27] See Waltke & O'Connor (1990:488-9), who consider this probable. Similarly Campbell (1975:151) and Witzenrath (1975:255).

[28] My translation. Waltke & O'Connor (1990:489) are correct in taking it as perfective of resolve. Gerleman (1965:35-6) explains the perfect as due to the legal context, where it stresses the definitive character of the act. So also Campbell (1975:143-4), Gow (1983:154, n. 15), Leggett (1974:222) and Sasson (1989:114). There is no need to follow e.g. Rudolph (1962:59, n. 3) in revocalizing it as a participle.

[29] A further indication of the legal force of Boaz' statement in vv. 9-10 is when he says that the elders and the people are witnesses *hayyôm*, "today". This is well-known as an indicator of legal proceedings, Gen 31:48; 47:23; Deut 4:26; 30:19; Jer 40:4. So Joüon (1953:88), Campbell (1975:152), Hubbard (1988:255) and Tucker (1966:42-5). Tucker draws a parallel to the Akkadian legal formula *ištu ūmi annîm*, "from this day". The two occurrences of the phrase "You are witnesses today" forms an inclusio around the statement in vv. 9-10, thus strengthening its legal force.

qĕnēh nā' 'et-śādî ...	Buy my field!
kî-lĕkā mišpaṭ hayruššâ	You have the right to inherit,
ûlĕkā haggĕ'ullâ	You have the right to redeem!
qĕnēh-lāk	Buy![30]

The imperative qĕnēh-lāk, known from Ruth 4:8, was apparently part of the technical terminology to be used at this kind of transaction. What is not found here is Jeremiah's formal declaration of purchase, but only the fact in v. 9 that he has bought the field. Jer 32:6-15 tells of a written contract being established, sealed and put away, whereas Ruth 4:8 describes a symbolic act apparently without anything written but a similar legal terminology. It is possible that this is an example of two different stages in the development of ratification of legal transactions in ancient Israel.

In vv. 4-5 it is the kinsman's prerogative to serve as kinsman-redeemer, but in v. 6 he declines from this prerogative and exhorts Boaz to serve as kinsman-redeemer instead. The only legal decision that is taken by the kinsman is thus to abstain from his right to act as kinsman-redeemer, or as stated formally in v. 8, to abstain from acquiring.[31] Since this is a prerequisite for Boaz' action, and the symbolic act occurs immediately before Boaz' pronouncement of purchase in vv. 9-10, the legal function of the symbolic act seems clear. It is to accomplish the kinsman's waiving of his right, to the benefit of Boaz. However, it would be a mistake to see the legal function as a transference of the right in question, since Boaz has already said in v. 4 that he is next in line after the kinsman.[32] It follows logically on the kinsman's decision that Boaz possesses the right instead, which might be the reason why the sandal was given to him, if indeed it was. The consequence of the legal symbolic act is then a transference of the right to act as kinsman-redeemer, but the legal function of the act itself

---

[30] My translation.

[31] McKane (1961-2:37), however, prefers to regard the two statements by the kinsman in vv. 4 and 6 as having the same force. In the light of the analysis made here, this would seem improbable.

[32] Boecker (1964:160-1), however, follows this interpretation and considers the acquisition closed by means of the symbolic act. He calls the positive statement by the kinsman in v. 4, 'ānōkî 'eg'āl, "I will serve as kinsman-redeemer" (my translation) a "Bereitschaftserklärung" and the negative statement in v. 6, lō' 'ûkal lig'ol-lî, "I cannot serve as kinsman-redeemer" (my translation) a "Verzichterklärung". The function of vv. 9-10 would then be to consolidate the agreement by the witnesses at the gate. This fails, however, to account for the fact that not until in vv. 9-10 does Boaz formally declare his purchase. From v. 6 it is only clear that he is able to serve as kinsman-redeemer and nothing more.

is restricted to the decision by the kinsman. This must now be tested against an analysis of v. 7, which seems to explain the act.

It is not often that an explanation is given to a legal symbolic act, indeed this is the only time that it occurs in the OT. The obvious reason for such an explanation is of course what the narrator says in v. 7, namely that the presumed readers would not have been acquainted with the act. Another, more literary reason has been advanced. Since v. 7 occurs just before the climax of the legal proceedings, it would be suitable with a reduced literary tempo, thus increasing expectations for what is to come.[33]

However, when v. 7 is looked at more closely, this supposed explanation does not really explain the context as clearly as it seemed to. There are several technical terms used, some of which are not very clear. Scholars also disagree as to the reference of the term *tĕʿûdâ*. The problematical terminology will be dealt with at first.

Some of the technical terms in v. 7 are in no need of further analysis, such as *gĕʾu(w)llâ*, "redeeming" and *tĕmûrâ*, "trading" or "exchanging". These terms, one from the legal institution of redemption[34] and the other from the sphere of commercial transactions, form a merismus, meaning "all forms of transactions."[35] This indicates that what is described in v. 7 is an act of a more general nature than the act which is performed in v. 8.

A more troublesome term, however, is the piel infinitive *qayyēm*, usually regarded as an aramaism and an example of late Biblical Hebrew.[36] It occurs seven times in Esther, 9:21, 27, 29, 31 (3) and 32, in Pss 119:28, 106, Ezek 13:6 and in the Aramaic pael form in Dan 6:8. In Dan 6:8 the Aramaic equivalent means to "establish" an edict, *lĕqayyāmâ qĕyām*.[37] In Esther it means to "establish" a royal edict. In Ps 119:28 it means to "restore", whereas in v. 106 it stands in parallelism with swearing an oath. In Ezek 13:6 it stands for the expectations which the false prophets have for

---

[33] So Hubbard (1988:248). See Berlin (1983:99), who calls v. 7 a 'frame-break', de Moor (1986:44, n. 44) and Sasson (1989:140-1). There is therefore no need to consider v. 7 as a later editorial comment, as e.g. Gow (1983:62-3) does.

[34] Cf. de Vaux (1961:166-7).

[35] So e.g. Hubbard (1988:248-9) and Sasson (1989:142). This may be confirmed by the expression *kol-dābār*, "any transaction."

[36] But see Campbell (1975:148), Hubbard (1988:249) and Sasson (1989:142) who question this assumption.

[37] See also the haphel forms in Dan 6:9 and 16 with apparently the same meaning. See Montgomery (1927:273).

their prophecies to be fulfilled. There is a parallel to Ruth 4:7 here in that
the object is *dābār*, lit. "word", meaning "transaction" in Ruth 4:7.[38]

> The Aramaic form also occurs in an ostraca-inscription from the 7th
> century, *KAI* 233:9, where it means to ratify a document, apparently
> equivalent to signing: *ydyhm ktbt wqymt qdmy*, "Their own hands have
> written and established (it) before my eyes."[39] There is also an occurrence
> in an undated Aramaic text from North Saqqâra, where it seems to mean "to
> be current" or "to be standing".[40]

The conclusion from this study of the word *qayyēm* is that it means to put
something, an agreement or a decree, into effect, i.e., "to ratify".

The term *tĕ'ûdâ* is difficult to understand. In the OT it occurs only here
in Ruth 4:7 and in Isa 8:16 and 20. In the Isaiah passages it stands for the
prophet's message that is to be wrapped up and sealed. The word *tĕ'ûdâ*
also stands in parallelism with *tôrâ*, "teaching". There it could be understood as "something preserved", since the act of witnessing means that
something is preserved in the memory of the witness. In Isa 8:16 and 20 it
might also point to the fact that Isaiah, as a prophet, looks upon himself as
a messenger of and witness to the divine revelation.

What is then referred to by means of *tĕ'ûdâ* in the proceedings of Ruth
4:7-9? It has been argued that there are two acts involved in Ruth 4:7-9.[41]
The first act would be the symbolic act itself, headed by the term *lĕqayyēm*.
The other act would the witnessing of the elders and the people standing by
at the gate, described in v. 9.[42] This act is then introduced by the term
tĕ'ûdâ. This would mean that since *tĕ'ûdâ* occurs at the end of v. 7 and the
witnesses are called upon in v. 9, there is a problem with v. 8, which does
not seem to fill any real function in its present position. The fact, however,
that a hypothesis cannot explain the presence of a verse in its context
makes the hypothesis itself questionable. A better solution can be reached
by taking a close view at the structure of v. 7:

---

[38] According to Niehr (1987:68), *dābār* is a term for "Rechtssache". Jackson
(1972:241) translates it "legal dispute". See also Exod 18:16; 22:8; 24:14; Deut 1:17;
16:19; 17:8; 19:15. This would apply to Ruth 4:7, which strengthens the impression of a
legal transaction in the text. A thorough analysis of this legal use of *dābār* can be found
in Bovati (1986:192-3).

[39] The translation is from Gibson (1975:104).

[40] Segal (1983), 19:2.

[41] So Tucker (1966:44) and Leeuwen (1976:212).

[42] Niehr (1987:108-9) holds that the elders hardly play any role in the legal process
described. It is rather the people who play the active part. He sees the mention of the
elders as a deliberate archaizing attempt. However, Boaz calls for the elders in v. 2, presumably to play a significant role in the legal proceedings.

a.   *wĕzôʾt lĕpānîm bĕyiśrāʾēl ʿal-haggĕʾu(w)llâ wĕʿal-hattĕmûrâ*
b.   *lĕqayyēm kol-dābār šālap ʾîš naʿālô wĕnātan lĕrēʿēhû*
c.   *wĕzôʾt hattĕʿûdâ bĕyiśrāʾēl*

a.   This was the custom in former times in Israel concerning
      redeeming and exchanging;
b.   to ratify a transaction, the one took off his sandal and
      gave it to the other;
c.   this was the custom of attesting in Israel.[43]

To begin with, the chiastic structure of the verse should be noted. The phrase *wĕzôʾt (lĕpānîm) bĕyiśrāʾēl*, lit. "and this was (earlier) in Israel" both begins and ends the verse.[44] There is also a clear case of assonance among *haggĕʾu(w)llâ*, *hattĕmûrâ* and *hattĕʿûdâ*, which works to hold the various parts of the verse together. This speaks strongly in favour of the view that *hattĕʿûdâ* refers back to what has been described in v. 7 and not forward, beyond v. 8 to v. 9. This would mean that the symbolic act of transferring one's sandal was a way in Israel of preserving, or better, attesting a legal transaction.[45] Naturally this implies the use of witnesses, since it goes with the constituent parts of the legal procedure.

According to v. 7, then, the reciprocal act of transferring sandals to each other was used as ratification of all forms of legal transactions. It also functioned as a way of preserving the agreements made. However, when this is joined with the conclusion above, namely that the legal function of the act in v. 8 was to abstain from a legal right, a problem immediately occurs. The two acts in vv. 7 and 8 are apparently not the same, and the legal transactions are not the same either. The kinsman is not engaged in a particular legal transaction, but instead he abstains from his prerogative to enter into a legal transaction. That is the reason why the act, as well as the transaction, is different in v. 8 from v. 7. Since it is a matter of not entering an agreement, the sandal is not transferred but only removed. The act in v. 8 should therefore be regarded as a negated version of the act in v. 7.

The conclusion is, then, that the legal function of the kinsman's act in Ruth 4:8 was for him to abstain from his right to act as kinsman-redeemer. The act made it clear, in a public manner, that the kinsman would not make use of his prerogative, to the benefit of Boaz. This legal function is accomplished by means of the act without any reference to a prior agreement.

---

[43] My translation.

[44] Noted by Campbell (1975:149).

[45] Hubbard (1988:251) calls it "attestation custom" which seems to convey the same sense.

The legal function of the act in v. 7, however, was meant to be ratifying, since it would refer to a prior agreement.

In relation to the following analysis of the act in Deut 25:9, it is important to note that it is a voluntary act on behalf of the kinsman. No trace of humiliation or punishment can be found as consequences of the act.

2.11.3.2 Deuteronomy 25:9.

Compared to Ruth 4:8, the symbolic act in Deut 25:9 seems rather straight-forward in its legal function. The context in vv. 7-10 concerns how the brother-in-law and the widow should behave in case the brother-in-law refused to perform his duty as levir.[46] The text makes it clear that it was possible to be exempted from this duty, but only at the cost of being humiliated by the widow in front of the elders of the town. When the brother-in-law refused marriage, he also lost his right to his brother's inheritance. This would have been his had he married, since in Israel a widow apparently could not inherit from her late husband.[47]

By looking at the text as a whole, it is clear that the legal function of the act is that the brother-in-law abstains from performing his duty as levir. This is stated in v. 7 by the narrator, in vv. 7 and 9 by the widow and by the brother-in-law himself in v. 8, standing before the elders. It is clear that the duty as levir cannot be forced upon him, but requires his acceptance.

The refusal by the brother-in-law in v. 8, *lōʾ ḥāpaṣtî lĕqaḥtāh*, "I have no desire to marry her" contains the suffix conjugation of *ḥāpaṣ*, "desire". It seems to function similarly to the suffix conjugation in Ruth 4:8, namely performatively.[48] The use of the suffix conjugation is due to the function of the statement within the legal proceedings, namely for the brother-in-law to declare that he refuses to fulfill his duty towards the widow. It can be contrasted with the widow's use of the prefix conjugation in v. 7, which

---

[46] Deut 25:5-10 is the only law in the OT concerning levirate marriage. For literature on the levirate in the OT, see Neufeld (1944:23-55), de Vaux (1961:37-8), Leggett (1974:42-62) and Kutsch (1982). Gen 38 is generally considered to contain an example of a levirate between Judah and Tamar. Whether the book of Ruth contains an example of a levirate marriage is a question that still awaits an adequate solution. Suffice it to say here that if the marriage in Ruth is a levirate, it must be of a very different kind than what is described in the deuteronomic law. For a recent and thorough discussion, see Hubbard (1988:48-63).

[47] However, from Ruth 4:3, where it is stated that Naomi is about to sell the field, many scholars have concluded that this was indeed possible. The laws in Num 27:5-11 and 36:5-9 do not seem to allow for widows to inherit, although it is not explicitly forbidden either. For further discussion, see Hubbard (1988:54-5).

[48] See Waltke & O'Connor (1990:488-9).

merely informs the elders without any legal force. Another similarity to Ruth 4:8 is that immediately after this performative statement by the brother-in-law in v. 8 comes the symbolic act in v. 9.[49] The fact that both the statement in v. 8 as well as the act in v. 9 are performed before the elders only strengthens their legal nature.

If these results are compared with what was found concerning the act in Ruth 4:8, the legal function seems clear. In Ruth 4:8 the kinsman abstained from his right willingly, thereby removing his own sandal. The brother-in-law in Deut 25:9, however, refuses to fulfill his duty as levir, which is the reason why the sandal is removed not by himself but by the widow. These two acts are then similar in the sense that the removal of the sandal functions as a way to abstain from performing a certain legal function. This means that the act here in Deut 25:9 as well as the act in Ruth 4:8, are negated variants of the act described in Ruth 4:7.

The legal function of the act is therefore to accomplish the decision of the brother-in-law to abstain from performing his duty as levir. The differences between Deut 25:9 and Ruth 4:8 are due to the different legal contexts. The most important difference is that the refusal in Deut 25:9 receives, through the accompanying act of spitting, a formal punishment. Spitting was an act of contempt and scorn, e.g. Num 12:14; Isa 50:6 and Job 30:10.[50] It is possible that the removal of the sandal was considered as a formal punishment, but this is uncertain.

Excursus: Amos 2:6; 8:6 and 1 Samuel 12:3

These texts have often been considered to contain references to similar legal symbolic acts as the ones found above in Ruth 4:8 and Deut 25:9. Amos 2:6 reads as follows: ʿal-mikrām bakkesep ṣaddîq wĕʾebyôn baʿăbûr naʿălāyim, "because they sell the righteous for silver, and the needy for a pair of sandals". Amos 8:6 has the same expression with the exception that the verb qānâ, "buy" is used instead of mākar, "sell".

It is particularly the phrase baʿăbûr naʿălāyim that has been interpreted in various ways and the most common alternatives will be presented here.

---

[49] A curious detail is that *Tg. Ruth* understands the symbolic act in Ruth 4:8 as pertaining to the glove and not the sandal. The reason for this is probably that the verb which is used in Deut 25:9, ḥālaṣ, "remove" was not used in Ruth 4:8, although *Tg. Ruth* says explicitly in 4:5 that it is a levirate marriage, see Levine (1973:36-7; 100-1). This is probably due to overly literalism on the part of the targumic author.

[50] See Kellermann (1990). Spitting in the face was a particularly severe symbolic act of showing contempt according to Num 12:14, where a daughter is supposed to feel shame for seven days if her father spits in her face. A similar case can be found in Ahiqar 133, where it is an act of contempt.

1. It is synonymous with the preceding phrase, and refers to the debt for which the poor are being sold into slavery or debt slavery.[51] Some even hold that *baʕăbûr* here has the meaning of *pretii*,[52] but that is not attested elsewhere.[53] It is also rather unlikely that sandals would be used as a means of payment in transactions.[54] One alternative is that a pair of sandals would be a surety, and when they cannot be restored, the poor man is forced into debt slavery.[55] The problem with this interpretation is the use of *qānâ*, which hardly fits in with the transference of a surety.

2. The phrase is used metaphorically for the very low sum of money which the poor owed but could not pay, and for which they were sold into debt slavery.[56]

3. The phrase refers to a legal symbolic act whereby a person entered debt slavery through transferring a pair of sandals, presumably to his debtor.[57] This is possible in the light of what has been found above regarding the legal symbolic acts in Ruth 4:8 and Deut 25:9. However, the sandals are not said to have been transferred, which would have to be considered implicit. Since the phrase seems to be idiomatic,[58] the legal symbolic act may very well be the proper historical explanation for the phrase, at the same time as there may be another explanation for its actual use. No reliable connection can therefore be found between the expression as it is used in Amos 2:6 and 8:6 and the performance of a legal symbolic act.

Some have claimed that there is a reference to a similar legal symbolic act in the LXX version of 1 Sam 12:3.[59] According to the MT Samuel says: *ûmîyad-mî lāqaḥtî kōper wĕʔaʕlîm ʕênay bô*, "From whom have I taken a bribe

---

[51] So e.g. Wolff (1969:163, 200), Botterweck (1971:226) and Bohlen (1986:285). Bohlen considers "a pair of sandals" as explanatory in relation to the earlier "money". Andersen & Freedman (1989:310-1) understand it similarly as a chiasmus where the parallelism forms a discontinuous construct phrase, "the price ... of a pair of sandals."

[52] So e.g. Wolff (1969:163).

[53] See Rudolph (1971:141), Lang (1981:482), Bohlen (1986:284, n. 4) and Kessler (1989:14-5).

[54] Against e.g. Speiser (1940:18).

[55] So Kessler (1989:20).

[56] See e.g. Rudolph (1971:141), Andersen & Freedman (1989:313), who also consider it possible to refer to a bribe, and Stuart (1987:316), who also deems it possible to refer to a legal symbolic act similar to the ones in Ruth 4:8 and Deut 25:9.

[57] So Lang (1981:483). The view of Speiser (1940:19), that it is a technical way to circumvent the law, seems to read too much of legal practices from Nuzi into the biblical text.

[58] So e.g. Dearman (1988:21).

[59] So Speiser (1940), who prefers to interpret the legal function of the act in the light of certain legal symbolic acts from Nuzi, and Lang (1981:483) who compares the legal proceeding with Ruth 4:7-8 and considers "sandals" in this case as a metonymy for a "Schuldvertrag".

to shut my eyes with it",[60] whereas the LXX reads, ἐκ χειρὸς τίνος εἴληφα ἐξίλασμα καὶ ὑπόδημα; ἀποκρίθητε κατ' ἐμου, "From whose hand have I taken a bribe and a sandal? Testify against me."[61] The problem is the occurrence of ὑπόδημα, "sandal". The best solution is that the Hebrew Vorlage to the LXX had the original reading.[62] What, then, caused the alternate reading of the MT? The simplest solution is to see it as a mechanical mistake in the transmission of the text, where the nun of nᵉly m, "sandals" was mistakenly read as an 'aleph, thus creating the form ʾaʿlīm, "I conceal". This, together with the following phrase, was then associated with a familiar expression, lit. "conceal the eyes from", although a new variant was created. The preposition min is used separatively in this expression in Lev 20:4 and Isa 1:15, whereas in Ezek 22:26 and Prov 28:27 no preposition is used. In the MT of 1 Sam 12:3, on the other hand, the preposition bĕ is used with the instrument, namely the bribe. This was caused by the alternate reading of ʿnw by, "testify against me", as ʿyny bw, "my eyes with it". The Hebrew expression ʿānâ bĕ, "testify against" is rather common in the OT,[63] and it is sometimes translated in the LXX with ἀπεκρίθην.[64] This expression also forms an inclusio, since it occurs at the beginning of the verse as well. The expression in the LXX is then familiar, in contrast to the one in the MT. It also seems to fit the context as against the phrase in the MT, which is followed rather abruptly by "I will restore it to you." This would be more understandable if it was preceded by "testify against me". The Hebrew Vorlage to the LXX would then have been as follows: mîyad mî lāqaḥû kōper wĕnaʿalayim ʿānû bî, "From whom have I received a bribe and sandals? Testify against me". This would then attest to the use of "sandal" in the context of a judge taking bribes. One alternative is to see "sandal" here as a figurative way of referring to something of insignificant value.[65] However, in the light of what has been concluded above

---

[60] My translation.

[61] This agrees in most parts with the Hebrew text of Sir 46:19 from the Cairo Geniza, kwpr wnᵉlm mm[y lqḥ]ty wkl ʾdm Pʿnh bw, "'From wh[om have] I [taken] a bribe or a pair of sandals?' But no one answered him."

[62] So Stoebe (1973:232), who refers to older literature, and McCarter (1980:209-10). Klein (1983:111) holds to the MT with an haplography of ʿānû bî, "testify against me". Andersen & Freedman (1989:311-3), after a lengthy discussion, leave the question undecided.

[63] E.g. Deut 19:18; 2 Sam 1:16; Jer 14:7; Ezek 22:10, 11; Mic 6:3; Prov 25:18; Ruth 1:21.

[64] E.g. Mic 6:3; 2 Sam 1:16. It is interesting that in 2 Sam 1:16 the LXX translates the MT pîkā ʿānâ bĕkā, "your own mouth has testified against you" with τὸ στόμα σου ἀπεκρίθη κατὰ σοῦ. This is the only occurrence, besides possibly 1 Sam 12:3, where the preposition bĕ is translated by κατὰ in this expression.

[65] Cf. Cassin (1987:306-7), who considers it likely that the sandal symbolizes the same in 1 Sam 12:3 as in Sir 46:19. She brings attention to an interesting parallel to this interpretation in a letter written by an Assyrian official, see Waterman (1930), 1285:26-28. He claims that he is innocent of taking bribery: "May Anu, Enlil and Ea, who establish

regarding Ruth 4:7-8 and Deut 25:9, it could be a reference to an agreement between an unjust judge and someone giving bribes. The agreement would then have included the transference of a sum of money, the *kōper*, and a ratification through the transference of a pair of sandals. It would then be likely that "sandal" is used metonymically for the agreement made,[66] and it might also have gone as far as becoming an idiom. However, it must be born in mind that this is hypothetical reasoning, based on a hypothetical Hebrew Vorlage to the LXX and the assumption that the MT has suffered some damage in its transmission.

Excursus: Walking Through the Land

According to Gen 13:17, Abram is told by God to walk through the land which lies in front of him. This act has often been claimed to describe a legal symbolic act whereby the change of ownership of a piece of land was ratified.[67] The structure of the argument in vv. 14b-17 is as follows:

v. 14b	Look at the land ...
v. 15a-16	because I will give it to you ...
v. 17a	Walk through the land ...
v. 17b	because I will give it to you.[68]

In v. 14b Abram is told to look at the land in all its width. This is followed in v. 15a by a promise by God that it will be given to him, which is the reason for viewing it so closely. Then, in v. 16, there is an extended description of the multitude of Abram's descendants, mentioned at the end of v. 15. In v. 17a there is a second command, this time to walk through the land. This is also followed by a promise, v. 17b, that it will be given to Abram, introduced as in v. 15a by *kî*, "because". The second occurrence of the promise is much shorter, leaving out the phrase *ʿad ʿôlām*, "forever", and reducing the subject to Abram only. These changes could be viewed as stylistic variations.

What seems strange about this text, especially v. 17a, is that God does not say that he has given the land, using the suffix conjugation, and that Abram should now travel through his land. Instead the prefix conjugation is used, as in v. 15. One possibility is to interpret this as a promise of a future gift, which would make Abram's tour around the country a way of proleptically being assured of the promise.[69] Another alternative is to view the

---

me at the head of the king my Lord, (curse me) if as much as a sandal or the wages of a kasir official (?) have restrained me."

[66] So Lang (1981:483). This is hard to determine from the context, however.

[67] So e.g. Daube (1947:37), Fitzmyer (1971:151), Westermann (1985:180) and Wenham (1987:298).

[68] My translation.

[69] So e.g. Hamilton (1990:395).

walk through the land as an act of taking possession. This would explain the use of the prefix conjugation, since the promise would then be fulfilled simultaneously with the act. But is there any reason to regard the act of walking through the land as a legal symbolic act? The only other texts in the OT that contain a similar expression, Deut 11:24 and Josh 1:3, do not shed any light on the problem, since they are merely similar examples.

From Nuzi a legal symbolic act is known, whereby a piece of land could change owner. The seller is said to lift his foot from the ground and place the foot of the buyer in its stead.[70] It was used in so-called 'sale-adoptions', which was a way of circumventing the legal restrictions on the sale of property, as well as in proper adoptions.[71] If the act in Gen 13:17 is to be considered as based on a legal symbolic act, it no doubt shares some symbolism with this act, but only from a historical point of view. The act from Nuzi is too different to be used as an argument for the existence of a legal symbolic act in Gen 13:17.

The conclusion is that as far as Gen 13:17; Deut 11:24 and Josh 1:3 are concerned, there is not enough evidence to claim that a legal symbolic act of walking through the land is described. The act in Gen 13:17 is best explained as a way of proleptically enhancing the promise of the land. The phrase in Deut 11:24 and Josh 1:3 concerns the promise of success in the entrance into the land.

2.11.4 Historical Explanation

Both examples of the legal symbolic act which have been studied above have involved the sandal. Here, however, the foot should be examined as well, since it is natural for the symbolic meaning to have been transferred from the foot to the sandal through metonymy.[72]

This can be seen in a recently published text from Emar.[73] Zadamma and his wife Ku'e have sold their four children to Ba'al-malik. The parents are said to have placed the feet of their children on clay in order to make an imprint of the soles of their feet. There is no further indication as to the possible legal nature of this act, although it is noteworthy that what appears to be three of these imprints are also found at Emar.[74] If this is a legal act

---

[70] See Lacheman (1937:53) and Malul (1988:382-4).

[71] So Lacheman (1937:54-5), Cassin (1987:294-5) and Malul (1988:379).

[72] See e.g. Keel (1982:535) and Stendebach (1990:342). For more elaborate analyses of the symbolic uses of the foot as well as the sandal, see e.g. Nacht (1915-16), Levy (1918), Dhorme (1923:157-60), Keel (1982) and Stendebach (1990:340-2). Cf. Sartori (1894) for the symbolism of the shoe in older European folklore and Deroy (1961) for ancient Greece.

[73] Arnaud (1986), 217. See also Tsukimoto (1989:17).

[74] Arnaud (1986), 218-20.

whereby the legal transaction was confirmed,[75] then the historical explanation would be based on a similar symbolic meaning as the one studied here, with the difference that it is the foot that is used and not the sandal. This would then be an example of how intimately related the symbolic meanings of the foot and the sandal were.

The foot is often used in contexts which display power and authority. This is illustrated in a concrete way when a person tramples with his foot on something, which is then regarded as under that person's authority.[76] The act would then symbolize subjugation and domination. This is found in the OT in Exod 23:27; Josh 10:24; 1 Kgs 5:3; Isa 51:23; Pss 8:7; 18:39; 47:4 and 110:1. An interesting expression can be found in Ps 60:10 (=108:10), where the sandal is instrumental in an aggressive act of taking possession over another land.

To fall down at the feet of someone is an act of prostration and subjugation, as, e.g., in 1 Sam 25:24; 2 Kgs 4:27 and Esth 8:3.

> The act of prostration by falling down at someone's feet is very common in the ancient Near East.[77] In e.g. *EA* 195:5-11, the author, writing to Pharaoh, calls himself the dust of Pharaoh's feet, the ground upon which he walks, the chair on which he sits and the stool for his feet. He also shows his subordination by saying that he falls down at the feet of Pharaoh.[78] There are illustrations from Egypt where Pharaoh is sitting on the knee of the god with his feet on a stool containing Egypt's enemies.[79]

According to Exod 3:5 and Josh 5:15, sandals may not be worn in the presence of God. Isaiah is told to remove his shoes, Isa 20:2 – a common way of treating prisoners of war, vv. 3-4. In Ezek 24:17 the prophet is told by God not to show himself to be in mourning, and therefore to keep his sandals on. To take off the sandals seems therefore to symbolize quite the opposite in relation to the act of trampling on the neck of the enemy, i.e., not to implement one's strength and authority, but to display one's weakness and submission.

---

[75] So Tsukimoto (1989:17).

[76] See Rühlmann (1971) for examples from Egypt. For an illustration of Thut-mose IV, treading upon his Asiatic enemies in the form of a sphinx, see *ANEP* no. 393. See also no. 308.

[77] See Gruber (1980:207-12).

[78] See also 84:4-6; 106:6; 141:40; 241:5-8. The text *EA* 369:29-32 characterizes a land as being under the feet of the king, i. e., under his authority. The theme is also known from Ugaritic treaty texts, e.g. PRU IV, 17.227:45.

[79] See Keel (1984:230-3).

To remove something from oneself would then symbolize the loss of something. So to remove the sandal would be to remove the authority and strength of that person. This is as far as the various symbolisms will take us.[80] However, it is enough to at least indicate the historical connection between the procedure of removing the sandal in the symbolic act and its legal function. When the kinsman removed his sandal in Ruth 4:8 he abstained from making use of the authority and power which accompanied his position as *gōʾēl*, "kinsman-redeemer". When the woman removes the sandal from her brother-in-law in Deut 25:9, he is cut off from his prerogative to act as levir.

It should be stressed at this point that there are no indications in these texts that any of these symbolic meanings would have been relevant for the understanding of the legal function of the act. The explanation which has been given here is merely an attempt to explain the relationship between the procedure and the act from a historical point of view.

Excursus: Removing the Sandals in *Testament of Zebulon* 3:2-7

There is an interesting example in *T. Zeb.* 3:2-7 of a further, symbolic use of the act in Deut 25:9. All the sons of Jacob, except Zebulon, are said to have used the money they got from selling Joseph to buy sandals and not food, v. 3. The reason is that the money "is the price of our brother's blood, but we will trample it underfoot in response to his having said he would rule over us." This is an example of the symbolic meaning of putting the foot on something in order to exercise authority. What is surprising here, however, is that the sandals, normally considered to have a similar symbolic meaning as the foot, are given the opposite meaning, namely that which is trampled upon. It is quite possible that the author is using a tradition from *Tg. Ps.-J.* Gen 37:28, which says that the brothers "sold Joseph to the Arabians for twenty mahin of silver; and they bought sandals of them." The fact that they are said to have bought sandals for the money might have seemed strange, and was therefore suitable for a midrashic explanation. Then, in vv. 4-7, a more lengthy midrashic expansion is given,

---

[80] Carmichael (1977:329-34) argues that in both Deut 25:5-10 and Ruth 4 the sandal symbolizes the male sexual organ. In Deut 25:9 the brother-in-law is then punished by the symbolic act which symbolizes his withdrawal from intercourse, and the spit from the widow symbolizes the semen that her brother-in-law has refused her. In Ruth 4 Carmichael sees two symbolic uses of the sandal. One is the legal symbolic use, described in 4:7, and the other is when the sandal symbolizes the male sexual organ. I fail, however, to find any contextual clues that point in the direction of the latter symbolic meaning. Indeed, according to Carmichael (1977:333) the reason why it is not explained in Ruth 4 is that is was so self-evident to the readers that it was not thought necessary, which seems to be arguing too much from silence.

based on the law in Deut 25:9-10.[81] In v. 4 the law is given, and in v. 5 it is applied to the case of Joseph and his brothers, with the rather cryptic statement, "the Lord removed Joseph's shoe from them." Joseph's brothers are said to have been exposed to the humiliating act of having their sandals removed in front of Joseph and being spat upon, vv. 6-7. The legal symbolic act of having one's sandals removed is here used symbolically for prostrating oneself in front of a superior, "they did obeisance to Joseph".

---

[81] De Jonge (1975:153) calls it a "super-midrash". It is interesting that *Pirqe R. El.* 38:77 shows an acquaintance with this tradition, probably influenced by *Tg. Pseudo-Jonathan*. There is, however, no elaboration in *Pirqe R. El.* 38:77 on the law in Deut 25:9-10. Instead, another thread is picked up by mentioning the reference to sandals in Amos 2:6.

2.11.5 Summary and Conclusions

1. It is probable that the kinsman did not transfer his sandal to Boaz in Ruth 4:8, but simply pulled it off. In Deut 25:9 the sandal is only pulled off as well, but this time by the widow.

2. The act described in Ruth 4:7 is not a strict description of what is said to be performed afterwards in v. 8. Instead, the act that is performed in v. 8 should be regarded as a variant of the act, which is described in v. 7.

3. The legal function of the symbolic act in Ruth 4:8 is to accomplish the kinsman's decision to rescind from his prerogative to serve as kinsman-redeemer. The legal function of the act in Deut 25:9 is to accomplish the decision of the brother-in-law to abstain from performing his duty as levir. Both these examples of the act accomplish the legal function without referring to a prior agreement. Both these examples are also negative counterparts to the act which is described in Ruth 4:7, which functioned as a ratification of an agreement which had been made.

4. The two examples of the act in Ruth 4:8 and Deut 25:9 are similar in that they both concern the abstention from a certain behaviour. This explains why in both cases the sandal was only pulled off and not transferred. The major difference between the two examples, however, is that whereas the kinsman abstained from a prerogative, the brother-in-law refused a duty. This explains why the widow pulled off the sandal of the brother-in-law and publicly punished him by an act of humiliation.

6. Historically speaking, the act in Ruth 4:8 and Deut 25:9 was created by means of the symbolic meaning of the foot, transferred to the sandal. This symbolic meaning was related to acts which display power and authority, such as putting the foot on the neck of a defeated enemy, or prostrating oneself before the feet of a superior or, which is more relevant, to remove the sandals in order to indicate submission and loss of authority. That would explain the connection with the legal function in Ruth 4:8, which meant abstaining from using a privileged position, and the legal function in Deut 25:9, which meant being cut off from performing a certain function.

2.12 Putting a Child on the Knees

2.12.1 Introduction

The text to be studied here is Ruth 4:16. Additional texts, however, have often been adduced to show the existence of this particular symbolic act, namely Gen 30:3 and 50:23. However, these texts do not describe a symbolic act, but contain an idiom, "give birth/be born on the knees of PN." The use of the phrase ʿal-birkayim, "on the knees" in this expression may suggest that the idiom developed out of a description of a symbolic act, where the new-born child was put on the knees of one of its parents. However, the idiomatic nature of the expression, and then especially its opacity, makes it too uncertain to be used as evidence for the existence of such an act.

Gen 48:12 has often been thought to describe an act of adoption or legitimation. However, according to v. 9 it is an affectionate act on behalf of the aging patriarch in order to bless the sons of Joseph who have been born in Egypt. Earlier in 48:5, however, a form of adoption is clearly described, using a terminology that has parallels from extra-biblical examples of adoption. This should not, however, be confused with what is described later in vv. 9-12.[1]

The two main problems with Ruth 4:16 are firstly, whether a legal symbolic act or simply an act of affection is described, and secondly, if a legal symbolic act is described, is it a matter of adoption or legitimation? Although adoption is not the primary objective in this study, it will inevitably be touched upon in the analysis that follows, in so far as it concerns the question of the legal function of the act.

> The categories adoption and legitimation are not used consistently among scholars. This has produced a great deal of confusion, as can be seen from the discussion of the views of various scholars, below. In this analysis, adoption is used when a child is given full status as child, including the right of heir, by parents other than the child's natural parents.[2] Legitimation, on the other hand, means for someone to acquire the particular legal

---

[1] This mistake is made by e.g. Speiser (1964:357), Phillips (1973:359) and de Vaux (1978:646). A better analysis can be found with Westermann (1982:207-11). Sarna (1989:327) regards vv. 8-9 as the second stage in the legal process, where the true identities of the candidates for adoption were established. The act which is alluded to in v. 12 then meant acceptance and legitimation as son and heir. It is evident that the text has been exposed to a redactional activity, which has caused the literary structure to be dischronologized.

[2] See Black (1979:45).

status of someone else.[3] In the case of legitimating a new-born child, it could, e.g. mean validating or confirming the child's status as heir. However, a legitimation of a child's legal status always presumes a previously existing blood-relationship between the party who legitimates and the child who is legitimated. Adoption, on the other hand, is considered as a legal act which transcends the boundaries of the family, whereas legitimation only functions within the family.[4]

A third problem is introduced in this study under Legal Function below, namely the relationship between the act of putting the child on the knees and the subsequent naming of the child. Extra-biblical texts, primarily Hittite, will be adduced to show that a connection between the act and the naming is likely, and that they together have a legal function.

2.12.2 Procedure

According to Ruth 4:13, Ruth gave birth to a son. The child was brought to Naomi, v. 16, who *wattĕšitĕhû bĕḥêqāh*, "put him on her lap".[5] It is then stated that Naomi became the child's nurse. She could not, however, have functioned as wet-nurse, since her age prevented her from having children of her own, 1:12.[6]

The word *ḥêq*, "lap" or "bosom" is often used in connection with a mother and her child, expressing the intimate relationship between the two.[7] In similar contexts, *ḥêq* is otherwise used with different verbs than in Ruth 4:13, such as *nāśâ*, "lift up", Isa 40:11; Ps 89:51, and *šakab*, "lie down", 2 Sam 12:3; 1 Kgs 3:20 and Mic 7:5. The verb *nāśâ* then refers to the lifting up of the child, whereas *šakab* refers to the subsequent placement of the child in the arms of its helper. Here in Ruth 4:16, however, is found the only occurrence of *ḥêq* in relation to the verb *šît*, "put". This verb was probably chosen because Naomi was not meant to be described as lifting up the child into her arms, as would have been the case with *nāśâ* and *šakab*, but as placing the child on her lap, i.e., on her knees. This was then caused by a desire to conform to the performance of a particular symbolic

---

[3] See Black (1979:811).

[4] See Black (1979:45).

[5] My translation.

[6] Therefore the translation of Hubbard (1988:269), "Then Naomi took the child and set him on her breast" is misplaced because of the wrong associations it brings with it.

[7] See 1 Kgs 3:20; 17:19; Lam 2:12. In a derived sense it is used in Num 11:12; 2 Sam 12:3; Isa 40:11.

act, since a new-born child is not usually put on the knees, but more naturally taken up into the arms.

The procedure of the act was then for Naomi to put the new-born child on her knees.

2.12.3 Legal Function

The legal function of the act in Ruth 4:16 is intimately connected with the question of whether adoption is ever described in the OT, a subject over which scholars continue to disagree.

Excursus: Adoption in the OT?

Older scholarship was generally more inclined to accept the concept of adoption in the OT.[8] Subsequently this view has persisted,[9] but not gone uncontested. The seminal study on the question was made by Donner, who differentiates between adoption which implies the right to inherit, arrogation, which excludes the right to inherit, a nursing relationship, where there is no such thing as receiving the status of proper child and finally acts of recognition within the family.[10] Donner then concludes that proper adoption was never referred to in the OT.[11] Boecker agrees with Donner regarding the texts discussed above, but not concerning Ps 2:7 and 2 Sam 7:14.[12] Paul claims that the institution of adoption actually occupied a central place in biblical theology. He deals with Ps 2:7 and 2 Sam 7:14, and his conclusion is that adoption could be found in the OT.[13] However, as far as Ruth 4:16 is concerned, Donner's view has not been challenged.

In narrowing down the focus to the legal function of the act in Ruth 4:16, it should be noted that scholars do not agree as to whether Ruth 4:16 describes a symbolic act with a legal function or whether Naomi is simply

---

[8] E.g. Köhler (1909) and Feigin (1931:193). See Paul (1979-80) for fuller bibliographical information.

[9] E.g. Mendelsohn (1959:181), de Vaux (1961:51) with certain restrictions, Würthwein (1969:23) and Phillips (1973:359-60). Phillips considers the placing of the child on the knee as an outward sign following the pronouncement of a legal formula. He explains the lack of attestation of adoption in the legal corpus of the OT as due to its nature as family law and therefore not a concern of the community at large.

[10] Donner (1969:88).

[11] Donner (1969:112). Blum (1984:252, n. 50) seems to agree with Donner, although he finds the OT occurrences to be very close to adoption. See also Westermann (1982:207-8) regarding Gen 48:5. Tigay (1971:300) doubts whether adoption was practised in Israelite families.

[12] Boecker (1974). See also Mettinger (1976:265-7).

[13] Paul (1979-80:173-5, 185).

displaying her most intimate feelings towards the child. The diversity of views available shows very clearly the difficulties which are inherent in the analysis of Ruth 4. Before proceeding to the analysis of this chapter, a short review of the different views among scholars will therefore be presented.

Excursus: Earlier Views on Naomi's Act in Ruth 4:16

The older view, that Naomi did indeed adopt the new-born Obed by this act,[14] was later countered by its opposite view, namely that there is no legal matter at all involved but merely a gesture of affection.[15] Some take into consideration that the act, although not describing an adoption, does have some function beyond mere affection, and one alternative is that the act had as its purpose to legitimate the child as a member of the family.[16] Still another alternative is that Ruth 4:16 contains a vestigial motif from Near Eastern mythology, showing a king as a descendant of divine parentage by making him suckle a deity.[17] This would then be an attempt to support David's claim to the throne of Saul.[18] However, it is doubtful whether this would have been readily understood by an ancient reader of the book of Ruth. Scholars have thus come to be more hesitant towards recognizing a legal function of the act done by Naomi, and especially that of adoption.

Ruth 4, and especially vv. 11-17, is a highly structured narrative. Careful attention must therefore be paid to the meaning inherent in the literary structure. This is particularly important since, as in most cases where a symbolic act is described, it does not receive an explicit explanation. The meaning of the act must therefore be sought in its function within the literary structure.

---

[14] So e.g. Köhler (1909:312), Falk (1964:163), Gerleman (1965:37-8) and Würthwein (1969:23). De Vaux (1961:51) calls it a case of adoption but with limited consequences, since it occurs within the family circle. Malul (1985b:201-2) also seems to argue that the act is an act of adoption.

[15] So e.g. Joüon (1953:94), Rudolph (1962:71), Leggett (1974:261-3), Campbell (1975:165) and Hubbard (1988:274). Donner (1969:111) concludes that since there is a levirate involved, adoption is out of the question. Instead, he regards the act as a legal act of recognition within the family.

[16] Gow (1983:73), while doubting that there is a full legal adoption described in this text, holds that at least "the child is thus shown to have been fully accepted into the family by Naomi." However, he finds it impossible to reach a point of certainty. Witzenrath (1975:280) considers an act of legitimation as possible.

[17] So Sasson (1989:233-9).

[18] Sasson (1989:240): "Those in a position to decipher the code would have understood *Ruth* as a vehicle to support David's claim to the throne of Saul, by showing that, decades previously, David's grandfather had already enjoyed divine protection."

The text is structured by means of direct speech in vv. 11-12 and vv. 14-15, both of which are followed by a narrative comment in vv. 13 and 16. The speech in vv. 11-12 looks forward to the offspring of Ruth and Boaz, which is fulfilled in the narrator's comment in v. 13 when it says that Ruth has given birth to a son. The speech in vv. 14-15 describes the happy circumstances which this child has brought about for Naomi. This is then described by the narrator in v. 16, where Naomi is said to put the boy on her knees and become his nurse.

It can readily be seen that the new-born child is central to the message of the text. What connects the speech in vv. 11-12 with the comment in v. 13 is the fact of the child's birth. The connection between the speech in vv. 14-15 and the comment in v. 16 takes the argument a step further, since they both concern the implications of the birth for Naomi. This can be seen by focusing on the contents of vv. 13 and 17. In v. 13 it is said that Ruth gave birth to a son, which is the climax to the first part, vv. 11-13 containing the fact of the birth of the child. In v. 17 it is said that a son has been born to Naomi, which is the climax of the second part, vv. 14-17 containing the implications of the birth of the son for Naomi.

The precise formulation in v. 17 is important, "A son has been born to Naomi", as over against the formulation in v. 13, "she bore a son."[19] These formulations show an awareness of the fact that whereas Ruth gave birth to the son, he apparently had some important implications for Naomi. This is evident from the fact that the child is described earlier in v. 14 as the *gōʾēl*, "redeemer" of Naomi.[20] How, then, has this been achieved? Two answers are given. According to v. 14, the divine initiative has led to Naomi's redemption, and according to v. 15 it is the human initiative, the very fact that Ruth bore the son, that has made it possible. Ruth was the step-daughter who married a distant relative to Naomi, thus achieving what Naomi had not thought possible, namely to keep the family property and the family name intact. Finally, it is significant that the climactic phrase "A son has been born to Naomi" comes after the symbolic act by Naomi in v. 16. The symbolic act in v. 16 is then found in that part of the text which deals with the implications of the new-born child for Naomi. The statement "A son has been born to Naomi" follows upon the act as an affirmation of these implications. This indicates that a turning-point occurs in v. 16. A

---

[19] This is similar to the traditional birth announcement in the OT, e.g. Isa 9:5; Jer 20:15; Job 3:3, so e.g. Hubbard (1988:275).

[20] My translation. Hubbard (1988a:296) might be right in regarding this expression as an ancient Israelite custom of notifying the father concerning a birth, but the evidence is slender.

connection can therefore be said to have been found between the implications of the child for Naomi and the act by Naomi.

The naming of the child also takes on an important role in explaining the legal background to the narrative at large, and to the symbolic act in particular. There are four formulations, more or less similar, which have caused some confusion to scholars in the past. They are *ûqĕrāʾ-šēm*, "call out a name" in v. 11, *wĕyiqqārēʾ šĕmô*, "and his name will be called out" in v. 14 and *wattiqreʾnâ lô haššĕkēnôt šēm*, "and the neighbouring women called him by a name" and *wattiqreʾnâ šĕmô ʿôbēd*, "and they called him by the name Obed" in v. 17.[21] Without entering into the discussion concerning the precise meaning of these phrases, it must be noted that they are similar and occur throughout the narrative, which gives them a cohesive role in the literary structure of vv. 11-17.[22] They also create expectancy, since the actual naming does not occur until v. 17, and then only in the second instance. A closer look at vv. 16-17 reveals that the actual naming of the child does not occur until the child has been put on Naomi's knees and, as was shown earlier, this is also the case with the expression "A son has been born to Naomi."

It would appear, therefore, that the symbolic act in v. 16 is a turning point in the literary structure; something is accomplished in v. 16 that invites both the expression "A son has been born to Naomi" and the naming of the child in v. 17. However, this still does not give a clear view of the legal function of Naomi's act, since it is still possible that it was an act of affection. By imitating the mother, Naomi's act would then symbolize the implications of the child for Naomi, namely that he would be her son, and there would be no legal function involved. Although this view could be held, there are some indications that point in another direction. Above, under Procedure, it was found that the act was not described as a normal act of taking the child up into the arms, but instead the child was put on the knees, an unusual act for showing affection for a new-born child. Furthermore, as Sasson points out, it would seem rather out of place for such an act of mere affection at this stage in the narrative.[23] A further indication is the naming and its occurrence precisely after the act. It would seem reasonable that the naming was placed there for some reason, and that reason might well have to do with what immediately preceded it, namely the act in v. 16. However, these indications do not lead all the way

---

[21] My translations.

[22] See Hubbard (1988a). Porten (1978:47) holds that the unit consists of vv. 13-17, and that the occurrences in vv. 14 and 17 bind the text together.

[23] Sasson (1989:171-2).

to a legal function, although some strong hints may have been given nonetheless.

Since nothing further is said in the text regarding the possible legal function of the act of Naomi in v. 16, some extra-biblical parallels will be brought forth to show how the act of putting the new-born child on the knees and naming it could have been used together with one particular purpose.

The symbolic act, and more importantly the combination of the symbolic act and the naming of the child, finds some striking parallels in certain Hittite texts.[24] The first example comes from a birth-ritual where the nurse describes her actions after the birth.[25] The woman that has given birth is apparently the queen.[26] After the nurse has dressed the queen she says, "[And] I place the child on her knees."[27]

The second example is from the story of Appu and the birth of his two sons. Appu is a wealthy man, but without a child. He seeks divine help and is told by the sun-god not to worry. Soon enough his wife is ready to give birth:

> Und die Gattin von Appu gebar einen Sohn. Die [Am]me hob den Sohn hoch, und setzte ihn dem Appu auf die Knie. Appu begann, sich über den Sohn zu freuen und ihn zu *schaukeln* und gab ihm den süßen Namen Schlecht: ... .[28]

Here the birth of the son is immediately followed by the act of putting the child on the knees of the father, who proceeds to name the child.[29]

The third example comes from the so-called song of Ullikummis. The situation is that Teshub, the storm-god, is now king among the gods. The former king, Kumarbi, opposes the change and by creating an adversary to Teshub he tries to regain his former position. To achieve this, Kumarbi has intercourse with a huge rock, which later bears him a son:

---

[24] Stamm (1939:8) concluded from analysing Akkadian texts that there the name-giving took place immediately after birth as well.

[25] See Berman (1972:466) and Beckman (1983:42-3). The text is KBo XVII.61:22.

[26] So Beckman (1983:53).

[27] Beckman (1983:42-3). Berman (1972:466) translates somewhat differently: "I put the child on his (i.e. the father's) knees."

[28] Siegelová (1971:10-1). The text is KUB XXIV.8+XXXVI.60, Rs. III:9-13.

[29] Regarding the use of this theme in Hittite literature, see Siegelová (1971:32-3). Hoffner (1968:199) describes the formal elements that are used in this standard formula.

> The [...] women brought him into the world; the Good-women and the
> Moth[er-goddesses lifted the child and] placed [him upon Kumarbis']
> knees. [Kumar]bis began to fondle his son [and] let him dance up and
> down. He proceeded to give [the child] a propitious name! Kumarbis
> began to say to his soul: "What name [shall I give] him? The child
> which the Good-women and the Mother-goddesses presented me, [for
> the reason that he] shot forth from (her) body (as) a shaft, let him go
> and [his] name be Ullikummis![30]

Again the birth is followed by the placing of the child by the nurse on the
knees of the father, who immediately proceeds to name the child.[31] This
symbolic act evidently serves to legitimate the new-born child[32] and it is
also part of the name-giving.[33]

There is also an interesting text in the Aqhat-story from Ugarit which
seems to deal with a similar subject. It tells of how the craftsman Kotharu-
and-Khasisu visits Dani'ilu to deliver a bow and arrows to him:

> In the hands of Dani'ilu he layed the bow, he put the arrows on his
> knees.[34]

Dani'ilu then proceeds to name the bow he has been given:

> And then Dani'ilu, the Saviour's man, then the hero, the Harnamite
> man, named (and) blessed the bow, yes, for Aqhatu he named it: ...[35]

Although this is a case of naming a weapon, the combination of the act and
the following naming of the weapon probably alludes to how a new-born
child was legitimated as a member of the family.[36]

These extra-biblical texts display a significant cultural parallel which is
hard to disregard. It is clear that extra-biblical parallels should be treated
with caution. However, the lack of any explicit reference to a legal function of the act, as well as the failure to find a reference to a legal function
of the act in the literary structure, make parallels in neighboring cultures all

---

[30] *ANET* (122).

[31] Hoffner (1968:200-1) claims that it was the nurse and not the mid-wife who presented the child to the parent, so also Beckman (1983:48).

[32] So Hoffner (1968:201), who also relates this to Ruth 4:16. There is an interesting
parallel to this in Homer *Iliad* 9:455-456, see Muhly (1965:586).

[33] So Berman (1972:467).

[34] *ARTU* (234). The text is *KTU* 1.17.V:26-28.

[35] *ARTU* (235). The text is *KTU* 1.17.V:33-36.

[36] De Moor, in *ARTU* (235, n. 72), may very well be right in that "The bow that is
placed on his lap now will take the place of his son, in a way it becomes a 'daughter' of
Dani'ilu."

the more relevant. These texts show that the symbolic act of placing the new-born child on the knees and the subsequent naming of the child could very well be taken together. They would then have a common legal function, namely to legitimate the status of the new-born child as a proper member of the family.

When this material is compared with the act in Ruth 4:16, there are some obvious differences that have to be dealt with. It is Naomi who puts the child on her knees and not one of the parents, i.e., Ruth or Boaz. However, as has been shown above, the main thrust of vv. 14-17 is to show the implications which the new-born child has for Naomi, namely that he would legally be considered as her son. However, this is a statement which should not be taken at face value, since Ruth and Boaz surely remain as the parents of the child.[37] It is more likely that what is described here is the fact that the child fulfils certain legal functions which only an heir of Naomi could fulfil. This is then described as if a son had been born to Naomi. This then actually means that a son has been born and an heir has been produced which has some profound consequences for Naomi. It is therefore consistent with the narrative at large that Naomi performs the act and not Ruth or Boaz.

Another problem that is encountered in this comparison with extra-biblical material is that it is the surrounding women who name the child in v. 17. This cannot be explained sufficiently, except to say that the literary artistry on the part of the author might well have provided him with the liberty of placing the naming of the child in the mouths of the women, as a matter of emphasis.

In spite of these differences, however, it would seem preferable to regard the act of putting the child on the knees in Ruth 4:16 as a legal symbolic act, as it occurs in connection with the naming of the child. This conclusion would then rely on the interpretation of a similar act in some Hittite texts above. The Ugaritic text, although more difficult to interpret, might indicate this practice as well. The fact that the legal function is achieved by relating to extra-biblical texts makes it less reliable and the view could still be held that it was only an act of affection. This is not likely, however.

On the basis of this comparison, it could not have been a matter of adoption on behalf of Naomi, since the matter was settled by the mere birth of Obed. What was needed, however, was for the child to be legitimated by Naomi by means of an act performed in public. This act of legitimation would then show that she recognized and accepted the child as being legally her son, in the derived sense that Obed would inherit the land as

---

[37] See e.g. Parker (1988:138).

well as the family name. It would not mean that the child ceased to be the proper child of Ruth and Boaz. When the women say that a son has been born to Naomi, it then means practically that she has gained someone who can fulfil certain functions of a son. This would then also comply with the legal function of the symbolic act in the Hittite texts above.

In conclusion, then, the legal function of the symbolic act of putting the child on the knees in Ruth 4:16 is to accomplish the legitimation of the new-born child as Naomi's son in a derived sense, which would imply the status of the child as heir to the family's name and land.[38] The legal function would only be relevant in so far as it occurs together with the naming of the child.

2.12.4 Historical Explanation

The basis for this legal symbolic act is the act of holding the new-born child as an expression of parental affection.[39] When it comes to relating this act of affection to the legal function it is not a case of either/or, but of both/and. It is an act of loving care for the child, which has gained the further function of also legitimating the child.

---

[38] This would come close to the view of Donner (1969:111), that the act is a legal act of recognition within the family.

[39] See Malul (1985b:201-2).

2.12.5 Summary and Conclusions.

1. The procedure of the act in Ruth 4:16 is to put the child on the knees, and not to lift it up to lie in the arms. This probably conforms with the procedure of a particular symbolic act. The act is performed together with the naming of the child by the surrounding women.

2. The legal function of the symbolic act in Ruth 4:16, in relation to the act of naming in 4:17, is to accomplish the legitimation of the child Obed as son in the derived sense of recognizing his right to the name and land of the family. The fact that it was Naomi who put the child on her knees was due to the fact that the child was considered legally to function in certain profound ways as a son to Naomi.

3. The legal function of the act was reached by comparing it with an act found in some Hittite texts and possibly one Ugaritic text. There the father, and possibly the mother, puts the new-born child on the knees and proceeds to name the child. This was an act by means of which the child was legitimated as a proper member of the family. However, the conclusion regarding the legal function of the act in Ruth 4:16 is less secure than had it been reached through the contextual analysis. This is due to its reliance on comparative material. However, the conclusion which has been reached seems most probable, nevertheless.

4. The act is explained historically as an act of parental affection. Since the act so clearly indicated that the parent recognized the child as his or hers, it also came to serve as the legitimation of the child.

3 Concluding Remarks

The time has now come to make some concluding remarks. Before the analysis was undertaken, some important theoretical aspects of legal symbolic acts were described in the introduction. It was also shown how these aspects would have to be taken into consideration, were the acts to be understood correctly. The most important of these aspects will briefly be taken up here again, in relation to some remarks which relate to legal symbolic acts in general. The conclusions regarding each act will not be repeated here, however, since they have been duly summarized under 'Summary and Conclusions'.

An important distinction should be made between the legal function of a legal symbolic act and its historical explanation. As in all etymological attempts, the historical explanation may very well come close to the truth, but, unfortunately, the opposite is true as well. Therefore, these acts have been studied in relation to how they function within their literary contexts, in order to reach a reliable understanding of their legal functions.

Legal symbolic acts are conventional, in the sense that the meaning of a legal symbolic act is the result of an agreement within the socio-cultural context in which it is known and performed. The meaning of the act is therefore not to be considered as resulting from its performance, as in the case of the symbolic acts of the prophets, but from its function within its context. Since the legal symbolic acts are only available in literary form, the relevant context then becomes the literary context.

This conventional character of the acts is particularly important for understanding the legal function, since that function is not to be perceived by merely understanding the performance of the acts. Instead, the acts are considered to be legal in the sense that they were the outworking of certain social norms, in this case legal norms. This particular form of law, both as norms and legal symbolic acts, is to be considered as customary law. This emphasis on the literary context then naturally leads to a contextual approach to the legal symbolic acts.

When this contextual approach was applied in the analysis of the acts, it resulted, for the most part, in discarding older interpretations because they were based on historical explanations and not on proper analyses of the literary contexts. In contrast, the contextual approach, as outlined above, provided a more reliable foundation for understanding these legal symbolic acts.

Sometimes, however, the literary context did not provide sufficient evidence to conclude that the act in question was indeed meant to be taken as a legal symbolic act. There are two items to be considered here from a more general perspective, namely the use of comparative material and the reuse of legal symbolic acts in non-legal contexts.

The extra-biblical material was used in two different ways in the analysis; one illustrative, which only emphasized what had already been found in the contextual analysis, and one explanatory. When the extra-biblical material was used in the explanatory sense, it provided an understanding of the act, which the analysis of the literary context had failed to do. It was particularly the case in the analysis of the act of transferring the mantle that the literary context was found to be insufficient, and in a lesser degree with the acts of covering a woman with the mantle and putting a child on the knees. In all the other cases, the literary contexts provided sufficient evidence to conclude that they were to be understood as legal symbolic acts.

The problem of identifying acts as legal symbolic acts was found to be tied in with the question of reuse in non-legal context. When a legal symbolic act is reused in a non-legal context, the legal function is often not referred to directly. Instead, it is by means of association to when the act is performed in a proper legal context that the legal function is to be perceived. Thus, it becomes harder to decide when an act is intended to be a reuse of a legal symbolic act, hence the problems with the act of transferring the mantle. Sometimes, however, the legal function is clearly emphasized even when it is a case of reuse, as in the case of the act of walking through a divided animal.

The acts which have been analysed then form the following three categories:

1. Acts in legal contexts only	*3. Acts in both legal and non-legal contexts*	*3. Acts in non-legal contexts only*
1. Shaking the hand	1. Raising the hand	1. Transferring the mantle
2. Putting the hand under the thigh	2. Walking through a divided animal	
3. Sharing a meal	3. Anointing the head with oil	
4. Piercing the ear of the slave		
5. Grasping the horns of the altar		
6. Removing the sandal		
7. Putting a child on the knees		
8. Covering a woman with the mantle		

The first category is naturally the least problematic, although the act of putting the child on the knees does present a particular problem. It was not possible to arrive at a sufficient conclusion regarding the legal nature of the act by means of the contextual approach, although the act appears to be performed in a proper legal context. The act of covering a woman with the mantle also presents a problem. The act is referred to in Ruth 3:9 in what appears to be a proper legal context, although the act is not described as performed.

The second category is somewhat more problematic, since it involves the question of reuse of legal symbolic acts in non-legal contexts. That these acts are indeed reused in non-legal contexts could be substantiated by the fact that they are also performed in proper legal contexts.

The third category is the most problematic, since this act only occurs in reused form in non-legal contexts.

A question which is related to the reuse of legal symbolic acts is why God is sometimes described as performing legal symbolic acts. Of the acts analysed here, God is described as raising his hand, walking through a divided animal, having the head of someone anointed with oil and, figuratively, covering a woman with the mantle. Why is God described in this way? The answer lies in recognizing the power of association. The association between God and the strong, legal force which these legal symbolic acts had in their proper legal use, provided the biblical authors with the emphasis which was felt to be needed in order to describe God sufficiently. This becomes particularly evident when God is described as making a covenant with Abram in Gen 15. In order to emphasize that God actually enters into a covenant relationship with Abram, as the party who plays the role of the suzerain, God is described as using a legal symbolic act. Since God is considered in the OT as the provider of law, it should come as no surprise that God is also described as interacting with men by means of law, in the form of legal symbolic acts.

4 Abbreviations and Technical Remarks

The abbreviations listed in *JBL* 107(1988):583–96 have been used. In addition to the abbreviations listed in *JBL* the following have also been used:

AP	Aramaic Papyri. (See: Bibliography: Sources)
ARTU	An Anthology of Religious Texts from Ugarit. (See: Bibliography: Sources)
BMAP	The Brooklyn Museum Aramaic Papyri. (See: Bibliography: Sources)
BRL	Biblisches Reallexikon. 2 ed.
EA	El Amarna Tablets. (See: Bibliography: Sources)
FS	Festschrift
IBoT	Istanbul arkeoloji Müzelerinde bulunan Boğazköy tabletleri
JPS	The Jewish Publication Society
KBo	Keilschrifttexte aus Boghazköy
KP	Der kleine Pauly. Lexikon der Antike von Pauly's Realencyclopädie der classischen Altertumswissenschaft
KTU	Die Keilalphabetischen Texte aus Ugarit. (See: Bibliography: Sources)
KUB	Keilschrifturkunden aus Boghazköi
MelT	Melita Theologica
MRS	Mission de Ras Shamra
NCBC	New Century Bible Commentary
NRSV	New Revised Standard Version. (See: Bibliography: Sources)
RS	Ras Shamra Tablet
StBoT	Studien zu den Boğazköy-Texten

References to biblical passages follow the numbering of the Hebrew text. Unless otherwise stated biblical quotations have been rendered according to the NRSV. Transliteration of Hebrew follow the system described in *JBL* 107(1988):582–83.

When sources and secondary literature have been quoted, they have been reproduced as faithfully as possible. This means that parentheses, square brackets, etc., except footnote references, are included as they appear in the original work. Ellipsis points, however, have sometimes been added to shorten the quotations.

5 Bibliography

5.1 Sources

(Note that the following sources are divided in two categories; those referred to by abbreviation or name only, and those referred to by name and year.)

[Ahiqar] *The Aramaic Proverbs of Ahiqar.* J. M. Lindenberger. JHNES. Baltimore. 1983.

[*ANEP*] *The Ancient Near East in Pictures Relating to the Old Testament.* J. B. Pritchard. 2 ed. Princeton. 1969.

[*ANET*] *Ancient Near Eastern Texts Relating to the Old Testament.* Ed. J. B. Pritchard. 3 ed. Princeton. 1969.

[*AP*] *Aramaic Papyri of the Fifth Century B.C.* A. Cowley. Oxford. 1923. (Reprint 1967).

[ARM:2] *Lettres diverses. Transcrites et traduites.* C.-J. Jean. Paris. 1955.

[ARM:8] *Textes juridiques.* G. Boyer. Paris. 1958.

[ARM:26] *Archives épistolaires de Mari I/1.* J.-M. Durand. Paris. 1988.

[*ARTU*] *An Anthology of Religious Texts from Ugarit.* J. C. de Moor. Religious Texts Translation Series. NISABA:16. Leiden. 1987.

[*BHS*] *Biblica Hebraica Stuttgartensia.* Eds. K. Elliger & W. Rudolph. Stuttgart. 1967-77.

[*BMAP*] *The Brooklyn Museum Aramaic Papyri. New Documents of the Fifth Century B.C. from the Jewish Colony at Elephantine.* E. G. Kraeling. New Haven. 1953.

[*EA*] *Die El-Amarna Tafeln.* J. A. Knudtzon. 2 vols. Vorderasiatische Bibliothek 2:1-2. Leipzig. 1907-15.

[*EA*] *El Amarna Tablets 359-379.* A. F. Rainey. AOAT:8. Neukirchen-Vluyn. 1970.

Herodotus, 4 vols. LCL. London. 1920-25.

Homer, The Iliad. 2 vols. LCL. London. 1924-25.

[*KAI*] *Kanaanäische und aramäische Inschriften.* H. Donner, W. Röllig. 3 vols. Wiesbaden. 1962-64.

[*KTU*] *Die Keilalphabetischen Texte aus Ugarit. Teil 1. Transkription.* M. Dietrich et al. AOAT:24. Neukirchen-Vluyn. 1976.

Livy, 14 vols. LCL. London. 1919-59.

[NRSV] *Holy Bible. New Revised Standard Version.* Grand Rapids. 1990.

The Old Testament in Greek. Eds. A. E. Brooke et al. 9 vols. Cambridge. 1906-40.

[Pirqe R. El.] *Pirķê de Rabbi Eliezer. (The Chapters of Rabbi Eliezer the Great) According to the Text of the Manuscript Belonging to Abraham Epstein of Vienna.* G. Friedlander. New York. 1916. (Reprint 1981).

Plato, Laws. 2 vols. LCL. London. 1926.

[PRU IV] *Le Palais royal d'Ugarit: IV. Textes accadiens des Archives Sud (Archives internationales).* J. Nougayrol. 2 vols. MRS:9. Paris. 1956.

Septuaginta. Ed. A. Rahlfs. 2 vols. Stuttgart. 1935.

Septuaginta. Vetus Testamentum graece auctoritate Societatis Göttingensis editum. Göttingen. 1931–.

Sirah, The Hebrew Text of. A. A. Di Lella. London. 1966.

[*Test. Zeb.*] "Testaments of the Twelve Patriarchs. (Second Century B.C.). A New Translation and Introduction". H. C. Kee. In: *The Old Testament Pseudepigrapha. Volume 1. Apocalyptic Literature and Testaments.* Ed. J. H. Charlesworth. New York. 1983, 775-828.

[*Tg. Onq.*] *The Bible in Aramaic Based on Old Manuscripts and Printed Texts.* A. Sperper. 4 vols. Leiden. 1959-73.

[*Tg. Ps.-J.*] *The Targums of Onkelos and Jonathan ben Uzziel on the Pentateuch with the Fragments of the Jerusalem Targum. Genesis and Exodus.* J. W. Etheridge. New York. 1862. (Reprint 1968).

Ugaritica V. Nouveaux textes accadiens, hourrites et ugaritiques des Archives et Bibliothèques privées d'Ugarit. Commentaires des textes historiques (1re partie). J. Nougayrol. MRS:16. Paris. 1968.

Arnaud, D., 1986. *Textes sumériens et accadiens. Texte.* Recherches au pays d'Aštata. Emar 6:3. Paris.

Beckman, G. M., 1983. *Hittite Birth Rituals.* 2 ed. StBoT:29. Wiesbaden.

Berman, H., 1972. "A Hittite Ritual for the Newborn". *JAOS* 92, 466-8.

Dalley, S. et al., 1976. *The Old Babylonian Tablets from Tell al Rimah.* Hertford.

Gibson, J. C. L., 1975. *Textbook of Syrian Semitic Inscriptions. Vol. 2. Aramaic Inscriptions.* Oxford.

— 1982. *Textbook of Syrian Semitic Inscriptions. Vol. 3. Phoenician Inscriptions.* Oxford.

Gurney, O. R., 1954. *The Hittites.* 2 ed. Harmondsworth.

Hoffner, H. A. Jr., 1969. See: Bibliography: Literature.

Huehnergard, J., 1983. "Five Tablets from the Vicinity of Emar". *RA* 77, 11-43.

Hulin, P., 1963. "The Inscriptions on the Carved Throne-Base of Shalmaneser III". *Iraq* 25, 48-69.

Kienast, B., 1978. *Die altbabylonischen Briefe und Urkunden aus Kisurra.* Freiburger altorientalische Studien:2. Wiesbaden.

Kümmel, H. M., 1967. *Ersatzrituale für den hethitischen König.* StBoT:3. Wiesbaden.

Levine, E., 1973. *The Aramaic Version of Ruth.* AnBib:58. Rome.

McCarthy, D. J., 1981. See: Bibliography: Literature.

Moran, W. L., 1987. *Les lettres d'El-Amarna. Correspondance diplomatique du pharaon.* Paris.

Segal, J. F., 1983. *Aramaic Texts from North Saqqâra. With Some Fragments in Phoenician.* Texts from Excevations:6. London.

Siegelová, J., 1971. *Appu-Märchen und Ḫedammu-Mythus*. StBoT:14. Wiesbaden.

Snell, D. C., 1983-84. "The Cuneiform Tablet From El-Qiṭār". *AbrN* 22, 159-70.

Speiser, E. A., 1928-29. "New Kirkuk Documents Relating to Family Laws". *AASOR* 10, 1-73.

Thureau-Dangin, F., 1937. "Trois contrats de Ras Shamra". *Syria* 18, 245-55.

Waterman, L., 1930. *Royal Correspondence of the Assyrian Empire. Part II*. University of Michigan Studies. Humanistic Series:18. Ann Arbor.

Wiseman, D. J., 1958. "Abban and Alalaḫ". *JCS* 12, 124-9.

5.2 Literature

Abela, A., 1986. "Genesis 15: A Non-Genetic Approach". *MelT* 37, 9-40.

Ackroyd, P. R., 1975. "The Verb Love - ᵓĀHĒB in the David-Jonathan Narratives - A Footnote". *VT* 25, 213-4.

— et al. 1982. "יָדַע *jād*'". *TWAT* 3, 421-55.

Aharoni, Y., 1974. "The Horned Altar of Beer-sheba". *BA* 37, 2-6.

Albertz, R., See: Westermann, C. & R. Albertz, 1971.

Allwood, J., 1987. *Linguistic Communication as Action and Cooperation. A Study in Pragmatics*. 2 ed. Gothenburg Monographs in Linguistics:2. Göteborg.

Alonso Schökel, L., 1988. *A Manual of Hebrew Poetics*. Subsidia Biblica:11. Rome.

Alt, A., 1953. *Kleine Schriften zur Geschichte des Volkes Israel*. Vol. 2. München.

— 1966. *Essays on Old Testament History and Religion*. Oxford.

Alter, R., 1981. *The Art of Biblical Narrative*. New York.

Anbar, M., 1982. "Genesis 15: A Conflation of Two Deuteronomic Narratives". *JBL* 101, 39-55.

Andersen, F. I., 1974. *The Sentence in Biblical Hebrew*. Janua linguarum. Series Practica:231. The Hague.

Andersen, F. I. & D. N. Freedman, 1980. *Hosea. A New Translation with Introduction and Commentary*. AB:24. New York.

— 1989. *Amos. A New Translation with Introduction and Commentary*. AB:24A. New York.

Anderson, A. A., 1989. *2 Samuel*. WBC:11. Dallas.

Austin, J. L., 1975. *How to Do Things with Words*. 2 ed. Eds. J. O. Urmson & M. Sbisà. Oxford.

Avishur, Y., 1988. "Treaty Terminology in the Moses-Jethro Story (Exodus 18:1-12)". *Aula Orientalis* 6, 139-47.

Bar-Efrat, S., 1989. *Narrative Art in the Bible*. JSOTSup:70. Sheffield.

Barr, J., 1977. "Some Semantic Notes on the Covenant". In: *Beiträge zur alttestamentlichen Theologie*. (FS W. Zimmerli). Göttingen, 23-38.

Barrick, W., B., 1982. "The Meaning and Usage of RKB in Biblical Hebrew". *JBL* 101, 481-503.

Barthélemy, D., 1986. *Critique textuelle de l'Ancien Testament. Vol. 2. Isaïe, Jérémie, Lamentations.* OBO 50:2. Fribourg.

Baumgartner, W. et al., 1967-90. *Hebräisches und aramäisches Lexikon zum Alten Testament.* 4 vols. 3 ed. Leiden. (Abbr. *HALAT*).

— See: Koehler, L. & W. Baumgartner.

Beattie, D. R. G., 1971. "Kethibh and Qere in Ruth 4:5". *VT* 21, 490-4.

Becker, U., 1990. *Richterzeit und Königtum. Redaktionsgeschichtliche Studien zum Richterbuch.* BZAW:192. Berlin. 1990.

Begg, C., 1987. "The Birds in Genesis 15,9-10". *Biblische Notizen* 36, 7-11.

Bellefontaine, E., 1987. "Customary Law and Chieftainship: Judicial Aspects of 2 Samuel 14,4-21". *JSOT* 38, 47-72.

Ben-Barak, Z., 1979. "The Mizpah Covenant (1 Sam 10 25) - The Source of the Israelite Monarchic Covenant". *ZAW* 91, 30-43.

Berlin, A., 1983. *Poetics and Interpretation of Biblical Narrative.* Bible and Literature Series:9. Sheffield.

Bettenzoli, G., 1979. *Geist der Heiligkeit. Traditionsgeschichtliche Untersuchung des QDŠ-Begriffes im Buch Ezechiel.* Quaderni di semitistica:8. Firenze.

Black, H. C., 1979. *Black's Law Dictionary. Definitions of the Terms and Phrases of American and English Jurisprudence, Ancient and Modern.* 5 ed. St. Paul.

Blenkinsopp, J., 1983. *Wisdom and Law in the Old Testament. The Ordering of Life in Israel and Early Judaism.* Oxford Bible Series. Oxford.

Blum, E., 1984. *Die Komposition der Vätergeschichte.* WMANT:57. Neukirchen-Vluyn.

— 1990. *Studien zur Komposition des Pentateuch.* BZAW:189. Berlin.

Boecker, H. J., 1964. *Redeformen des Rechtslebens im Alten Testament.* WMANT:14. Neukirchen-Vluyn.

— 1974. "Anmerkungen zur Adoption im Alten Testament". *ZAW* 86, 86-9.

— 1984. *Recht und Gesetz im Alten Testament und im Alten Orient.* 2 ed. Neukirchen-Vluyn.

Bohlen, R., 1986. "Zur Sozialkritik des Propheten Amos". *TTZ* 95, 282-301.

Botterweck, G. J., 1971. "'Sie verkaufen den Unschuldigen um Geld'". *BibLeb* 12, 215-31.

Bovati, P., 1986. *Ristabilire la giustizia. Prozedure. vocabolario, orientamenti.* AnBib:110. Rome.

Brauner, R. A., 1974. "'To Grasp the hem' and 1 Samuel 15:27". *JANESCU* 6, 35-8.

Brekelmans, C. H. W., 1954. "Exodus XVII and the Origins of Yahwism in Israel". *OTS* 10, 215-24.

Brettler, M. Z., 1989. *God is King. Understanding an Israelite Metaphor.* JSOTSup:76. Sheffield.

Bright, J., 1965. *Jeremiah. A New Translation with Introduction and Commentary.* AB:21. New York.

Brinkman, J. A., 1968. *A Political History of Post-Kassite Babylonia 1158-722 B.C.* AnOr:43. Rome.

Brongers, H. A., 1982. "Die metaphorische Verwendung von Termini für die Kleidung von Göttern und Menschen in der Bibel und im Alten Orient". In: *Von Kanaan bis Kerala*. (FS J. P. M. van der Ploeg). AOAT:211. Neukirchen-Vluyn, 61-74.

Brownlee, W. H., 1986. *Ezekiel 1-19*. WBC:28. Waco.

Brueggemann, W., 1970. "Of the Same Flesh and Bone (Gn 2,23a)". *CBQ* 32, 532-42.

Campbell, A. F., 1986. *Of Prophets and Kings. A Late Ninth-Century Document (1 Samuel 1 - 2 Kings 10)*. CBQMS:17. Washington.

Campbell, E. F. Jr., 1975. *Ruth. A New Translation with Introduction and Commentary*. AB:7. New York.

Caqout, A., 1962. "L'alliance avec Abram (Genèse 15)". *Semitica* 12, 51-66.

Cardellini, I., 1981. *Die biblischen "Sklaven"-Gesetze im Lichte des keilschriftlichen Sklavenrechts. Ein Beitrag zur Tradition, Überlieferung und Redaktion der alttestamentlichen Rechtstexte*. BBB:55. Bonn.

Carena, O., 1981. *La communicazione non-verbale nella Bibbia. Un approccio semiotico al ciclo di Elia ed Eliseo:1 Re 16,29-2 Re 13,25*. Turin.

Carlson, R. A., 1964. *David the Chosen King. A Traditiohistorical Approach to the Second Book of Samuel*. Stockholm.

Carmichael, C. M., 1977. "A Ceremonial Crux: Removing a Man's Sandal as a Female Gesture of Contempt". *JBL* 96, 321-36.

— 1980. "'Treading' in the Book of Ruth". *ZAW* 92, 248-66.

Carroll, R., 1986. *Jeremiah. A Commentary*. OTL. London.

Cassin, E. M., 1987. *Le semblable et le différent. Symbolismes du pouvoir dans le proche-orient ancien*. Paris.

Childs, B. S., 1974. *Exodus. A Commentary*. OTL. London.

Clements, R. E., 1967. *Abraham and David. Genesis XV and its Meaning for Israelite Tradition*. SBT 2nd. ser:5. London.

— (ed.), 1989. *The World of Ancient Israel. Sociological, Anthropological and Political Perspectives*. Cambridge.

Clines, D. J. A., 1984. *Ezra, Nehemiah, Esther*. NCBC. Grand Rapids.

— 1989. *Job 1-20*. WBC:17. Dallas.

Cody, A., 1968. "Exodus 18,12: Jethro Accepts a Covenant with the Israelites". *Bib* 49, 153-66.

Cogan, M. & H. Tadmor, 1988. *II Kings. A New Translation with Introduction and Commentary*. AB:11. New York.

Condamin, A., 1936. *Le livre de Jérémie. Traduction et commentaire*. 3 ed. Paris.

Conrad, D., 1969. "Samuel und die Mari Propheten. Bemerkungen zu 1 Sam 15:27". In: *XVII Deutscher Orientalistentag*. Ed. W. Voight. ZDMG suppl. 1, 273-80.

Conroy, C., 1985. "A Literary Analysis of 1 Kings I 41-53, with Methodological Reflections". *VTSup* 36, 54-66.

Craigie, P. C., 1976. *The Book of Deuteronomy*. NICOT. Grand Rapids.

— 1983. *Psalms 1-50*. WBC:19. Waco.

Crown, A. D., 1963-64. "Aposiopesis in the O.T. and the Hebrew Conditional Oath". *AbrN* 4, 96-111.

Dahood, M., 1966. *Psalms I. 1-50. Introduction, Translation and Notes.* AB:16. New York.

Daube, D., 1947. *Studies in Biblical Law.* Cambridge.

Davies, E. W., 1983. "Ruth IV 5 and the Duties of the GŌʾĒL". *VT* 33, 231-4.

Dearman, J. A., 1988. *Property Rights in the Eighth-Century Prophets. The Conflict and its Background.* SBLDS:106. Atlanta.

Deroy, L., 1961. "Un symbolisme juridique de la chaussure". *L'Antiquité Classique* 30, 371-80.

DeVries, L. F., 1987. "Cult Stands. A Bewildering Variety of Shapes and Sizes". *BARev* 13, 27-37.

DeVries, S. J., 1975. *Yesterday, Today and Tomorrow. Time and History in the Old Testament.* London.

— 1985. *1 Kings.* WBC:12. Waco.

Dhorme, É., 1923. *L'Emploi métaphorique des noms de parties du corps en hébreu et en akkadien.* Paris. (Reprint 1963).

Dommerhausen, W., 1984. "כָּנָף *kānap*". *TWAT* 4, 243-6.

Donner, H., 1969. "Adoption oder Legitimation? Erwägungen zur Adoption im alten Testament auf dem Hintergrund der altorientalischen Rechte". *OrAnt* 8, 87-117.

Doré, J., 1981. "La rencontre Abraham-Melchisédech et le problème de l'unité littéraire de Genèse 14". In: *De la Tôrah au Messie* (FS H. Cazelles). Paris, 75-95.

Draffkorn, A. E., 1957. "ILĀNI/ELOHIM". *JBL* 76, 216-24.

Draffkorn Kilmer, A., 1974. "Symbolic Gestures in Akkadian Contracts from Alalakh and Ugarit". *JAOS* 94, 177-83.

Driver, G. R., 1937-38. "Linguistic and Textual Problems: Jeremiah". *JQR* 28, 97-129.

Durham, J. I., 1987. *Exodus.* WBC:3. Waco.

Edelman, D. V., 1991. *King Saul in the Historiography of Judah.* JSOTSup:121. Sheffield.

Eilberg-Schwartz, H., 1990. *The Savage in Judaism. An Anthropology of Israelite Religion and Ancient Judaism.* Bloomington.

Eisenhut, W., 1964. "Clavus". *KP* 1, 1220-1.

Eitrem, S., 1947. "A Purificatory Rite and Some Allied *rites de passage*". *Symbolae Osloenses* 25, 36-53.

Eslinger, L. M., 1985. *Kingship of God in Crisis.* Bible and Literature Series:10. Sheffield.

Falk, Z. W., 1959. "Exodus 21:6". *VT* 9, 86-8.

— 1959a. "Gestures Expressing Affirmation". *JSS* 4, 268-9.

— 1964. *Hebrew Law in Biblical Times. An Introduction.* Jerusalem.

— 1967. "Hebrew Legal Terms: II". *JSS* 12, 241-4.

Feigin, S., 1931. "Some Cases of Adoption in Israel". *JBL* 50, 186-200.

Fensham, F. C., 1959. "New Light on Exodus 21₆ and 22₇ from the Laws of Eshnunna". *JBL* 78, 160-1.

— 1964. "The Treaty Between Israel and the Gibeonites". *BA* 27, 96-100.

— 1964a. "Did a Treaty between the Israelites and the Kenites Exist?" *BASOR* 175, 51-4.

— 1982. *The Books of Ezra and Nehemiah*. NICOT. Grand Rapids.

Fiensy, D., 1987. "Using the Nuer Culture of Africa in Understanding the Old Testament: An Evaluation". *JSOT* 38, 73-83.

Finet, A., 1969. "Les symboles du cheveu, du bord du vêtement et de l'ongle en Mésopotamie". In: *Eschatologie et cosmologie*. Eds. A. Abel et al. Annales du Centre d'Étude des Religions:3. Bruxelles, 101-30.

Firmage, E. B. et al. (ed.), 1990. *Religion and Law. Biblical-Judaic and Islamic Perspectives*. Winona Lake.

Firth, R., 1973. *Symbols. Public and Private*. London.

Fitzmyer, J. A., 1971. *The Genesis Apocryphon of Qumran Cave I. A Commentary*. 2 ed. BibOr 18:A. Rome.

Fohrer, G., 1968. *Die symbolischen Handlungen der Propheten*. 2 ed. ATANT:54. Zürich. 1968.

Fokkelman, J. P., 1981. *Narrative Art and Poetry in the Books of Samuel. A Full Interpretation Based on Stylistic and Structural Analyses. Vol. I: King David (2 Sam. 9-20 & 1 Kings 1-2)*. SSN:20. Assen.

— 1990. *Narrative Art and Poetry in the Books of Samuel. A Full Interpretation Based on Stylistic and Structural Analyses. Vol. III: Throne and City (II Sam. 2-8 & 21-24)*. SSN:27. Assen.

Fowler, W. W., 1899. *The Roman Festivals of the Period of the Republic. An Introduction to the Study of the Religion of the Romans*. New York. (Reprint 1969).

Frankena, R., 1965. "The Vassal-Treaties of Esarhaddon and the Dating of Deuteronomy". *OTS* 14, 122-54.

— 1972. "Some Remarks on the Semitic Background of Chapters 29-31 of the Book of Genesis". *OTS* 17, 53-64.

Freedman, D. N. See: Andersen, F. I. & D. N. Freedman, 1980 and 1989.

Freedman, D. N. & B. E. Willoughby, 1986. "עִבְרִי *ʿibrî*". *TWAT* 5, 1039-56.

Freedman, R. D., 1976. "'Put Your Hand Under My Thigh' - The Patriarchal Oath". *BARev* 2, 3-4, 42.

GAG. See: Soden, W. von.

Galling, K., 1956. "Die Ausrufung des Namens als Rechtakt in Israel". *TLZ* 81, 65-70.

Gaster, T.H., 1969. *Myth, Legend and Custom in the Old Testament*. New York.

Geertz, C., 1973. *The Interpretation of Cultures*. New York.

Gerleman, G., 1965. *Ruth. Das Hohelied*. BKAT:18. Neukirchen-Vluyn.

Gesenius, W., 1910. *Gesenius' Hebrew Grammar as Edited and Enlarged by the Late E. Kautsch*. Transl. A. E. Cowley. 2 English ed. Oxford. (Abbr. GKC).

Giesebrecht, F., 1907. *Das Buch Jeremia*. 2 ed. HKAT III 2:1. Göttingen.

Giesen, G., 1981. *Die Wurzel שׁבע "schwören" . Eine semasiologische Studie zum Eid im Alten Testament*. BBB:56. Bonn.

Gitin, S., 1989. "Tel Miqne-Ekron: A Type-Site for the Inner Coastal Plain in the Iron Age II Period". In: *Recent Excavations in Israel: Studies in Iron Age Archeology*. AASOR:49. Winona Lake, 23-55.

GKC. See: Gesenius, W.

Goff, B. L., 1963. *Symbols of Prehistoric Mesopotamia*. New Haven.

Goldingay, J. E., 1989. *Daniel*. WBC:30. Dallas.

Gordis, R. A., 1974. "Love, Marriage and Business in the Book of Ruth: A Chapter in Hebrew Customary Law". In: *A Light Unto My Path* (FS J. M. Myers). Philadelphia, 241-64.

Gordon, C. H., 1935. "אלהים in its Reputed Meaning of *Rulers, Judges*". *JBL* 54, 139-44.

Gordon, R. P., 1980. "David's Rise and Saul's Demise: Narrative Analogy in 1 Samuel 24-26". *TynBul* 31, 37-64.

— 1986. *I and II Samuel. A Commentary*. Grand Rapids.

Gorman, F. H. Jr., 1990. *The Ideology of Ritual. Space, Time and Status in the Priestly Theology*. JSOTSup:91. Sheffield.

Gow, M. D., 1983. *Structure, Theme and Purpose for the Translation of the Book of Ruth*. Unpubl. diss. Cambridge.

— 1984. "The Significance of Literary Structure for the Translation of the Book of Ruth". *BT* 35, 309-20.

— 1990. "*Ruth quoque* - a Coquette? (Ruth 4:5)". *TynBul* 41, 302-11.

Graesser, C. F., 1972. "Standing Stones in Ancient Palestine". *BA* 35, 34-63.

Gray, J., 1967. *Joshua, Judges and Ruth*. NCBC. London.

Greenberg, M., 1959. "The Biblical Conception of Asylum". *JBL* 78, 125-32.

— 1983. *Ezekiel 1-20. A New Translation with Introduction and Commentary*. AB:22. New York.

Greenfield, J. C., 1986. "An Ancient Treaty Ritual and its Targumic Echo". In: *Salvacion en la palabra. Targum-Derash-Berith*. (FS A. D. Macho). Madrid, 391-7.

Greengus, S., 1966. "Old Babylonian Marriage Ceremonies and Rites". *JCS* 20, 55-72.

— 1969. "The Old Babylonian Marriage Contract". *JAOS* 89, 505-32.

Greenstein, E. L., 1982. "'To Grasp the Hem' in Ugaritic Literature". *VT* 32, 217-8.

Groß, W. H., 1964. "Nagel". *KP* 3, 1562-3.

Gruber, M. I., 1975. "Akkadian laban appi in the Light of Art and Literature". *JANESCU* 7, 73-83.

— 1978. "The Tragedy of Cain and Abel: A Case of Depression". *JQR* 69, 90-1.

— 1980. *Aspects of Nonverbal Communication in the Ancient Near East*. 2 vols. Studia Pohl 12:1-2. Rome.

— 1983. "The Many Faces of Hebrew ns' pnym, Lift Up the Face". *ZAW* 95, 252-60.

Gunn, D. M., 1978. *The Story of King David. Genre and Interpretation*. JSOTSup:6. Sheffield.

Güterbock, H. G., 1951. "The Song of Ullikummi. Revised Text of the Hittite Version of a Hurrian Myth". *JCS* 5, 135-61.

Ha, J., 1989. *Genesis 15. A Theological Compendium of Pentateuchal History.* BZAW:181. Berlin.

Habel, N. C., 1985. *The Book of Job. A Commentary.* OTL. London.

HALAT. See: Baumgartner, W. et al.

Hallo, W. H. & W. K. Simpson, 1971. *The Ancient Near East. A History.* New York.

Halpern, B., 1981. *The Constitution of the Monarchy in Israel.* HSM:25. Chico.

Hamilton, V. P., 1990. *The Book of Genesis. Chapters 1-17.* NICOT. Grand Rapids.

Hamp, V., 1977. "חֲלָצִים *ḥᵃlāṣajim*". *TWAT* 2, 1008-11.

Hanell, K., 1946. *Das altrömische eponyme Amt.* Lund.

Hartley, J. E., 1988. *The Book of Job.* NICOT. Grand Rapids.

Hasel, G. F., 1981. "The Meaning of the Animal Rite in Genesis 15". *JSOT* 19, 61-78.

— 1984. "כָּרַת *kāraṯ*". *TWAT* 4, 355-67.

Haulotte, E., 1966. *Symbolique du vêtement selon la Bible.* Lyon.

Hayes, J. H. & P. K. Hooker, 1988. *A New Chronology for the Kings of Israel and Judah and Its Implications for Biblical History and Literature.* Atlanta.

Held, M., 1970. "Philological Notes on the Mari Covenant Rituals". *BASOR* 200, 32-40.

Henninger, J., 1953. "Was bedeutet die rituelle Teilung eines Tieres in zwei Hälften? Zur Deutung von Gen. 15, 9 ff." *Bib* 34, 344-53.

Hillers, D. R., 1964. *Treaty-Curses and the Old Testament Prophets.* BibOr:16. Rome.

— 1990. "*Rite*: Ceremonies of Law and Treaty in the Ancient Near East". In: Firmage, 351-64.

Hobbs, T. R., 1985. *2 Kings.* WBC:13. Waco.

Hoebel, E. A., 1954. *The Law of Primitive Man. A Study in Comparative Legal Dynamics.* Cambridge, Mass.

Hoffner, H. A. Jr., 1968. "Birth and Name-Giving in Hittite Texts". *JNES* 27, 198-203.

— 1969. "Some Contributions of Hittitology to Old Testament Study". *TynBul* 20, 27-55.

— 1973. "The Hittites and Hurrians". In: *Peoples of OT Times.* Ed. D. J. Wiseman. Oxford, 197-228.

Hofmann, I. & A. Vorbichler, 1981. "'Gottes Bund mit Abraham' in religionswissenschaftlicher Sicht". *ZMR* 65, 139-47.

Hoftijzer, J., 1956. *Die Verheissungen an die drei Erzväter.* Leiden.

Høgenhaven, J., 1990. *Den gamle pagt. En introduktion til den nyere debat om pagten i det Gamle Testamente.* Tekst og Tolkning:8. Århus. (Cop. 1989).

Holladay, W. L., 1989. *Jeremiah 2.* Hermeneia. Minneapolis.

Hönig, H. W., 1957. *Die Bekleidung des Hebräers. Eine biblisch-archäologische Untersuchung.* Zürich.

Hooker, P. K., See: Hayes, J. H. & P. K. Hooker, 1988.

Horn, K., 1977. "Das Kleid als Ausdruck der Persönlichkeit: Ein Beitrag zum Identitätsproblem im Volksmärchen". *Fabula* 18, 75-104.

Horst, F., 1957. "Der Eid im Alten Testament". *EvT* 17, 366-84.

Hoskisson, P., 1992. "The *Nīšum* 'Oath' in Mari". In: *Mari in Retrospect. Fifty Years of Mari and Mari Studies*. Ed. G. D. Young. Winona Lake, 203-10.

Hossfeld, J.-L., 1982. *Der Dekalog. Seine späten Fassungen, die originale Komposition und seine Vorstufen*. OBO:45. Göttingen.

Houtman, C., 1990. *Het altaar als asielplaats. Beschouwingen over en naar aanleiding van Exodus 21:12-14*. Kamper Cahiers:70. Kampen.

Höver-Johag, I., 1982. "טוֹב *ṭôb*". *TWAT* 3, 315-39.

Hubbard, R. L. Jr., 1988. *The Book of Ruth*. NICOT. Grand Rapids.

— 1988a. "Ruth IV 17: A New Solution". *VT* 38, 293-301.

Huehnergard, J., 1985. "Biblical Notes on Some New Akkadian Texts from Emar (Syria)". *CBQ* 47, 428-34.

Ishida, T., 1977. *The Royal Dynasties in Ancient Israel. A Study on the Formation and Development of Royal-Dynastic Ideology*. BZAW:142. Berlin.

— (ed.), 1982. *Studies in the Period of David and Solomon and Other Essays*. Winona Lake.

Jackson, B. S., 1972. *Theft in Early Jewish Law*. Oxford.

— 1988. "Biblical Laws of Slavery: A Comparative Approach". In: *Slavery and Other Forms of Unfree Labour*. Ed. L. J. Archer. London, 86-101.

— 1989. "Ideas of Law and Legal Administration: A Semiotic Approach". In: Clements, 185-202.

— 1990. "Legalism and Spirituality. Historical, Philosophical, and Semiotic Notes on Legislators, Adjudicators, and Subjects". In: Firmage, 243-61.

Jacobsen, T., 1987. "Pictures and Pictorial Language (The Burney Relief)". In: *Figurative Language in the Ancient Near East*. Eds. M. Mindlin et al. London, 1-11.

Jakob-Rost, L., 1965. "Beiträge zum hethitischen Hofceremoniell (IBoT I 36)". *Mitteilungen des Instituts für Orientforschung* 11, 165-225.

Janzen, J. G., 1973. *Studies in the Text of Jeremiah*. HSM:6. Cambridge, Mass.

Jeremias, J., 1977. *Theophanie. Die Geschichte einer alttestamentlichen Gattung*. 2 ed. WMANT:10. Neukirchen-Vluyn.

Jirku, A., 1917-18. "Zur magischen Bedeutung der Kleidung in Israel". *ZAW* 37, 109-25.

Jobling, D., 1986. *The Sense of Biblical Narrative: Structural Analyses in the Hebrew Bible II*. JSOTSup:39. Sheffield.

Jones, G. H., 1984. *1 and 2 Kings*. 2 vols. NCBC. London.

— 1990. *The Nathan Narratives*. JSOTSup:80. Sheffield.

Jonge, M. de, 1975. *Studies on the Testaments of the Twelve Patriarchs. Text and Interpretation*. SVTP:3. Leiden.

Joüon, P. P., 1935. "Notes de lexicographie hébraique. VI. כָּנָף 'aile', employé figurément". *Bib* 16, 201-4.

— 1953. *Ruth: Commentaire philologique et exégétique*. Rome.

— 1923. *Grammaire de l'hébreu biblique*. Rome.

Jüngling, H.-W., 1981. *Richter 19 - Ein Plädoyer für das Königtum*. AnBib:84. Rome.

Kalluveettil, P., 1982. *Declaration and Covenant. Formulae from the Old Testament and the Ancient Near East.* AnBib:88. Rome.

Kapelrud, A. S., 1982. "The Interpretation of Jeremiah 34, 18ff." *JSOT* 22, 138-40.

Kautzsch, E. See: Gesenius, W. & E. Kautzsch, 1910.

KB. See: Koehler, L. & W. Baumgartner.

Keel, O., 1981. "Zeichen der Verbundenheit. Zur Vorgeschichte und Bedeutung der Forderungen von Deuteronomium 6, 8f und Par." In: *Mélanges Dominique Barthélemy* (FS D. Barthélemy). OBO:38. Freiburg, 159-240.

— "Symbolik des Fußes im Alten Testament und seiner Umwelt". *Orthopädische Praxis* 18, 530-8.

— 1984. *Die Welt der altorientalischen Bildsymbolik und das Alte Testament. Am Beispiel der Psalmen.* 3 ed. Darmstadt. (Unchanged from 2 ed. 1977).

Keil, C. F., 1873. *Jeremiah, Lamentations.* Grand Rapids. (Reprint 1986).

Kellermann, D., 1982. "יָרַק *jāraq*". *TWAT* 3, 948-53.

Kessler, R., 1989. "Die angeblichen Kornhändler von Amos VIII 4-7". *VT* 39, 13-22.

Kittay, E. F., 1987. *Metaphor. Its Cognitive Force and Linguistic Structure.* Oxford.

Klein, R. W., 1983. *1 Samuel.* WBC:10. Waco.

Knutson, F. B., 1975. "Political and Foreign Affairs". In: *Ras Shamra Parallels. The Texts from Ugarit and the Hebrew Bible.* Vol. 2. Ed. L. R. Fisher. AnOr:50. Rome, 109-29.

Köhler, L., 1909. "Die Adoptionsform von Rt 4[16]". *ZAW* 29, 312-4.

Koehler, L. & W. Baumgartner, 1953. *Lexicon in Veteris Testamenti libros.* 1 ed. Leiden. (Abbr. *KB*).

Korpel, M. C. A., 1990. *A Rift in the Clouds. Ugaritic and Hebrew Descriptions of the Divine.* Ugaritisch-biblische Literatur:8. Münster.

Koschaker, P., 1940. "Kleidersymbolik in Keilschriftrechten". In: *Actes du XXe congrès international des orientalistes, Bruxelles 5-10 Sept. 1938.* Louvain, 117-9.

— 1942. "Persönlichkeitszeichen". *Forschungen und Fortschritte* 18, 246-8.

Kraus, H.-J., 1978. *Psalmen. 1. Teilband. Psalmen 1-59.* 2 ed. BKAT 15:1. Neukirchen-Vluyn.

Kruger, A., 1984. "The Hem of the Garment in Marriage. The Meaning of the Symbolic Gesture in Ruth 3:9 and Ezek. 16:8". *JNSL* 12, 79-86.

— 1986. "The Symbolic Significance of the Hem (*KĀNĀF*) in 1 Samuel 15.27". In: *Text and Context.* (FS F. C. Fensham). JSOTSup:48. Sheffield, 104-16.

— 1988. "Prophetic Imagery. On Metaphors and Similes in the Book Hosea". *JNSL* 14, 143-51.

— 1989. "On Non-Verbal Communication in the Baal Epic". *Journal for Semitics* 1, 54-69.

Kuan, J. K., 1990. "Third Kingdoms 5.1 and Israelite-Tyrian Relations during the Reign of Solomon". *JSOT* 46, 31-46.

Kühne, C., 1986. "Hethitisch *auli-* und einige Aspekte altanatolischer Opferpraxis". *ZA* 76, 85-117.

Kutsch, E., 1963. *Salbung als Rechtakt im Alten Testament und im Alten Orient.* BZAW:87. Berlin.

— 1973. *Verheißung und Gesetz. Untersuchungen zum sogennanten 'Bund' im Alten Testament.* BZAW:131. Berlin.

— 1979. "Wie David König wurde. Beobachtungen zu 2. Sam 2,4a und 5,3". In: *Textgemäß. Aufsätze und Beiträge zur Hermeneutik des Alten Testaments.* (FS E. Würthwein). Göttingen, 75-93.

— 1982. "יבם *jbm*". *TWAT* 3, 393-400.

Lacheman, E. R., 1937. "Note on Ruth 4 7-8". *JBL* 56, 53-6.

Lang, B., 1981. "Sklaven und Unfreie im Buch Amos (II 6, VIII 6)". *VT* 31, 482-8.

Leeuwen, C. van, 1973. "Die Partikel אם". *OTS* 18, 15-48.

— 1976. "עֵד *ʿēd* Zeuge". *THAT* 2, 209-21.

Leggett, D. A., 1974. *The Levirate and Goel Institutions in the Old Testament with Special Attention to the Book of Ruth.* Cherry Hill.

Lehmann, M. R., 1969. "Biblical Oaths". *ZAW* 81, 74-91.

Lemche, N. P., 1975. "The 'Hebrew Slave'. Comments on the Slave Law Ex. xxi 2-11". *VT* 25, 129-44.

— 1979. "Hebrew as a National Name for Israel". *ST* 33, 1-23.

— 1985. *Early Israel. Anthropological and Historical Studies on the Israelite Society Before the Monarchy.* VTSup:37. Leiden.

Levine, B. A., 1974. *In the Presence of the Lord. A Study of Cult and Some Cultic Terms in Ancient Israel.* SJLA:5. Leiden.

— 1983. "In Praise of the Israelite *mišpaḥā*: Legal Themes in the Book of Ruth". In: *The Quest For the Kingdom of God.* (FS G. E. Mendenhall). Winona Lake, 95-106.

Levy, L., 1918. "Die Schuhsymbolik im jüdischen Ritus". *MGWJ* 62, 178-85.

Liedke, G., 1971. "אֹזֶן *ʾōzæn* Ohr". *THAT* 1, 95-8.

Lindström, F., 1983. *God and the Origin of Evil. A Contextual Analysis of Alleged Monistic Evidence in the Old Testament.* ConBOT:21. Lund.

Lipiński, E., 1970. "'Se battre la cuisse'". *VT* 20, 495.

— 1990. "קָנָה *qānāh*". *TWAT* 7:1-2, 63-71.

Loewenstamm, S. E., 1968. "Zur Traditionsgeschichte des Bundes zwischen den Stücken". *VT* 18, 500-6.

Lohfink, N., 1967. *Die Landverheißung als Eid. Eine Studie zu Gn 15.* SBS:28. Stuttgart.

— 1982. "חָפְשִׁי *hopšî*". *TWAT* 3, 123-8.

Long, B. O., 1987. "Framing Repititions in Biblical Historiography". *JBL* 106, 385-99.

Longacre, R. E., 1989. *Joseph: A Story of Divine Providence. A Text Theoretical and Textlinguistic Analysis of Genesis 37 and 39-48.* Winona Lake.

Loretz, O., 1984. *Habiru-Hebräer. Eine sozio-linguistische Studie über die Herkunft des Gentiliziums ʿibrî vom Appellativum ḫabiru.* BZAW:160. Berlin.

Lust, J., 1967. "Ez. XX, 4-26 une parodie de l'histoire religieuse d'Israël". *ETL* 43, 488-527.

— 1969. *Traditie, redactie en kerygma bij Ezechiel. Een analyse van Ez. XX, 1-26*. Verhandelingen van de koninklijke vlaamse academie voor wetenschappen, letteren en schone kunsten van België. Klasse der letteren. Jaargang XXXI:65. Brussel.

Lyons, J., 1968. *Introduction to Theoretical Linguistics*. Cambridge.

— 1977. *Semantics*. 2 vols. Cambridge.

Lys, D., 1954. "L'onction dans la Bible". *ETR* 29:3, 3-54.

Löhr, M., 1930. *Das Asylwesen im Alten Testament*. Schriften der Königsberger Gelehrten Gesellschaft 7:3. Halle.

Malina, B. J., 1986. *Christian Origins and Cultural Anthropology: Practical Models for Biblical Interpretation*. Atlanta.

Mallowan, M. E. L., 1966. *Nimrud and Its Remains*. Vol. 2. London.

Malul, M., 1985. "More on PAḤAD YIṢḤĀQ (Genesis XXXI 42, 53) and the Oath by the Thigh". *VT* 35, 192-200.

— 1985a. "The *bukannum*-Clause – Relinquishment of Rights by Previous Right Holder". *ZA* 75, 66-77.

— 1985b. "Studies in Biblical Legal Symbolism – A Discussion of the Terms *kānāph, chēq*, and *ḥoṣen/ḥeṣen*. Their Meaning and Legal Usage in the Bible and the Ancient Near East". *Shnaton* 9, 191-210. (Hebr.)

— 1986. "'Sissiktu' and 'sikku' – Their Meaning and Function". *BO* 43, 19-37.

— 1987. "Touching the Sexual Organs as an Oath Ceremony in an Akkadian Letter". *VT* 37, 491-2.

— 1987a. "gag-rú: sikkatam maḫāṣum/retûm. 'To Drive in the Nail'. An Act of Posting a Public Notice". *OrAnt* 26, 17-35.

— 1988. *Studies in Mesopotamian Legal Symbolism*. AOAT:221. Neukirchen-Vluyn.

— 1990. *The Comparative Method in Ancient Near Eastern and Biblical Legal Studies*. AOAT:227. Neukirchen-Vluyn.

— 1990a. "Adoption of Foundlings in the Bible and Mesopotamian Documents. A Study of Some Legal Metaphors in Ezekiel 16.1-7". *JSOT* 46, 97-126.

Martin, W. J., 1969. "'Dischronologized' Narrative in the OT". *VTSup* 17, 179-86.

Masson, O., 1950. "A propos d'un rituel hittite pour la lustration d'une armée: le rite de purification par le passage entre les deux parties d'une victime". *RHR* 137, 5-25.

Mayes, A. D. H., 1979. *Deuteronomy*. NCBC. London.

Mazar, A., 1990. *Archeology of the Land of the Bible 10,000–586 B.C.E.* The Anchor Bible Reference Library. New York.

McAlpine, T. H., 1987. *Sleep, Divine and Human, in the Old Testament*. JSOTSup:38. Sheffield.

McCarter, P. K. Jr., 1980. *1 Samuel. A New Translation with Introduction, Notes and Commentary*. AB:8. New York.

— 1984. *2 Samuel. A New Translation with Introduction, Notes and Commentary*. AB:9. New York.

McCarthy, D. J., 1964. "Three Covenants in Genesis". *CBQ* 26, 179-89.
— 1981. *Treaty and Covenant. A Study in Form in the Ancient Oriental Documents and in the Old Testament.* 3 ed. AnBib:21A. Rome.
— 1982. "Compact and Kingship: Stimuli for Hebrew Covenant Thinking". In: Ishida, 75-92.
McCree, W. T., 1926. "The Covenant Meal in the Old Testament". *JBL* 45, 120-8.
McKane, W., 1961-62. "Ruth and Boaz". *Transactions of the Glasgow University Oriental Society* 19, 29-40.
— 1970. *Proverbs. A New Approach.* OTL. London.
Mendelsohn, I., 1959. "A Ugaritic Parallel to the Adoption of Ephraim and Manasseh". *IEJ* 9, 180-3.
Mendenhall, G. E., 1990. "The Suzerainty Treaty Structure: Thirty Years Later". In: Firmage, 85-100.
Mettinger, T. N. D., 1976. *King and Messiah. The Civil and Sacral Legitimation of the Israelite Kings.* ConBOT:8. Lund.
— 1988. *In Search of God. The Meaning and Message of the Everlasting Names.* Philadelphia.
Milgrom, J., 1976. *Cult and Conscience. The Asham and the Priestly Doctrine of Repentance.* SJLA:18. Leiden.
— 1983. *Studies in Cultic Theology and Terminology.* SJLA:36. Leiden.
Miller, P. D. Jr., 1984. "Sin and Judgment in Jeremiah 34:17-19". *JBL* 103, 611-3.
Minokami, Y., 1989. *Die Revolution des Jehu.* GTA:38. Göttingen.
Montgomery, J. A., 1927. *A Critical and Exegetical Commentary on the Book of Daniel.* ICC. Edinburgh.
Moor, J. C. de, 1986. "The Poetry of the Book of Ruth (Part II)". *Or* 55, 16-46.
— 1990. *The Rise of Yahwism. The Roots of Israelite Monotheism.* BETL:91. Leuven.
Moore, S. F. & B. G. Myerhoff (eds.), 1977. *Secular Ritual.* Assen.
Muffs, Y., 1969. *Studies in the Aramaic Legal Papyri from Elephantine.* Studia et Documenta:8. Leiden.
— 1982. "Abraham the Noble Warrior: Patriarchal Politics and Laws of War in Ancient Israel". *JJS* 33, 81-107.
Muhly, J. D., 1965. Review: "M. C. Astour. Hellenosemitica. 1965". *JAOS* 85, 585-8.
Munn-Rankin, J. M., 1956. "Diplomacy in Western Asia in the Early Second Millenium B.C." *Iraq* 18, 68-110.
Myerhoff, B. G., 1977. "We Don't Wrap Herring in a Printed Page: Fusion, Fictions and Continuity in Secular Ritual". In: Moore & Myerhoff, 199-224.
— See: Moore, S. F. & B. G. Myerhoff, 1977.
Na'aman, N., 1986. "Ḫabiru and Hebrews: The Transfer of a Social Term to the Literary Sphere". *JNES* 45, 271-88.
Nacht, J., 1915-16. "The Symbolism of the Shoe with Special Reference to Jewish Sources". *JQR* 6, 1-2.

Neufeld, E., 1944. *Ancient Hebrew Marriage Laws. With Special References to General Semitic Laws and Customs.* London.

Nicholson, E. W., 1986. *God and His People.* Oxford.

Nicolsky, N. M., 1930. "Das Asylrecht in Israel". *ZAW* 48, 146-75.

Niehr, H., 1987. *Rechtsprechung in Israel. Untersuchungen zur Geschichte der Gerichtsorganisation im Alten Testament.* SBS:130. Stuttgart.

— 1990. *Der höchste Gott. Alttestamentlicher JHWH-Glaube im Kontext syrisch-kanaanäischer Religion des 1. Jahrtausends v. Chr.* BZAW:190. Berlin.

Nilsson, M. P., 1906. *Griechische Feste von religiöser Bedeutung.* Stuttgart. (Reprint 1957).

North, C. R., 1932. "The Religious Aspects of Hebrew Kingship". *ZAW* 50, 8-38.

Noth, M., 1930. *Das System der zwölf Stämme Israels.* BWANT:52, Stuttgart.

— 1950. "Gott, König, Volk im Alten Testament. Eine methodologische Auseinandersetzung mit einer gegenwärtigen Forschungsrichtung". *ZTK* 47, 157-91.

— 1957. "Das alttestamentliche Bundschließen im Lichte eines Mari-Textes". In: *Gesammelte Studien zum Alten Testament.* Theologische Bücherei:6. München, 142-54.

— 1968. *Könige. 1.1-16. 1 Teilband.* BKAT 9:1. Neukirchen-Vluyn.

Nyberg, H. S., 1952. *Hebreisk grammatik.* Stockholm.

O'Connor, M. See: Waltke, B. K. & M. O'Connor, 1990.

Oelsner, J., 1960. *Benennung und Funktion der Körperteile im hebräischen Alten Testament.* Unpubl. diss. Leipzig.

Osumi, Y., 1991. *Die Kompositionsgeschichte des Bundesbuches Exodus 20,22b-23,33.* OBO:105. Freiburg.

Otto, E., 1988. *Wandel der Rechtsbegründungen in der Gesellschaftsgeschichte des antiken Israel. Eine Rechtsgeschichte des "Bundesbuches" Ex XX 22 – XXIII 13.* StudBib:3. Leiden.

— 1991. *Körperverletzungen in den Keilschriftrechten und im Alten Testament. Studien zum Rechtstransfer im Alten Testament.* AOAT:226. Neukirchen-Vluyn.

Pardee, D., 1977. "A New Ugaritic Letter". *BO* 34, 3-20.

Parker, S. B., 1988. "The Birth Announcement". In: *Ascribe to the Lord. Biblical and Other Studies in Memory of Peter C. Craigie.* JSOTSup:67. Sheffield, 133-49.

Patrick, D., 1985. *Old Testament Law.* Atlanta.

Paul, S. M., 1970. *Studies in the Book of the Covenant in the Light of Cuneiform and Biblical Law.* VTSup:18. Leiden.

— 1979-80. "Adoption formulae: A Study of Cuneiform and Biblical Legal Clauses". *Maarav* 2, 173-85.

Petersen, D. L., 1977. "Covenant Ritual: A Traditio-Historical Perspective". *BR* 22, 7-18.

Phillips, A., 1970. *Ancient Israel's Criminal Law.* Oxford.

— 1973. "Some Aspects of Family Law in Pre-Exilic Israel". *VT* 23, 349-61.

— 1984. "The Laws of Slavery: Exodus 21.2-11". *JSOT* 30, 51-66.

— 1986. "The Book of Ruth - Deception and Shame". *JJS* 37, 1-17.

Plöger, O., 1984. *Sprüche Salomos. (Proverbia)*. BKAT:17. Neukirchen-Vluyn.

Polzin, R., 1969. "*HWQY'* and Covenantal Institutions in Early Israel". *HTR* 62, 227-40.

— 1989. *Samuel and the Deuteronomist. A Literary Study of the Deuteronomic History. Part Two. 1 Samuel*. San Francisco.

Porten, B., 1978. "The Scroll of Ruth: A Rhetorical Study". *Gratz College Annual* 7, 23-49.

Potts, D. T., 1990. "Notes on Some Horned Buildings in Iran, Mesopotamia and Arabia". *RA* 84, 33-40.

Reventlow, H. G., 1963. "Kultisches Recht im Alten Testament". *ZTK* 60, 267-304.

Reviv, H., 1989. *The Elders in Ancient Israel. A Study of a Biblical Institution*. Jerusalem.

Richter, H.-F., 1979. "'Auf den Knien eines andern gebären'? (Zur Deutung von Gen 30:3 und 50:23)". *ZAW* 91, 436-7.

— 1983. "Zum Levirat im Buch Ruth". *ZAW* 95, 123-6.

Ricoeur, P., 1981. *Hermeneutics and the Human Sciences. Essays on Language, Action and Interpretation*. Ed. J. B. Thompson. Cambridge.

Riesener, I., 1979. *Der Stamm עבד im Alten Testament. Eine Wortuntersuchung unter Berücksichtigung neuerer sprachwissenschaftlicher Methoden*. BZAW:149. Berlin. (Cop. 1978).

Rowley, H. H., 1947. "The Marriage of Ruth". *HTR* 40, 77-99.

— 1976. *Job*. 2 ed. NCBC. London.

Rudolph, W., 1962. *Das Buch Ruth. Das Hohe Lied. Die Klagelieder*. KAT 17:1-3. Gütersloh.

— 1968. *Jeremia*. HAT:12. 3 ed. Tübingen.

— 1971. *Joel - Amos - Obadja - Jona*. KAT 13:2. Gütersloh.

Rummel, S., 1976. "Clothes Maketh the Man - An Insight from Ancient Ugarit". *BARev* 2, 6-8.

Ruprecht, E., 1980. "Exodus 24,9-11 als Beispiel lebendiger Erzähltradition aus der Zeit des babylonischen Exils". In: *Werden und Wirken des Alten Testaments*. (FS C. Westermann). Göttingen, 138-73.

Rühlmann, G., 1971. "'Deine Feinde fallen unter deine Sohlen'". *Wissenschaftliche Zeitschrift*. 20, 62-84.

Römer, T., 1990. *Israels Väter. Untersuchungen zur Väterthematik im Deuteronomium und in der deuteronomistischen Tradition*. OBO:99. Freiburg.

Sæbø, M. et al., 1982. "יום *jôm* ". *TWAT* 3, 559-86.

Sakenfeld, K. D., 1978. *The Meaning of Ḥesed in the Hebrew Bible: A New Inquiry*. HSM:17. Missoula.

Salmon, J. M., 1969. *Judicial Authority in Early Israel: A Historical Investigation of Old Testament Institutions*. Unpubl. diss. Princeton.

Sarna, N. M., 1989. *Genesis. The Traditional Hebrew Text with the New JBS Translation*. The JPS Torah Commentary. Philadelphia.

— 1991. *Exodus. The Traditional Hebrew Text with the New JBS Translation*. The JPS Torah Commentary. Philadelphia.

Sartori, P., 1894. "Der Shuh im Volksglauben". *Zeitschrift des Vereins für Volkskunde* 4, 41-54; 148-80; 282-305; 412-27.

Sasson, J. M., 1989. *Ruth. A New Translation with a Philological Commentary and a Formalist-Folklorist Interpretation.* 2 ed. The Biblical Seminar. Sheffield.

Schatz, W., 1972. *Genèse 14. Une Recherche.* Europäische Hochschulschriften. Reihe 23. Theologie:2. Berne.

Schedl, C., 1982. "Zur logotechnischen Struktur von Jeremia 34, 18". *BZ* 26, 249-51.

Schmidt, L., 1970. *Menschlicher Erfolg und Jahwes Initiative. Studien zu Tradition, Interpretation und Historie in Überlieferungen von Gideon, Saul und David.* WMANT:38. Neukirchen-Vluyn.

Schoors, A., 1977. "Isaiah, the Minister of Royal Anointment?" *OTS* 20, 85-107.

Schwienhorst-Schönberger, L., 1990. *Das Bundesbuch (Ex 20,22-23,33). Studien zu seiner Entstehung und Theologie.* BZAW:188. Berlin.

Seybold, K., 1986. "מָשַׁח *māšaḥ*". *TWAT* 5, 46-59.

Simpson, W. K. See: Hallo, W. H. & W. K. Simpson, 1971.

Sittl, C., *Die Gebärden der Griechen und Römer.* Leipzig.

Smend, R., 1977. "Essen und Trinken – ein Stück Weltlichkeit des AT". In: *Beiträge zur alttestamentlichen Theologie.* (FS W. Zimmerli). Göttingen, 446-59.

Smith, S. H., 1990. "'Heel' and 'Thigh': The Concept of Sexuality in the Jacob-Esau Narratives". *VT* 40, 464-73.

Snijders, L. A., 1958. "Genesis XV. The Covenant with Abram". *OTS* 12, 261-79.

— 1977. "זוּר/זָר *zûr/zār*". *TWAT* 2, 556-64.

Soden, W. von, 1969. *Grundriss der akkadischen Grammatik.* AnOr:33/47. Roma. (Abbr. *GAG*).

Soggin, J. A., 1981. *Judges. A Commentary.* OTL. London.

— 1984. *A History of Israel. From the Beginnings to the Bar Kochba Revolt, AD 135.* London.

— 1987. *The Prophet Amos. A Translation and Commentary.* London.

Sonsino, R., 1980. *Motive Clauses in Hebrew Law. Biblical Forms and Near Eastern Parallels.* SBLDS:45. Chico.

Speiser, E. A., 1934. "A Figurative Equivalent for Totality in Akkadian and West-Semitic". *JAOS* 54, 200-3.

— 1940. "Of Shoes and Shekels". *BASOR* 77, 15-20.

— 1964. *Genesis.* AB:1. New York.

Stamm, J. J., 1939. *Die akkadische Namengebung.* MVAG:44. Leipzig.

Stendebach, F. J., 1990. "רֶגֶל *ræḡæl*". TWAT 7:3-5, 330-45.

Sternberg, M., 1985. *The Poetics of Biblical Narrative. Ideological Literature and the Drama of Reading.* Indiana Studies in Biblical Literature. Bloomington.

Stoebe, H. J., 1973. *Das erste Buch Samuelis.* KAT 8:1. Gütersloh.

Stuart, D., 1987. *Hosea-Jonah.* WBC:31. Waco.

Stulman, L., 1985. *The Other Text of Jeremiah. A Reconstruction of the Hebrew Text Underlying the Greek Version of the Prose Sections of Jeremiah with English Translation*. Lanham.

Tadmor, H., 1982. "Treaty and Oath in the Ancient Near East. A Historian's Approach". In: *Humanizing America's Iconic Book. Society of Biblical Literature Centennial Addresses 1980*. Eds. G. M. Tucker & D. A. Knight. Biblical Scholarship in North America:6. Chico, 127-52.

— 1982a. "Traditional Institutions and the Monarchy: Social and Political Tensions in the Time of David and Solomon". In: Ishida, 239-57.

— See: Cogan, M. & H. Tadmor, 1988.

Talmon, S., 1978. "The Presentation of Synchroneity and Simultaneity in Biblical Narrative". *ScrHier* 27, 9-26.

— 1978a. "The 'Comparative Method' in Biblical Interpretation – Principles and Problems". *VTSup* 29, 320-56.

Tambiah, S., J. 1985. *Culture, Thought, and Social Action. An Anthropological Perspective*. Cambridge, Mass.

Thiel, W., 1981. *Die deuteronomistische Redaktion von Jeremia 26-45. Mit einer Gesamtbeurteilung der deuteronomistischen Redaktion des Buches Jeremia*. WMANT:52. Neukirchen-Vluyn.

Thompson, J. A., 1974. "The Significance of the Verb *Love* in the David-Jonathan Narratives in 1 Samuel". *VT* 24, 334-8.

— 1980. *The Book of Jeremiah*. NICOT. Grand Rapids.

Thompson, T. & D., 1968. "Some Legal Problems in the Book of Ruth". *VT* 18, 79-99.

Thorion, Y., 1984. *Studien zur klassischen hebräischen Syntax*. Marburger Studien zur Afrika- und Asienkunde. Serie B: Asien Band 6. Berlin.

Tigay, J. H., 1971. "Adoption". *EncJud* 2, 298-301.

Tosato, A., 1982. *Il matrimonio israelitico. Una teoria generale*. AnBib:100. Rome.

Tsukimoto, A., 1989. "Emar and the Old Testament – Preliminary Remarks –". *AJBI* 15, 3-24.

Tucker, G. M., 1966. "Witnesses and 'Dates' in Israelite Contracts". *CBQ* 28, 42-5.

Turner, V. W., 1977. "Symbols in African Ritual". In: *Symbolic Anthropology. A Reader in the Study of Symbols and Meanings*. Eds. J. L. Dolgin et al. New York. 183-94.

Ullendorff, E., 1979. "The Bawdy Bible". *BSOAS* 42, 425-56.

Vannoy, J. R., 1974. "The Use of the Word *hā'ᵉlōhîm* in Exodus 21:6 and 22:7, 8". In: *The Law and the Prophets*. (FS O.T. Allis). Nutley, 225-41.

Van Seters, J., 1975. *Abraham in History and Tradition*. New Haven.

Vaux, R. de, 1961. *Ancient Israel. Its Life and Institutions*. London.

— 1978. *The Early History of Israel*. Philadelphia.

Veenhof, K. R., 1966. Review: Kutsch (1963). *BO* 23, 308-13.

Volz, D. P., 1922. *Der Prophet Jeremia übersetzt und erklärt*. KAT:10. Leipzig.

Vorbichler, A. See: Hofmann, I. & A. Vorbichler, 1981.

Vorster, W. S., 1985. "Meaning and Reference: The Parables of Jesus in Mark 4". In: *Text and Reality. Aspects of Reference in Biblical Texts.* Eds. B. C. Lategan & W. S. Vorster. Atlanta, 27-65.

Vorwahl, H., 1932. *Die Gebärdensprache im Alten Testament.* Berlin.

Vriezen, T. C., 1972. "The Exegesis of Exodus xxiv 9-11". *OTS* 17, 100-33.

Walkenhorst, K.-H., 1969. *Der Sinai. Im liturgischen Verständnis der deuteronomistischen und priesterlichen Tradition.* BBB:33. Bonn.

Wallis, G., 1952. "Eine Parallele zu Richter 19,29ff. und 1 Sam. 11,5ff. aus dem Briefarchiv von Mari". *ZAW* 64, 57-61.

Waltke, B. K. & M. O'Connor, 1990. *An Introduction to Biblical Hebrew Syntax.* Winona Lake.

Weidner, E., 1966. "Nimrud". *AfO* 21, 150-2.

Weimar, P., 1973. *Untersuchungen zur priesterschriftlichen Exodusgeschichte.* FB:9. Würtsburg.

Weinel, H., 1898. "משׁח und seine Derivate". *ZAW* 18, 1-82.

Weinfeld, M., 1970. "The Covenant of Grant in the Old Testament and in the Ancient Near East". *JAOS* 90, 184-203.

— 1972. *Deuteronomy and the Deuteronomic School.* Oxford.

— 1973. "בְּרִית". *TWAT* 1, 781-808.

— 1988. "Initiation of Political Friendship in Ebla and its Later Developments". In: *Wirtschaft und Gesellschaft von Ebla.* Eds. H. Hauptmann & H. Waetzoldt. Heidelberger Studien zum Alten Orient:2. Heidelberg, 345-8.

Weippert, H., 1973. *Die Prosareden des Jeremiabuches.* BZAW:132. Berlin.

Weippert, H., 1977. "Kleidung". *BRL* 2 ed., 185-8.

Weisman, Z., 1976. "Anointing as a Motif in the Making of the Charismatic King". *Bib* 57, 378-98.

Weiss, D. H., 1964. "The Use of קנה in Connection with Marriage". *HTR* 57, 244-8.

Wellhausen, J., 1904. "Zwei Rechtriten bei den Hebräern". *ARW* 7, 33-41.

Wenham, G. J., 1982. "'The Symbolism of the Animal Rite in Gen 15': A Response to G. F. Hasel, JSOT 19 (1981) 61-78". *JSOT* 22, 134-7.

— 1987. *Genesis 1-15.* WBC:1. Waco.

Westbrook, R., 1971. "Redemption of Land". *Israel Law Review* 6, 367-75.

— 1985. "Biblical and Cuneiform Law Codes". *RB* 92, 247-64.

— 1988. *Studies in Biblical and Cuneiform Law.* CahRB:26. Paris.

— 1989. "Cuneiform Law Codes and the Origins of Legislation". *ZA* 79, 201-22.

— 1990. "Adultery in Ancient Near Eastern Law". *RB* 97, 542-80.

Westermann, C., 1981. *Genesis. 2. Teilband. Genesis 12-36.* BKAT 1:2. Neukirchen-Vluyn.

— 1982. *Genesis. 3. Teilband. Genesis 37-50.* BKAT 1:3. Neukirchen-Vluyn.

Westermann, C. & R. Albertz, 1971. "גלה glh aufdecken". *THAT* 1, 418-26.

Whitelam, K. W., 1979. *The Just King: Monarchical Judicial Authority in Ancient Israel.* JSOTSup:12. Sheffield.

— 1986. "The Symbols of Power. Aspects of Royal Propaganda in the United Monarchy". *BA* 49, 166-73.

Whybray, R. N., 1987. *The Making of the Pentateuch. A Methodological Study.* JSOTSup:53. Sheffield.

Williamson, H. G. M., 1982. *1 and 2 Chronicles.* NCBC. Grand Rapids.

Willoughby, B. E. See: Freedman, D. N. & B. E. Willoughby, 1986.

Wilson, R. R., 1980. *Prophecy and Society in Ancient Israel.* Philadelphia.

— 1990. "Ethics in Conflict: Sociological Aspects of Ancient Israelite Ethics". In: *Text and Tradition. The Hebrew Bible and folklore.* Ed. S. Niditch. Atlanta, 193-205.

Witzenrath, H. H., 1975. *Das Buch Rut. Eine literaturwissenschaftliche Untersuchung.* SANT:40. München.

Wolff, H. W., 1969. *Dodekapropheton 2. Joel und Amos.* BKAT 14:2. Neukirchen-Vluyn.

Woude, A. S. van der, 1971. "יָד *jād* Hand". THAT 1, 667-74.

Wright, D. P., 1987. *The Disposal of Impurity. Elimination Rites in the Bible and in Hittite and Mesopotamian Literature.* SBLDS:101. Atlanta.

— 1987a. "Deuteronomy 21:1-9 as a Rite of Elimination". *CBQ* 49, 387-403.

Würthwein, E., 1969. "Ruth". In: *Die fünf Megilloth.* HAT I:18. 2 ed. Tübingen, 1-24.

— 1984. *Die Bücher der Könige. 1 Kön. 17-2 Kön. 25.* ATD 11:2. Göttingen.

— 1985. *Die Bücher der Könige. 1 Kön. 1-16.* ATD 11:1. 2 ed. Göttingen.

Yaron, R., 1961. *Introduction to the Law of the Aramaic Papyri.* Oxford.

Zimmerli, W., 1969. *Ezechiel. 1 Teilband. Ezechiel 1-24.* BKAT 13:1. Neukirchen-Vluyn.

Zobel, H.-J., 1973. "גָּלָה". *TWAT* 1, 1018-31.

Zwickel, W., 1990. *Räucherkult und Räuchergeräte. Exegetische und archäologische Studien zum Räucheropfer im Alten Testament.* OBO:97. Freiburg.

6 Indexes

6.1 Biblical, Apocryphal and Jewish Sources

(Note that the index of biblical referenses is selective.)

Genesis				*Exodus*	
13:14	160	26:29	71	3:5	162
13:14-17	160	**26:30**	10, 70, **71-72,**	6:2ff.	30
13:15	160		74, 75, 76	6:8	27, 30
13:16	160	26:31	71, 72, 74	18	70
13:17	**160-61**	28:18	91	18:1-12	70
14:11	22	30:3	166	18:12	70
14:16	22	31:36-42	73	21:2	77, 78, 84
14:18-20	25	31:42	49	21:2-4	77, 85
14:20	24-25	31:43-44	73	21:2-6	77, 78, 80, 84
14:21	22	31:44	73	21:3-4	77
14:22	18, **21-25**, 26,	31:44-46	73, 74	21:5	77-78, 80, 85
	27, 29, 30, 32	31:44-54	73	21:5-6	77, 81, 83, 85
14:23	22	31:45	73	**21:6**	17, **77-86**, 88
14:23-24	22, 23	31:45-46	73	21:7-11	143
15	53, 55, 56, 57,	**31:46**	10, 70, **73-**	21:12	121
	58, 59, 63,		**74,** 75, 76	**21:12-14**	120, **121-**
	65, 68, 69	31:47-54	73		**22,** 126
15:7	63	31:48	73	21:13	121
15:7-21	63	31:48-53	73	21:13-14	121
15:8	63	31:49	74	21:14	120, 121
15:9	58	31:52	73		123, 124
15:9-11	63	31:53	49, 74	23:27	162
15:10	58, 65	31:53-54	74	24:11	70
15:12	58	**31:54**	10, 70, **73-**	28:41	116
15:12-16	63		**74,** 75, 76	28:42	45
15:13	63	32:1	74	29:7	91, 116
15:13-16	63	32:26	45	29:36	116
15:17	58, 59,	32:33	45	29:44	117
	63-65, 67	38	156	30:22-33	116
15:17-18	63	38:17-20	41-42	30:25	115
15:18	63	39:5	73	30:30	117
15:18-21	63	44:30	128	32	60
24:1	47, 48	**47.29**	4, 46, 47,		
24:1-9	47		**48-49,** 51	*Leviticus*	
24:2	4, 46, 47,	47:31	49	8:12	116
	48, 49, 51	48:5	166, 168	14:27	20
24:3	47, 48	48:8-9	166	18:7	140
24:7-8	47	48:9	166	18:8	140
24:9	4, 46, **47-48,**	48:9-12	166	20:11	140
	49, 51	48:12	166	25	84
24:10	47	48:13	20	25:39	83, 84
26:28	71	48:17	20	25:44-46	83
		50:23	166		

| 25:39-46 | 83 |
| 25:46 | 84 |

Numeri

5:21	46, 47
5:22	46, 47
5:27	46, 47
12:14	157
14:21	27
14:28	27
14:30	27
27:5-11	156
35:9-29	121
36:5-9	156

Deuteronomy

4:41-43	121
6:9	80
10:11	29
11:24	161
15:12	84
15:12-17	17
15:12-18	77, 80, 81, 84
15:16	85
15:17	**77-86**
19:1-13	121
19:11-12	121
21:1-9	4
23:1	139, 140
25	78
25:5-10	156, 163
25:7	156
25:7-10	156
25:8	156, 157
25:9	17, 146, **147-48, 156-57**, 163, 165
27:20	139, 140
32:11	143
32:40	20, **26-27** 29, 30, 32
32:41	27
32:41-42	26

Joshua

1:3	161
5:15	162
6:4	33
9:14	70

| 10:24 | 162 |

Judges

3:27	33
7:20	20
9	99
9:2	94, 101
9:3	94
9:6	94
9:8	**94-95**
9:8-15	95
9:15	**94-95**
9:16	94
9:20	94
16:29	20
19	66
19:29	**65-67**, 69
19:29-30	16, 66
20	16
20:1	66
20:1-11	66
20:8	66

1 Samuel

3:14	23
8	96
8:6	95
8:19-20	95
8:22	95
9:1-10:15	95, 96
9:12-13	103
9:16	95, 109
9:17	96
9:19	103
9:22-24	103
9:25	96
10:1	5, 91, **95-97**, 98, 99, 115, 118, 119
10:2	97
10:6-7	97
10:9-13	97
10:10	98
10:16	95, 96
10:24	96, 115
10:24-25	97
11	66
11:5	66
11:7	**65-67**, 69
11:15	96

12:3	96, **158-60**
12:13	96
15:1	96
15:17	96
15:27	127, 136
16:1	97
16:3	103
16:5	103
16:11	103
16:13	5, 91, **97-98**, 99, 118, 119
16:21	128
18	128, 129
18:1	128, 131
18:1-3	130
18:1-5	131
18:2	128, 131
18:3	128, 129, 130, 131
18:3-4	131
18:4	3, 4, 7, **127-134**, 135
18:5	128-29, 131
18:13	129
18:16	128
18:20	128
18:22	128
19:24	128
20:7-8	130
20:8	130
20:12-13	130
20:14	130
20:14-15	130, 131
20:16	130
20:17	130
20:23	130
20:42	130
23:17	131
23:18	130
24:5	127
25:24	162
30:26	98

2 Samuel

1:16	159
1:26	130
2:4	**98-99**, 100, 101, 102, 103, 113, 118, 119

2:7 98, 99
3:12 74
3:13 74
3:13-16 74
3:17-19 74
3:20 10, 70, **74-75**, 76
3:21 74, 75
3:22 75
3:23 75
3:24 75
3:27 100
3:39 98
4:6-7 100
5:1 100, 101
5:1-2 100, 101
5:1-3 99, 100, 101, 102, 103
5:2 100, 102
5:3 98, **99-102**, 113, 118, 119
5:12 102
5:17 112
7 100
7:14 168
9 130
9:3 130
12:7 98, 115
15:1-12 103
15:10 103
15:11 103
19:8 24
19:11 **103**, 113, 118, 119
21:7 130

1 Kings

1 97, 103, 106, 108, 109, 122
1-2 123
1:5 107
1:9 103
1:11 107
1:18 107
1:19 107
1:21 104
1:24 107
1:25 70, 107, 115
1:29 23
1:30 107
1:32-35 103
1:34 **104-5**
1:35 90, 106
1:37 105
1:38-40 104
1:39 90, 91, 99, **103-9**, 115, 116, 118, 119
1:41 103, 122
1:43 107
1:43-48 104, 122
1:44 104, 105
1:45 **104-5**
1:46 106
1:47 105
1:48 105
1:49 122
1:50 120, **122-23**, 124, 126
1:51 122
1:52 122
1:53 122
2:28 120, **123-24**, 126
2:28-34 123
2:30 123
2:31 123
2:31-33 123
2:34 123, 124
3:1 113
5:3 162
5:15 113
9:16-17 113
19:15 109
19:15-16 **109-110**, 118, 119
20:33 36
22:4 36

2 Kings

3:7 36
4:27 162
8:13 109
9:1 91
9:3 91, **109-110**
9:6 91, **109-110**
9:13 109
10 36
10:12-14 36
10:12-16 36
10:15 33, 34, **36-37**, 44
10:15-16 36
11 103
11:4 110
11:4-19 110
11:7 110
11:8 110
11:11 110
11:12 99, **110-13**, 114, 115, 118, 119
11:13 112
11:14-19 110
11:15 122
11:17 101
23:1-3 39
23:30 **113-14**, 118, 119
24:17 38

Isaiah

8:16, 20 154
13:2 24, 31
20:2 147, 162
20:3-4 162
41:10 20
45:1 116
47:2-3 140
51:23 162
55:12 33
62:8 20

Jeremiah

17:1 125
31:19 50
32:6-15 152
32:8 **151-52**
34 53, 55, 56, 57, 58, 59, 65, 68, 69, 84
34:8 58
34:8-10 57
34:8-11 57, 58
34:8-16 77
34:8-22 57
34:9 83
34:14 83, 84
34:11 58
34:12-22 57

34:13-14	57	*Hosea*		144:8	19
34:15	60	2	144	144:11	19
34:16	58	2:3	140		
34:17-22	57, 58	2:8-9	143	*Job*	
34:18	58, 59, 60,			17:3	33, 35,
	61, 62, 63	*Amos*			**42-43**, 44
34:18-19	57, 58, **59-**	**2:6**	**157-58**	40:24	86
	63, 64, 67	**8:6**	**157-58**	40:26	86
34:19	60, 61, 62	3:14	124, 125	40:28	86
34:18-20	61				
34:19	58	*Obadiah*		*Proverbs*	
34:20	62	7	70	1:24	24, 31
34:20-22	62			2:17	139
37:1	38	*Nahum*		**6:1**	33, 35, **40-42**, 44
		3:19	33	6:2	41
Ezekiel				6:3	41
13:6	153-54	*Habakkuk*		11:15	33, 35, 40, 44
16:8	136, 137, **138-**	3:13	116	11:21	33
	39, 142,			16:5	33
	143, 144	*Haggai*		17:18	33, 35, 40, 44
17:1-10	37	1:6	82	20:16	40, 41
17:1-21	37			22:26	33, 35, 44
17:11-21	37	*Zecharaiah*		27:13	41
17:13	37	8:17	19-20		
17:15	37	8:23	127	*Ruth*	
17:16	37			1:12	167
17:18	33, 34, 35,	*Malachi*		2:12	143
	37-39, 44	2:14	139	2:20	141
17:19	37			3:4	136, 142
20	30	*Psalms*		3:7	136, 142
20:3	28	2:7	168	**3:9**	136, 137, 138,
20:5	27, 28,	8:7	162		**141-42**, 143,
	29, 30	18:3	125		144, 179
20:5-6	23, **27-31**	18:39	162	3:10	142
20:6	20, 27, 28,	45:2	114, 115	3:10-13	142
	29, 30	45:3	114, 115	3:13	148
20:7	29	45:4-6	115	4	16, 148, 150,
20:10	28	45:7	114, 115		163, 169
20:15	27, 31	**45:8**	**114-15**	4:2	154
20:23	27, 31	47:2	33	4:3	150, 151, 156
20:28	27, 29, 31	47:4	162	4:4	148, 150,
20:42	27, 31	60:10	162		151, 152
21:17	50	**89:21**	**115**	4:4-5	152
24:17	162	98:8	33	4:4-10	149, 150
25:6	33	105:6	115	4:5	148, 150, 151
36:6	29	105:11-12	115	4:6	148, 151, 152
36:7	27, 29	**105:15**	**115-16**	**4:7**	145, 146, 147,
36:8	29	106:26	27		150, 153, 154,
44:12	27, 29, 31	110:1	162		**155**, 156, 157,
47:14	27, 31	119:28, 106	153		163, 165

4:7-8	158
4:7-9	154
4:8	5, **145-47,** **148-56**, 157, 163, 165
4:9	145, 148, 154, 155
4:9-10	150, 151, 152
4:10	84, 148, 150
4:11	171
4:11-12	170
4:11-13	170
4:11-17	169, 171
4:13	167, 170
4:13-17	171
4:14	170, 171
4:14-15	170
4:14-17	170, 174
4.15	170
4:16	**166-75**, 176
4:16-17	171
4:17	170, 171, 174

Lamentations
| 5:6 | 35, 43, 44 |

Esther
| 8:3 | 162 |
| 9:21, 27, 29, 31, 32 | 153 |

Daniel
6:8	153
10:6	142
12:7	20, 21, **25-26**, 27, 29

Ezra
10:1	39
10:3	39
10:5	39-40
10:11	40
10:14	34
10:19	33, 34, 35, **39-40,** 43, 44

Nehemiah
| 9:15 | 27 |

1 Chronicles
| 11:1-3 | 100 |

| 29:23 | 105 |
| 29:24 | 34, 35, 43, 44 |

2 Chronicles
| 22:7 | 109 |
| 30:8 | 34, 35, 43, 44 |

| 1 Macc 6:58 | 35 |
| Sir 46:19 | 159 |

Tg. Onq. Exod 21:6	85
Tg. Ps.-J. Gen 37:28	163
Tg. Ruth 4:8	157
Pirqe R. El. 38:77	164
T. Zeb. 3:2-7	163-64

6.2 Ancient Near Eastern Sources

6.2.1 Syro-Palestine and Mesopotamia

Abba-AN and Yarimlim, treaty	53-54
Ahiqar	
133	157
171	127
AP 14:5	30
ARM	
2.37:6-8, 11, 13-14	53
2.48	66-67
8.13:11'-12'	72
8.85:5'	72
26.251:16-18	137
Ashurnirari VI and Mati'ilu, treaty	54
BMAP	
5:3	82
8:5-9	82
Descent of Ishtar	50
EA	
34:50-51	92

51:6-7	93, 118
84:4-6	162
106:6	162
141:40	162
195:5-11	162
241:5-8	162
369:29-32	162
El-Qiṭār, Snell (1963-64), ll. 16-17	133
Emar	
Arnaud (1986)	
5:21	133
30:9	133
31:15	132
217	161
218-20	161
Huenergard (1983)	
2:21-22	133
3:16	133
Esarhaddon, treaties, ll. 547-54	55
Hadad, Gibson (1975) 13:28-29	26
Hammurapi, law of, §282	81

KAI
  215:11   127
  233:9   154
Kisurra, Kienast (1978)   47
KTU
  1.2.IV:30-40   92
  1.2.IV:32   92
  1.2.IV:37-38   92
  1.2.IV:39   92
  1.6.II:9-11   127
  1.17.V:26-28   173
  1.17.V:33-36   173
Middle Assyrian Laws
  §40   82
  §44   81
Nimrud, throne-base inscription,   38
  Hulin (1963)
PRU IV
  17.159:8-10   132
  17.159:22-31   132
  17.159:26   132
  17.159:27-31   132
  17.227:45   162
  17.340:31   22
Tell al Rimah, Dalley (1976),   53
  1:10-12
RS 8.145   132
Saqqâra, Segal (1983)
  3:1-2   82
  5:8   82
  9:2   8

  10a:5   82
  19:2   154
  97a:1   82
  164a:1   82
Sefire I.A:39-40   54-55
Shalmanezer III, chronicles   110
Ugaritica V, 83 (20.146)   132
Waterman (1930), 1285:26-28   159-60

6.2.2 Hatti

Appu   172
KBo
  XVI.25, obv. 54´-55´   93
  XVII.61:22   172
KUB
  XVII.28.IV:45-55   56
  XXIV.5+IX.13, obv. 19´   93
  XXXVI.119:3´-5´   93
The Mešedi-Protocol   147
Ullikummis   173

6.3 Classical Sources

Herodotus II.139   52
Homer, Iliad 9:455-56   173
Livy
  I.XXIV   54
  VII.3   87
  XL.6.1-2   57
Plato, Laws VI.753.D   57

Itero

www.ehs.se/itero

1. Åke Viberg, *Symbols of Law: A Contextual Analysis of Legal Symbolic Acts in the Old Testament.* 2021. First published 1992 by Almqvist & Wiksell International.

2. Thomas Kazen, *Jesus and Purity* Halakhah: *Was Jesus Indifferent to Impurity?* 2021. First published 2002 by Almqvist & Wiksell International. Corrected reprint edition published 2010 by Eisenbrauns.

3. Åke Viberg, *Prophets in Action: An Analysis of Prophetic Symbolic Acts in the Old Testament.* 2021. First published 2007 by Almqvist & Wiksell International.

4. Thomas Kazen, *Issues of Impurity in Early Judaism.* 2021. First published 2010 by Eisenbrauns.

5. Rikard Roitto, *Behaving as a Christ-Believer: A Cognitive Perspective on Identity and Behavior Norms in Ephesians.* 2021. First published 2011 by Eisenbrauns.